Best Wishes!

"Dr. B's"

More Praise for
Where the Money Is

"Technology, politics, globalization . . . Powerful forces are shaping the future, but how is the investor to make sense of it all? Do what the pros do. Turn to Dr. Bob! I know no one better at distilling the key trends shaping our future and translating them into actionable advice. This book will get you thinking and will introduce you to a host of great investment opportunities."

Don Phillips, Managing Director, Morningstar, Inc.

"Finally, someone on Wall Street has joined me in figuring out the role demographics can play on the global markets and economies. Dr. Bob's *Where the Money Is* is a must read for any long-term investor."

Harry S. Dent, Jr., Investment Strategist and author,
The Roaring 2000s and *The Roaring 2000s Investor*

"In turbulent, uncertain markets, one searches for an experienced guide like Bob Froehlich who well knows the pitfalls and, importantly, the opportunities."

Steve Forbes, President and CEO, Editor-in-Chief, *Forbes*

"Bob Froehlich has written a useful and readable guidebook for the potentially treacherous investment journey. He takes you through virtually every theme, concept, industry, and region in a lively and insightful narrative. The novice investor will gain confidence from his explanations and the professional will find some stimulating revelations in his conclusions."

Byron R. Wien, Chief U.S. Investment Strategist, Morgan Stanley

"Once you read this book you will enjoy talking about and referring others to BobSpeak™. He cuts through the jargon and gives more than a one-line explanation of important investment terms. I know you will enjoy this book as much as I did. Happy reading!"

Ralph J. Acampora, CMT, Managing Director, Director of Technical Research, Prudential Securities Inc.

"A wonderful treatment of 'iceberg investment trends' that should determine the core holdings in any long-term portfolio. Once again Dr. Bob demonstrates an exceptional talent to present complex subjects in understandable and entertaining terms."

Elizabeth J. Mackay, CFA, Chief Investment Strategist,
Bear, Stearns & Co., Inc.

"Bob Froehlich is dead-on with his Sectornomics™ strategy. Fast changing market conditions make diversification prudent. However, recognizing key economic trends that will drive some sectors more than others is the definitive approach to achieving superior equity returns. This book promises a fast payback to investors."

Thomas M. Galvin, Chief Investment Officer,
Credit Suisse First Boston

"*Where the Money Is* provides the long-term investor a complete survey of today's investment opportunities in straightforward language. BobSpeak™ cuts through jargon to inform (and amuse) the reader."

Joseph V. Battipaglia, Executive Vice President,
Chairman of Investment Policy, Gruntal & Co.

"Dr. Bob's *Where the Money Is* dispenses a lot of essential knowledge and great wit. The top ten things to remember at the end of every chapter make this a worthwhile book."

A. Michael Lipper, CFA, President, Lipper Advisory Services, Inc.

"Bob Froehlich has given us a witty, entertaining, and insightful look into the major economic trends of our time—focusing on the long-term factors that are likely to motivate investors and drive markets for years to come. *Where the Money Is* rises above the day-to-day din of the trading floor to address the fundamental forces influencing the economy and money flows. You will both enjoy it and learn from it."

Robert Hormats, Vice Chairman, Goldman Sachs International

"*Where the Money Is* is a refreshing, well-written, and forward-thinking primer for investors by one of the best forward-thinking investment strategists in the business."

Dr. Edward Yardeni, Chief Investment Strategist,
Deutsche Banc Alex Brown

"Dr. Bob's notes provide a seasoned practitioner's insights on how one should invest in the increasingly interrelated global economy and marketplace."

Mario J. Gabelli, Chairman and CEO, Gabelli Asset Management Inc.

"Not surprisingly, Bob Froehlich's book is both entertaining and informative. Long-term investors take notice!"

Michael F. Holland, Chairman, Holland & Company L.L.C.

"In *Where the Money Is* Bob Froehlich provides investors with a thought-provoking yet amusing guide to personal money management."

Jeffrey M. Applegate, Chief Investment Strategist, Lehman Brothers

"One thing guaranteed, anyone who completes *Where the Money Is* will know a lot more about finance and investments than before starting. In his upbeat, positive-thinker style, Froehlich covers seven mega-themes, blending macro and micro analysis. Along the way he guides the reader with his "Top Ten Things to Remember" bringing each chapter into focus. Froehlich's guidance is worth taking under consideration."

Robert H. Stovall, CFA, Market Strategist, Prudential Securities

"Wow, did I enjoy reading *Where the Money Is*. Bob Froehlich gives us an invaluable guide to the new, global, Internet economy, a practical guide to financial planning, and a brilliant, spirited primer on the power of free markets to increase both wealth and freedom around the world—all rolled into one. And he does it with common sense, good humor, and crystal clear prose. A must-read for anyone planning to live, work, and invest in the 21st century."

Jack Kemp, Founder and Co-Director, Empower America,
Former Congressman, Secretary of Housing and Urban Development,
and Republican candidate for Vice-President of the United States

"Bob Froehlich's top-down trip around the world is an eye and mind opener. Step aboard for an enjoyable and memorable trip! *Where the Money Is* helps span a notable chasm; by providing insight into important themes, Bob helps investors develop the ideas that should add significant value to their portfolios. Bob's Top Ten lists and investment principles are praiseworthy in their own right."

Thomas M. McManus, Equity Portfolio Strategist,
Banc of America Securities

"*Where the Money Is* covers a wide range of topics that are necessary for success in today's fast-paced markets. It is important not only because of its coverage of many little understood but essential investment themes, but also because of the solid advice provided in understanding and investing in many key industries. An added dividend is its lucidity and humor. Must reading for individual and professional investors alike."

David Dreman, Chairman and CIO, Dreman Value Management, L.L.C., author of the best selling *Contrarian Investment Strategies: The Next Generation*

"In *Where the Money Is*, Dr. Bob uses his analysis of demographic trends to construct some broad investment themes that individuals can use for building portfolios designed for long-term investment results. He discusses these trends in terms that anyone can understand. All in all, the book is a great guide to some very important issues. These pages will give those that try to build portfolios for their retirement plans a very good backdrop in which to make decisions and stay the course. The book is a handy tool as we go through the turbulent and volatile markets that we seem to find ourselves in these days."

Greg A. Smith, Chief Investment Strategist, Prudential Securities

"Bob Froehlich presents a compelling case for thinking sector by sector and long-term as an investor in the global marketplace."

General Alexander M. Haig, Jr., Former White House Chief of Staff and Secretary of State, Chairman, Worldwide Associates, Inc.

"*Where the Money Is* provides an in-depth view of what really drives the market. Dr. Froehlich looks behind the popular conceptions to give a clear view of where money can be made over the next decade. An excellent read for all investors!"

Erik Gustafson, Portfolio Manager, Liberty Growth Stock Fund, Stein Roe & Farnham

"This book is a must-have for investors. Comprehensive, engaging, and unique, it will definitely make you think! I found Froehlich's insights on free trade, technology, and government downsizing, particularly valuable. Froehlich is a maestro at presenting essential information on how to make money."

Ed Hyman, Chairman, International Strategy & Investment Group Inc.

"Is there life after Nasdaq? 'Absolutely,' says Bob Froehlich. In this thoughtful and far reaching review he argues persuasively that a myriad of important investment opportunities will flow from the aging of the population, global restructuring and privatization, and, yes, even from the continuing information technology revolution. A must read for anyone who's been in the market in the past few years."

Peter J. Canelo, Investment Strategist, Managing Director, Morgan Stanley

"Make this one of your top picks for your investment bookshelf. Dr. Bob not only shows you *Where the Money Is*, he shows you how to make money as well."

Michael R. Bloomberg, CEO and founder Bloomberg L.P.

"Bob Froehlich simply exudes passion and useful insights in *Where the Money Is*. He is one of our truly dedicated and knowledgeable investment professionals and should be read by anyone interested in the thoughts of someone who holds no punches. Very enjoyable, very informative, very useful."

Hugh Johnson, Chief Investment Officer, First Albany Corporation

"As a firm believer that the Internet is the greatest invention in our lifetime and that demographics will shape our markets dramatically for many years to come, it was a true joy to read *Where the Money Is*. The art of blending an intense amount of information with humor, lay-speak, great stories, and amazing insight is truly a gift and Froehlich has that gift. Bob brings unmatched warmth, understanding, simplicity, and honesty to all who have a thirst for learning. Though I make my living as an investor, I also learned a lot reading this wonderful book. I think he's dead-on with this one!"

Liz Ann Sonders, Managing Director, Campbell, Cowperthwait
(A Division of U.S. Trust)

"Bob Froehlich is truly one of those rare strategists on Wall Street who understands that the future of investing will be significantly determined by demographics."

John Naisbitt, Futurist and author, *Megatrends*

Where the money is

How to Spot Key Trends to Make Investment Profits

DR. BOB FROEHLICH

John Wiley & Sons, Inc.

New York • Chichester • Weinheim • Brisbane • Singapore • Toronto

Published by John Wiley & Sons, Inc.
Published simultaneously in Canada.

Library of Congress Cataloging-in-Publication Data:

Froehlich, Robert J.
   Where the money is : how to spot key trends to make investment
profits / by Bob Froehlich.
      p. cm.
   Includes index.
   ISBN 0-471-39317-7 (cloth : alk. paper)
   1. Investment analysis. 2. Investments. 3. Securities. I. Title.
HG4529 .F76 2001
332.6—dc21   2001026188

Printed in the United States of America

10 9 8 7 6 5 4 3 2 1

To the three most important
women in my life, the true treasures
of my life, who already know
"Where the Money Is"

Cheryl
My wonderful wife

Marianne
My precious, elder daughter

Stephanie
My darling, younger daughter

With these three women to inspire
my thoughts, I am thankful for the
gift of each precious day together.

Foreword

One Sunday morning almost five years ago, I was working on my book *The 9 Steps to Financial Freedom* while the radio played in the background. It was tuned to one of the many investment advice programs that hit the airwaves on weekend mornings. Though I was thoroughly engaged in my own work, my attention kept wandering to the radio show. The host, Cynthia Oti, was bursting with enthusiasm about a recent trip to London. She wasn't describing Big Ben or the quaint pubs she'd visited, however. She was raving about an investment speech she'd heard by the creator of a wonderful new way of identifying investment opportunities called "Sectornomics."

For the remainder of the show, Oti described virtually every concept and strategy that had been presented during that speech in London. By the end of the show I wasn't writing anymore, I was listening. I was mesmerized by what I heard and by the realization that there was someone on Wall Street who actually gets it—who understands how changing demographics and globalization will rule the markets in the years to come. That person was and is Dr. Bob Froehlich.

The next day I got on the phone, tracked down Dr. Froehlich in Chicago, and talked to him. We debated with each other, analyzed, argued, and laughed. When I hung up, I knew that Bob Froehlich was one of the best-kept secrets on Wall Street.

Since that first phone call, I have made it a practice to watch Dr. Froehlich's insightful and even amusing appearances on CNBC's *Squawk Box*. After reading his latest book, there's one thing I'm certain of: My initial impression of Bob was correct. He is one of the best big-picture thinkers in the investment world today. If you are looking for someone to show you where the money is on Wall Street, that person is Bob Froehlich.

Investing is an art, a science—and a necessity. As I wrote in *The 9 Steps to Financial Freedom*, to increase your wealth you *must* invest—both through your 401(k) and other retirement plans and on your own. Over the long term, investing in the stock market is a time-tested strategy for achieving the best possible returns on your money. Although the stock market may be highly volatile over the short term—as the renowned Wharton School professor Jeremy Siegel pointed out in his classic book, *Stocks for the Long Run*—with time enough (10 years or more) the volatility evens out into fairly consistent, reliable, and beneficial gains. Professor Siegel's analysis was based on almost 200 years of market returns—no short-term study!

Clearly, you must be invested in the stock market. And you can do this. I firmly believe that most investors have it within themselves to choose and manage their own investments. Your knowledge of what's best for you—your inner voice—can be a powerful guide in helping you to find investment opportunities that suit your own financial needs and time horizon, whether you choose to put your money in mutual funds, exchange-traded funds, individual stocks, or all three. However, you also need dependable information. And that is exactly where this book comes in. If the biggest risk of all is not being in the stock market, where, exactly, should you be?

This is a question that Dr. Froehlich helps to answer in plain language, with broad-based knowledge and with imagination and an understanding of the most important global trends. Truly valuable investment advice doesn't just direct you to buy a particular stock but helps you to think about investment opportunities within sectors—specifically, in the industries that are poised for growth over the next years and decades. Bob's solid guidance helps you target long-term opportunities.

Over the years, some of the best investment guidance of all has come from futurists who accurately predicted major trends. Savvy investors could have profited greatly by heeding the guidance of John Naisbitt's blockbuster *Megatrends*, originally published in 1982, on major economic, political, demographic, and sociological trends. Faith Popcorn's

1992 *The Popcorn Report* identified important trends for the 1990s, including the growth of child care and domestic services in general. As the creator of the "Sectornomics" investment theme, Dr. Froehlich may go down in history for having devised one of the most significant forward-looking investment discoveries of our time.

Increasingly in this volatile market environment, what particular stocks you buy may be less important than what sectors you choose to invest in—and what sectors you choose to avoid. Attention to global trends—be they demographic, economic, political, or technological in nature—will get you into the right sectors and, just as important, will keep you out of sectors and industries that are headed for problems. Understanding major global trends can help you confirm what you already know—that with increasing energy costs on the horizon, for example, the transportation sector may not be the best place to put your money. That, given an aging population, pharmaceuticals may be a good bet, particularly in the industrialized world, where medicines are considered a necessity of life, and that financial services will be an increasingly important sector as more people near retirement. That technology is still the most powerful engine driving economic growth around the world. And, yes, that there are opportunities in energy.

Where the Money Is combines the best of futurist thinking with smart investment guidance. Dr. Froehlich points out where the money is by highlighting the major trends that will shape our world in the coming decade—reminding us all the while that we should keep our eye tuned to the big picture over the long term rather than to the short-term blips on the ticker at the bottom of the television screen.

Bob explains the broad themes and then drills down to the specific opportunities that these trends present for investors. If we understand what trends will move our world in the next decade, we will be better able to identify the markets, sectors, and, yes, even companies, that are best positioned to benefit from seismic shifts in our ever-changing world.

Bob's enthusiasm for the future and the opportunities it represents is boundless. Yet he keeps us grounded by reminding us that the single most important ingredient for success is time. Quoting from Maya Angelou, he poignantly reminds readers that "we cannot influence, neither speed up or slow down" time. Pick the sectors that seem poised for growth, invest in them through mutual funds or by selecting a broad basket of stocks on your own, and then hold on. If you follow his guidelines, you will be picking an investment that will be viable for at least a decade.

Where the Money Is provides a tonic: a much-needed view of the big picture in our noisy, short-term, volatility-fixated world. Bob offers *excellent* information we can put to use in our investment portfolios. If we can see and understand the engines that drive growth and in turn propel the markets, we will be smarter investors. If you take the time to read *Where the Money Is*, you'll be the richer for it.

Suze Orman
Author, *The 9 Steps to Financial Freedom,*
The Courage to Be Rich, and *The Road to Wealth*

Acknowledgments

Gratitude is the memory of the heart.

J. B. Massieu

I am grateful to so many people—friends, colleagues, and family—who each in his or her own special way helped me with this book. To each of you I say thank you from the bottom of my heart.

While my name appears as the author, this book could not have been written without the assistance of thousands of stockbrokers all across the United States. Over the years they have let me become part of their business. They have shared their most valuable asset with me, their clients. But most important, they gave me the forum to develop, debate, and challenge the way the investment world looks at things. The brokers that I have worked with are some of the hardest working, loyal, and devoted people you will find anywhere. Throughout my career they have provided me with guidance, insights, and critical analyses that have been invaluable to me. I do not have words to adequately convey my gratitude to them.

I also heartily acknowledge a series of intellectual debts to my investment colleagues at Scudder Investments, who under the leadership of Farhan Sharaff, our Global Chief Investment Officer, helped me explore avenues that were new to me and always provided innovative investment insights and analysis that helped me to think "outside the box." I am especially grateful to Mark Casady and Lin Coughlin, who have both provided me with countless opportunities and unwavering support at Scudder. And to my fellow colleagues on the Leadership Team of the U.S. Retail Distribution Group, I thank each of you for helping and supporting my efforts in your own unique way. It's a privilege for me to be a part of such a great team. An extra special thanks goes to Susan Crawshaw, our marketing guru, and her colleagues Bill Barsanti and Peggy Doherty, who together with our top-notch advertising agency, Foote, Cone & Belding, actually created a "cottage" industry around me that included a national advertising campaign as well as the best trinkets in the mutual fund industry. My face has been embraced on coffee mugs, flashlights, candy bars, mouse pads, baseballs, and even a deck of cards. It has been more fun than I ever imagined.

Possibly no one has had more fun with my trinkets than the gang at CNBC's hit program *Squawk Box*. It is a real privilege for me to have the opportunity once a month to go to New York and be the guest cohost on that show. One of the greatest things in life is getting a chance to work with people who really know the business and who are enthusiastic and passionate about what they do—and that pretty much sums up the *Squawk Box* crew. In addition to that they are witty, insightful, and fun to work with. Many of my best thoughts have come to me when I was bantering about on *Squawk Box*. Special thanks to Mark Haines, the best financial news anchor in the business, and to his sidekicks, Joe Kernen, David Faber, Maria Bartiromo, and Kathleen Hays. It's fun working with all of you. I enjoy being your colleague.

One of the best things that has happened to me in my career has been the opportunity to be involved with my alma mater, the University of Dayton. I would first like to thank Tom Burkhardt, the head of finance at the University of Dayton, for giving me the opportunity to serve on the Investment Committee for the Board of Trustees. I would also like to thank my fellow members on the Investment Committee. I am proud to be part of a group where the dialogue, the insights, and the discussions we have rival the investment committees and the discussions that are had at some of the top firms on Wall Street. I especially want to thank Sam Gould, Dean of the Business School, and David

Sauer, Professor of Finance, for letting me get involved with the students. Both Sam and Dave took me under their wings and let me take part in helping to create U.D.'s state-of-the-art Center for Portfolio Management and Securities Analysis. I am truly grateful for the vision and support that both of them provided to this important project. However, first and foremost I am indebted to the students at U.D., who have welcomed me into their classroom as a teacher, advisor, mentor, and friend. One of the secrets to my success has been to not lose sight of where the youth in this country are going to take us. If you want to see the future, go to a college campus and learn how the young people think and feel. I am grateful to the students at U.D. for providing me with a peek of what the future holds for us.

No one has done a better job of motivating and encouraging investors so they can change their investment future than best-selling author and CNBC Personal Finance Editor Suze Orman. I am excited, honored, and humbled that she agreed to write the Foreword for my book. No one in the world has done a better job of or worked harder at demystifying, explaining, and motivating individuals regarding their investments. She may go down in history as the greatest investment educator ever, educating Main Street and Wall Street alike.

I also want to thank all of my colleagues from Wall Street who took the time to both review my manuscript and provide an endorsement. I owe special thanks to my good friend and colleague Ed Lynch, who is now the head of sales for Seligman Financial Services. Ed and I worked together at Van Kampen Merritt. He is the best and brightest sales and marketing person in the business today. He understands the investment side of our business better than any other sales and marketing person. It was Ed who first challenged me and then helped and encouraged me to learn and understand the sales and marketing side of our business. It was Ed's bright idea that led the two of us to create a quarterly tape for stockbrokers over five years ago. After that first tape I did with Ed, I have been recording a quarterly CD (compact disc—times change, no more cassette tapes) ever since . . . 20 and counting. I don't think Ed had any idea of the marketing monster he was creating five years ago. It is a privilege to call myself a friend and a colleague of his.

A book like this is not just the product of current research and colleagues. Any person's views are the product of a lifetime. In that vein I owe special thanks and gratitude to my loving and caring mother and father, who have both passed away. They left me with a restless curiosity that has always guided me in my research, and most important they instilled in me a self-belief that I could do anything that I set out to do. I am also blessed with a wonderful older sister, Mary Ann, who has always been a constant source of love, friendship, and support. And with the passing of my parents, she has taken up their cause and is not only my number-one promoter but also the head of my unofficial fan club in my hometown of Pittsburgh.

After writing my first investment book, *The Three Bears Are Dead*, which was published by Forbes in 1998, I had no intention of ever writing another one. That was until John Wiley & Sons pitched the idea to me after a keynote address I gave while they were in the audience. Our business relationship blossomed from there. I am particularly grateful to my new publisher at John Wiley & Sons, who believed there was merit in my book; to my editor at John Wiley & Sons, Pamela van Giessen, who handled this project with just the right touch by providing constant encouragement and insightful comments; and finally to Peter Knapp, who handled the creative packaging and marketing components of the book.

I am especially grateful to my executive assistant, Michelle Pilota. She participated in every step of the research, writing, editing, and creative process. Her long hours of dedication and commitment are unparalleled. Michelle is a cheerful, productive, efficient assistant who also played a key role in the production (she typed every single one of my sometimes illegible handwritten words) of this book, and I thank her for that as well.

As a father I am truly blessed with two loving and caring daughters, Marianne and Stephanie, who have grown up to become beautiful and intelligent young women. I am so proud of everything that both of them have accomplished. Throughout their young lives they have shown me such unbelievable wisdom at such a young age as both of them juggled the priorities of academics, athletics (tennis), and social life. They are so prepared to take on the world that it scares me. They are both ready for all of what life has to offer. Watching them grow and mature and change has been a great joy to me. An even greater joy is watching what hasn't changed, like their infectious laughter and hearts of gold. They still find humor in the smallest everyday happenings, which is usually at the dinner table when everyone has a mouthful of food. I knew for sure that God loved me when he sent both of you to me. I am proud to be your father.

Finally, I saved the best for last. I could have never written this book without the love and support of my wife, Cheryl. The creativity, enthusiasm, and energy I invested in writing this book were fueled by her unfailing belief in me. It has made all the difference in this book. It has made all the difference in my life. Cheryl is always there for me with a brilliant insight, a clever turn of a phrase, or wise judgment about the right thing to say or do. Without her I would be simply reading a book instead of writing one. I am thankful every day that I have you as my wife.

DR. BOB FROEHLICH
Chicago, Illinois

Contents

We have no sense of direction.

Edna St. Vincent Millay
Poet (1940)

This table of contents will give you some sense of the direction I am about to take in order to show you exactly "Where the Money Is."

2   The Globalization of Economies and Markets   49

3   The Technology Revolution Is Creating the "I" (Information Age) Generation   89

4   Government Downsizing and Privatization   121

Introduction

Money is something you got to make in case you don't die.

Max Asnas
Russian-American Restaurateur

Most people who are looking to make money look to the stock market. And once into the stock market, they are hoping to run with the bulls. You see, that is because most stock market investors are well aware of the analogies we use to describe the events and the mood of the stock market. In the most basic terms, a "bull" market is when the stock market is going up, and a "bear" market is when the market is going down. The origins of why these animals were chosen to depict these different markets lie in the way these animals kill their prey. A bull uses its horns and tosses its prey upward (hence we call an "up" market a bull market). A bear meanwhile uses its massive claws and slashes downward on its prey (hence we call a "down" market a bear market).

The Butterfly Effect

I would like to introduce another analogy to you to go along with the bulls and the bears . . . butterflies. The global investment trends that have been driving the markets can be traced back to what is known as the "butterfly effect."

The butterfly effect theory goes like this: In the early 1960s Edward Lorenz, a meteorologist, attempted to model the weather for the entire globe in a comprehensive computer program. This model was programmed with certain initial conditions based on accurate data and was then instructed to predict the weather. Finally, the initial conditions were very, very slightly altered in what would appear to be a very, very insignificant amount, especially from a global weather perspective; however, the results from these insignificant changes produced wildly dramatic impacts in weather patterns around the globe. The phenomenon became known as the "butterfly effect" because it was theorized that the simple movement of a butterfly's wings in the Amazon basin could change the wind current in South America, which would alter cloud formations over the Pacific Ocean, which would cause it to snow in Russia . . . all because a butterfly flapped its wings in the Amazon.

The global trends that have been driving the stock markets today can best be explained by this same butterfly effect. There are two very important lessons to be learned from the butterfly effect. First, the entire world is connected by some fiber in some way. There is no longer any corner of the earth in which you can hide. Second, something that on the surface may appear insignificant can set off a chain reaction that produces dramatic results.

Let's shift the butterfly effect from the weather to the markets. First, there is no longer any market anywhere that isn't connected. Markets may be connected from a direct or an indirect economic perspective or from a political or a social perspective or even a psychological perspective. It doesn't matter what fiber connects the market; the fact remains that we are all interconnected. In the New World order, globalization has turned previously isolated problems (and opportunities) into everyone's problems. There is nowhere to hide.

Second, because the markets are all connected, the impact of what appears on the surface to be a somewhat minor isolated event—like Thailand devaluing its local currency (or a butterfly flapping its wings)—may first be felt by countries in close proximity—like Southeast Asia—but it is eventually felt around the globe in the world's largest market, the U.S. stock market.

Think of it this way: Every event around the globe will at some point in time impact any market—it may take a minute, a day, or even a year, but it will happen. Because all markets are now interconnected, there is no longer such a thing as an irrelevant or isolated event. There was a time when investors in the U.S. stock market didn't need to worry about what was happening in Mexico or Poland or Indonesia. Not anymore! Everything that happens anywhere around the globe will eventually have an impact either positive or negative on all markets.

Finally, don't forget the role technology is playing. Because of the information superhighway, we find out about things faster, which makes markets move even quicker, which makes them even more volatile. While the market pundits continue to argue whether this record bull market will continue or if we are now heading for a bear market, I would encourage you to forget about the bulls and the bears and to focus on the butterflies. For it is these global trends that will ultimately drive the markets over the next decade.

Remember, the long-term direction of the stock market is not determined by the economic releases that we worry about every week, nor is it determined by the never-ending stream of earnings reports with which we are bombarded on what at times seems like a daily basis. Now I do not mean to diminish the impact that these indicators do have on the markets. Their impact, however, is short term. These economic releases and earnings reports that we worry about every minute of every day simply help determine the short-term direction and the volatility of the market. The longer-term direction in the market is determined by global trends that impact the markets for decades, unlike these economic and earnings reports whose market impact diminishes after only a few short days.

Thus, if you can figure out what the next economic release or earnings report will be, you can probably figure out the direction of the market for the next few days. If, however, you can figure out the underlying global trends that are driving the markets, you just may be able to figure out the direction of the markets for the next decade or longer.

I think that the butterfly effect will create five dominant global trends in the next decade; and if you can identify and understand these trends, you will be able to understand why the greatest bull market is just beginning. These five global trends serve as the real foundation to move the markets forward. These global trends help identify markets, economies, and sectors that are best positioned to benefit from the ever-changing social, political, and economic trends.

Demographic Trends

The first global trend, which I explore in Chapter 1, focuses on the evolving demographic trends around the globe and their potential impact on the markets. I begin by looking at the demographic trends in the United States, first by looking at the "senior boom" in the United States. Sometimes we forget about the explosion of senior citizens, those aged 65 and over, when in fact two-thirds of all the people who have ever celebrated a 65th birthday in the history of time are still alive somewhere today. And in the United States the crossroads was hit in 1983. That was the year when, for the first time in U.S. history, there were more senior citizens than there were teenagers. That trend will not reverse itself for the next quarter of a century. Second, I will explore what I like to call the "birth bust" trend. In other words, there are not enough babies to replace all of these aging senior citizens. In fact, 25 percent of the baby boomers' families will be made up with just one child in the entire family, while another 20 percent of the baby boomers' families will be made up with no children at all. Third and finally, I explore the "baby boomers"—without a doubt, the most historic demographic trend the United States has ever witnessed. One out of every three people in the United States, myself included, is a baby boomer; they are 76 million strong.

Those of the "baby boom" generation have dramatically changed everything that they encountered as they moved along their life cycle. Think about it: In the 1950s the diaper industry came into existence to keep the boomers comfortable. Then in the 1960s the fast-food explosion was being fueled by 76 million teenagers who wanted their french fries and wanted them now! In the 1970s, as the boomers were becoming young adults, they fueled the real estate boom. Then in the 1980s, as they were trying to figure out how to get ahead in the business world, they supported the explosion of financial and business news. And in the 1990s, when they began focusing on saving and investing for their retirement, they fueled the U.S. stock market. In the next decade, their impact will continue to drive the markets and may even become more significant as saving and investing habits explode.

Next I explore the demographic trends in Europe. Although in general European demographics tend to mirror U.S. demographics, in many ways they also have their unique characteristics. For example, generation X will have a much greater impact in Europe than anywhere else. Generation Xers (teenagers) have two sources of income: a part-time job and an allowance from their parents. Together these two sources can combine to create tremendous spending power, especially when we realize that the economic impact of this money takes on even greater significance because teens do not have to pay the mortgage or the heating bill. Generation Xers spend their rising income entirely on discretionary items like clothes, cosmetics, fast food, and entertainment. And unlike their parents, generation Xers are not jaded, time-pressed consumers for whom shopping is a chore; on the contrary, going to the mall is actually a form of entertainment. I do consider myself somewhat of an expert on this because I have not one but two grown daughters who have logged their fair share of time and credit card receipts at our local mall. And because when teens are deciding what to buy they are shaping their personal appearance and personal identity during a very formative period in their lives, brands matter to teens more than prices.

Finally, I conclude Chapter 1 by analyzing the demographics of Asia and Latin America. Without a doubt the most historic demographic trend that Asia has ever faced is one I fondly refer to as the "Asian Roller Blade Generation." There are one billion Asians aged 10 to 24 (granted, not all will be on roller blades) at the start of the new millennium. And remember what it was like when you were aged 10 to 24? You bought beverages and food, you bought cosmetics, you bought cigarettes, you bought automobiles, you bought clothes, and you saved nothing. Thus these conditions set the stage for what could become one of the greatest consumption bubbles in the history of time. And last, I touch on Latin America, one of the world's key emerging markets, by focusing on how both children and senior citizens are now enjoying longer life expectancies.

Globalization Trends

In Chapter 2, I explore the second global trend, the globalization of economies and markets. There was a time when the focus regarding our global economy centered entirely on two regions: the United States (the world's largest economy) and Japan (the world's second-largest economy). However, with the fall of communism and the rise of capitalism around the world, we have witnessed a new economic and market force, emerging markets. And with the recent creation of the European Economic and Monetary Union (EMU), the 11 European countries that have joined together to create Euroland now have an economy larger than Japan's, and a population base larger than that of the United States.

Thus in the new global marketplace we can segment the world into four key regions: the United States, Euroland, Japan, and emerging markets. For each of these regions we will explore their unique trends, issues, developments, and opportunities, starting with the United States where I analyze workforce and employment shifts, with a focus on wage inflation. I then expand into how compensation changes could be driving the equity markets. Next I unlock the mystery of the U.S. trade deficit and explain why it is not a problem. I also look at some of the benefits to investors when the U.S. dollar weakens. The segment on the United States ends with a closer look at the consumer credit explosion and the supposedly poor savings rate in the United States.

Chapter 2 then moves on to Euroland, where I begin by setting the foundation with the new Economic and Monetary Union. I then focus on the European equity markets and discuss the emergence of a new shareholder focus just in time for the stock ownership boom that is being created in part by an explosion in retirement savings. I then take a closer look at reforms in Euroland: one that has happened, tax reform in Germany; and one that needs to happen, labor market reform. The section on Euroland ends with my warning about the Internet in Europe.

The third region that I explore in Chapter 2 is Japan. I begin with a brief historical perspective and evolve to two key influences in Japan, the aging demographics and the population density. No discussion of Japan would be complete without looking at its trading patterns. I will give you a perspective on why their trade surplus is nothing to be proud of. The section on Japan closes with a brief analysis of the changes in its banking system and a new source of money for the equity markets that was discovered at, of all places, the post office.

Chapter 2 concludes with my insights on emerging markets. After putting this vast market into perspective for you, I discuss one of the key safety features to this market, namely the International Monetary Fund (IMF). I then explore in detail the two largest of all emerging markets, China and Mexico. Chapter 2 ends by looking at how a non-financial risk (HIV/AIDS) may pose the greatest long-term financial risk to certain emerging markets.

Technology Trends

In Chapter 3, I explore the impact of the technology revolution, a revolution that will have an even more profound impact on our lives than the industrial revolution. At the center of this technology revolution is the Internet, probably the single greatest invention in our lifetime.

The impact of the Internet will be so great because its uses are so wide-range in scope. Most inventions improve our quality of life in some way, shape, or form; however, some have a greater impact than others. Airbags are a very useful product, especially if you're in a car crash; however, they have not had the same impact as the invention of the telephone or the television. The wheel, the steam engine, the harnessing of electricity—they have all been landmark inventions that have changed our lives forever with very far-reaching effects.

This wide-ranging potential is why the Internet will be the greatest invention in history. A new website is launched each minute on the Internet. The growth of the Internet will not be constrained by scarcity. Recall that *scarcity* was one of the key economic principles that formulated the concept from the "old school" of economic thinking that population will always increase faster than food supply. It was this theory, which was actually formulated by Thomas Malthus, that led academia to dub economics "the dismal science." But unlike food or clothing or other resources, the Internet is not constrained by scarcity. The Internet is an intellectual resource, not a physical one; and as such, it can be copied, downloaded, and recopied ad infinitum. Its supply of intellectual information will far exceed the demand. Thus there are no growth constraints on what the Internet or technology can accomplish.

Later in Chapter 3, I explore in detail the impact that our technology revolution is having on five key issues. First, I explore how technology is changing the retail sector. The basic cost for the traditional retailer continues to trend higher. Those traditional costs are bricks and mortar, real estate, people, and benefits and taxes. Meanwhile the key costs for Internet retailing—computer hardware, computer database software, and communications—are all going down. This divergent trend will change the face of the retail sector as we know it.

Second, I look at the global infrastructure needed to support this technology revolution. These infrastructure needs are the very basic needs of both developing countries and fully developed countries embracing the technology revolution. Thus, we will see an explosion of global infrastructure when basic telecommunication needs in developing countries converge with the information superhighway needs of developed countries.

Third, I look at productivity in the technology revolution. Remember this revolution is very different from the industrial revolution because it's less capital intensive, less energy intensive, and less labor intensive. Thus, it has dramatically different economic implications for productivity than we have ever experienced. Productivity traditionally has been defined as "output divided by input." Economic models of growth focused on labor and capital—an increase in both would increase output. The increased rate of investment, however, eventually ceased to yield greater returns on economic growth, hence the economic principle "the theory of diminishing returns." This model did not account for technological advancing investment.

Fourth, I analyze the impact that the technology revolution will have on the employment market. Technology is playing a key role in the downsizing and restructuring certain sectors. I explore whether technology is eliminating jobs or simply changing the economic structure so fast that even as technology makes some jobs obsolete it also creates new ones, with the net effect being adding jobs, not eliminating them.

Fifth and finally, I explore the impact that technology will have on the markets, focusing on how the technology revolution's foundation is really the increased capital outlay for more and improved computer hardware and software. This increased use of the latest and greatest hardware and software eventually increases productivity. When productivity increases, profits tend to rise. When profits rise, the prices of stocks as well as the overall market also rises. Could the real fuel behind this bull market be capital outlays for technology?

Government Trends

In Chapter 4, the focus shifts to government downsizing and privatization of traditional government functions around the globe. It was a confluence of three separate fronts that have combined to push government spending downward.

The first front was in 1994 in the United States with the Republican Party's sweep of the congressional elections. This election changed the playing field regarding the size of government. Prior to 1994 the debate centered on whether the size of government should be reduced. Now the debate focuses only on how much to reduce and how to go about it. Downsizing has made its transition from the private business sector to the public sector. As the political landscape will continue to change, it will be increasingly difficult to forecast exactly how much government will be cut. One thing is sure, however, and that is the fact that government spending will not be the engine of growth that it has been to the U.S. domestic economy since the 1960s.

The second front came from Europe on January 1, 1999, when 11 European countries—Austria, Belgium, Finland, France, Germany, Ireland, Italy, Luxembourg, the Netherlands, Portugal, and Spain—joined together to create the EMU. In order to be eligible for membership in the EMU, one of the key economic measures was that a country's budget deficit as a percent of its gross domestic product (GDP), the broadest measurement of an economy, must be only 3 percent or less. The target for EMU membership set a new benchmark for all governments to be judged against, whether they are a part of the EMU or not. With this new global benchmark, I simply cannot imagine the United States ever slipping back to where it was in 1943 when the budget deficit as a percent of GDP was an astounding 31 percent.

The third front came from the end of the Cold War in the 1990s. The beginning of the end started with the Soviet Communist Party relinquishing exclusive power on February 7, 1990. Next the Berlin Wall came tumbling down, and West Germany and East Germany were united on October 3, 1990. Finally, the Soviet Union was dissolved during December 1991 when the Soviet Republics became independent states. Without the Cold War threat, government outlays for defense spending began a major reversal.

It is also important to note the ripple effect of these events. When government downsizing occurs at the national level, it tends to work its way down to the state and local levels as well. All of a sudden, a wealth of capital is freed up for use in the private sector, not in a public spending program.

Business Trends

In Chapter 5, I explore the changing landscape of the size, the shape, and the form of companies in this New World order. It seems as though a day doesn't go by without a major corporate merger announcement. In fact, starting in 1991, every single year in the 1990s saw more mergers and acquisitions completed than the year prior did.

There are two major forces at work that are driving these mergers and acquisitions. First is the combination of global competition and no pricing power (or at the most, very limited pricing flexibility), which has put pressure on corporate profits as their results have fallen below investors' expectations. To offset these issues, companies are buying and merging with their competitors in order to build scale, cut overhead cost, and provide more pricing flexibility.

The second force is the desire to provide full-service, one-stop shopping to consumers. Think about it this way: If you are a bank, why not provide a mutual fund as well? And after you do that, what about life insurance and property and casualty insurance? And if you are going to do that, why not include an investment-banking arm for your corporate clients? This move to providing a full-service, umbrella-like solution to customer needs will continue to be a driving force for mergers and acquisitions.

Although there has been tremendous consolidation in some sectors, others have been left virtually untouched. There are more mergers and acquisitions in front of us than there are behind us. In addition, mergers are no longer restricted within country boundaries; in our global marketplace, different companies from all around the globe can potentially get together.

Sector Strategies

Then in Chapter 6, I share my latest investment discovery with you, *Sectornomics*™. *Sectornomics* means that the *sector* that you invest in will have the greatest *economic* impact on your investment performance, even greater than the impact of the individual company or the region of the world that you invest in.

I then put this new discovery to use as I explore which specific sectors are most likely to be the winners as a result of the global trends that I have discussed. Identifying global trends before they emerge is easy once you quit trying to convince yourself that the future will tend to look a lot like the past. Translating those global trends into specific strategies that highlight sector winners, however, is quite another matter.

I will reveal my top five investment strategies and sector winners:

> Strategy #1: We're not getting any younger!
>> Sector Winner: Pharmaceuticals.
> Strategy #2: Pretty soon the only road will be the information superhighway.
>> Sector Winner: Technology.
> Strategy #3: We're all connected.
>> Sector Winner: Telecommunications.
> Strategy #4: It doesn't hurt to save.
>> Sector Winner: Financial Services.
> Strategy #5: Plug it in and turn it on!
>> Sector Winner: Energy.

Investment Principles

Finally, in Chapter 7, I discuss the challenge that you will face trying to be a long-term investor in a short-term world. To help you stay a long-term investor, I reveal my six principles of long-term investing:

Principle #1: Fear and Greed.
Principle #2: You Are Going to Lose Money . . . I Guarantee It!
Principle #3: You Didn't Sell the House, Did You?
Principle #4: The Woodshop Syndrome.
Principle #5: There's Only One Way to Make a Billion Dollars.
Principle #6: Is Everything a Buy?

I close out the book with a quick look at the next generation of investors and then I disclose the most guarded secret to investing . . . Vitamin C!

At the end of each chapter I have a one-page notebook where I have captured for you what I feel are the most important insights from the preceding chapter. I call this "Dr. Bob's Notes—Top 10 Things to Remember."

And don't forget to look at the Glossary, where you will find one of the book's most unique features: *BobSpeak*™. Instead of your traditional, boring investment glossary, *BobSpeak* is actually a unique glossary of not simply investment terms, but also my opinions regarding the importance, the significance, and the relevance of those terms. I think it just might be the first opinionated glossary of investment terms. You won't want to miss it.

What you do next is up to you. I liken your decision to the story of two hunters deep in the forest who were getting ready to turn in for the night when suddenly a grizzly bear appeared in the distance and was fast approaching. One of the hunters jumped up out of his sleeping bag and immediately began putting on his Nike running shoes. The other hunter screamed at him, "You don't really think those running shoes will make you run faster than that grizzly bear, do you?" To which the other hunter replied, "I don't have to outrun the grizzly bear. I simply have to outrun you!" I want you to think of *Where the Money Is* as your pair of running shoes that can keep you ahead of other investors in the ever-changing social, economic, and political environment. Staying ahead means you can keep your eyes on identifying global trends that will help you develop a strategy that will recognize the specific sectors best poised to benefit from the changes affecting society in the next decade.

Don't forget to tie your running shoes!

Chapter 1

The Evolving Demographics Trends around the Globe

The man who views the world at 50 the same as he did at 20 has wasted 30 years of his life.

Muhammad Ali
Former World Heavyweight Boxing Champion

The words of wisdom from Muhammad Ali are an eloquent way of saying that demographics have the power to change the way we think. I on the other hand simply want to change the way you think about demographics.

Demographic Bias

Typically when investors such as yourself begin to think about what is going to drive the markets, they focus on the short-term topic of the week, whether it's interest rates, earnings reports, or the latest public policy proposal coming out of Washington, D.C. Few, if any, would say that they focus on demographics. Yet demographics just might be one of the most powerful long-term forces driving the markets. They also happen to be one of the least understood forces.

Part of the reason is that demographics are not one of the sciences that are looked up to anywhere in the world. You probably have your own bias against demographics, and you do not even realize it. Think of your bias against demographics this way. If someone in your neighborhood told you that she was going off to college to study medicine, you would be excited for her. Or if a friend told you that he was going away to study business or law, you would be equally excited. (Let me take that law part back; we already have too many lawyers.) Now think for a minute what your reaction would be when your neighbor told you that he was going away to college to study demographics. You would probably roll your eyes back and think to yourself, "Uh, demographics, isn't that where the people sit on the street corners and count how many cars turn left?"

Because the study of demographics is misunderstood, so too is their long-term impact on the markets and on investments. If you can step back from your bias regarding demographics, you will quickly realize that they just may be one of the most dynamic influences driving the markets.

Age Characteristics

Just think for a moment about the factors on which demographics and your age characteristics exert a major influence. First, like it or not, your age characteristics are a key determinant of your consumption patterns. Not many 16-year-olds buy reading glasses. Likewise, not many 60-year-olds buy acne cream. I've yet to see a 20-year-old searching for just the right hair product to wash the gray away.

Second, your level of savings and investing is greatly influenced by your age characteristics. Even though you may have great self-discipline and motivation to invest when you are younger, it is very difficult because there are higher priorities, whether it's raising your family or buying your first home. However, as you approach your fifties, you suddenly seem to be able to save and to invest more. It's not because you are more motivated; it's because your age characteristics are now playing in your favor to help you save and invest. When you are 50, your children are grown and about to leave home and start life on their own. This frees up a great deal of cash. Also, that home that you have been paying a mortgage on for what seems like forever is just about paid off, which also frees up your cash flow. And finally, at age 50, your employer pays you the financial rewards that you thought you deserved at age 22. Your age characteristics just might be the most important factor you need to understand saving and investing.

Third, your age characteristics will determine both the size and the makeup of your household. Very few 60-year-olds think of starting a family, whereas that is on the top of the list for most young adults in their twenties.

Fourth and finally, the age characteristics of a nation have a very strong influence on government policy. When a nation is driven by younger age characteristics, it spends money on schools and recreational programs. Meanwhile a nation that is driven by older age characteristics tends to spend its money on retirement and medical benefits.

And you thought that the demographic makeup of population didn't matter. Think about this for a minute. If you are an investor and you know what people are going to buy, what they are going to save and invest, how many houses there are going to be and how many people live in those houses, as well as what the government policies are going to be, why would you need to know anything else? Why are you so worried about a stock's price/earnings ratio or beta? Does it really matter if the Federal Reserve Board moves interest rates at their next meeting?

If I had a choice of something to focus on to drive investments, it certainly would not be price/earnings ratios. Instead, tell me what people are going to buy, what they are going to save and invest, how many houses there are going to be and how many people live in the houses, as well as what government policies are going to be. I then would be able to take these factors and determine the outlook for the overall market as well as the specific sectors that comprise the markets.

Before I try to convince you that demographics can drive the overall markets, let me start with smaller steps by showing you what the demographic trends have done to certain sectors in the United States. As these few sector examples will show, age characteristics will have a major impact on which sectors are investment winners and losers.

Discount Stores

When discount stores first appeared in the United States in the early 1980s as an investment, they were both very volatile and only marginally successful. Now they are one of the hottest investment themes anywhere. And they are making money. Why the change? Were they doing a better job of marketing? No. Were they doing a better job with inventory control? No. Did they develop some secret strategic plan for success? No. The fact of the matter is that they aren't doing anything different today than they were in the 1980s. Why are they profitable all of a sudden?

Well, one major thing did change . . . demographics. You see, when discount stores first appeared on the scene 15 to 20 years ago, baby boomers like myself didn't shop discount stores. Now that my wife and I have two daughters in college, we shop at discount stores, as do a lot of other baby boomers. You see, fundamentally the buying power of this younger generation is no longer so young, nor is it any longer so freespending. When this age group starts worrying about saving for their children's college or paying off their mortgage, they usually end up at discount stores.

Fundamentally this accounts for only one of the two major shifts on the demographic front that are driving the success of discount stores. The second has to do with senior citizens. When discount stores first appeared, senior citizens wanted no part of them, and why would they. You have worked hard your entire life, and now you get to shop in some cement floor warehouse where everything is packed so high to the sky you cannot even read the labels? I don't think so, and neither did they. Something amazing has happened to those senior citizens of 15 years ago who boycotted the discount stores. They are still alive today—many of them didn't count on that. In addition to still being alive, many of them are still living on that same fixed income of 15 years ago. The number-one shopper in discount stores today is aged 65 and older. And why not? If the older generation is now living longer on its same fixed income, it would make sense that as part of the aging process, senior citizens are becoming even more selective in their spending habits. In other words, they too are becoming discount shoppers.

It's all about demographics. Even though the underlying theme and target of discount stores has not changed, the people who fit into the cost-conscious-buyer category are greatly expanding. Both of these demographic shifts with the baby boomers and senior citizens are creating an expanding universe of potential customers for discount stores.

Food

In the investment world, the food sector is perceived as one of the more boring sectors in the United States market. If you are a young investment analyst, you want to cover technology or financial services or telecommunications—anything but the food group. In fact, if you are an analyst and find yourself assigned to the food group, you'd better get your resume together—your next move is usually out the door. All of that is about to change, however. The food sector is about to become one of the more exciting and dynamic sectors because of one simple fact—demographics.

For the first time in the United States, there is a group of 18-to-24-year-olds coming into their adult years as the first generation to be raised by "working moms." In other words, 18-to-24-year-olds were raised with "meals on the run."

Think about how this generation goes grocery shopping. They stroll right past all of the meat, raw baking ingredients, and other basic cooking materials and head straight for the precooked ham or prebaked turkey or the ready-to-go salad bar deluxe. This generation knows that an oven can be used for something—they are just not sure what. This is the microwave generation. The food sector must reach out to this group who are much more proficient using microwaves than traditional ovens.

Fifty years ago the average homemaker spent over 2.5 hours (150 minutes) preparing the family dinner. Today the average homemaker spends less than 20 minutes preparing the family dinner. Remember the Saturday morning cartoons you watched growing up as a kid—the way the Jetsons prepared meals in one second and that seemed as if it were light-years away? Well, guess what! It's almost here. We have only another 19 minutes and 59 seconds to go. If you don't think demographics can turn a sector on its head, consider this fact: By the year 2005 a majority of homemakers (over 50 percent) will have never ever cooked a meal from basic ingredients. This demographic shift will change the food sector forever. Even though the food sector has been besieged by years of slow growth. Look for consumer spending on ready-made food to accelerate in the next 10 years. This growth again will be driven by demographics.

Health Clubs

Did you ever wonder why health clubs began popping up everywhere? All of a sudden there are health clubs in hotels. Heck, there are even health clubs in most major office buildings today.

As a nation, did the United States all of a sudden decide that it needed health clubs everywhere, or did demographics play the key role? First, when you get older, your metabolism slows down. And when your metabolism slows down, something that you used to be able to eat without it ever showing is suddenly appearing on your waist-line. Second, when you were younger, you always seemed to have more time on your hands to exercise and to keep fit. As you grow older, the demand on your time becomes even greater, and thus the opportunity to find time to exercise is less and less frequent.

Think about it: The boomers in their forties all of a sudden putting on those extra pounds and taking on that shape that they thought only affected their parents, never them. Combine this with the fact that they are so busy, stretched between business and personal commitments, that there is no time left for them to exercise and stay fit.

What jumps up to fill this demographic need? You guessed it, the health club. Now you can go to the club at 5 A.M. before you leave for work. Or you can go to the club in your office complex during lunch hours. Traveling? No problem, just swing by the hotel health club. If the hotel doesn't have one on site, I'm willing to bet that they have made arrangements for their hotel guests to use the facilities at a nearby health club. It's not just about getting fit; it's about getting older.

Drugs

I have no idea which drug company is going to discover the next wonder drug. Nor do I know which drug company will merge with which to create the new global leader. What I do know is that demographics are making the pharmaceutical sector a great place to invest. In the United States, from the time of birth until children celebrate their fifth birthday, parents give their children on average eight different prescription drugs a year. For the next 40 years, however, that trend line is on a downward slope and never breaks trend. And no one is exactly sure just why. Are they simply healthier? Or did they just stop going to visit the doctor? Or do they no longer listen to their parents when it comes to health matters? It is most likely a combination of the three.

Something magical, however, happens at age 45. At age 45 the worm turns and that trend reverses itself. For the rest of their lives, the amount of prescription drugs they use each year will accelerate. This trend currently plateaus at age 75. The average 75-year-old in the United States currently uses 18 different prescription drugs a year. That trend helps to explain why with only 5 percent of the world's population the United States accounts for over 40 percent of the world's pharmaceutical sales. Meanwhile Africa, which has over 13 percent of the world's population, accounts for less than 1% of the world's pharmaceutical market.

Retirement and Nursing Homes

As the graying of America takes hold, it becomes pretty simple to figure out what is going to be the next sector that is impacted. After all, those baby boomers that overcrowded the nation's school systems in the 1950s and the 1960s have to go somewhere.

And where they are going is where we all eventually go as we get older and can no longer take care of ourselves—a retirement or nursing home. As the United States gets older, industry must prepare to take care of this baby boom generation in a very different way. The aging demographics in the United States should spell a real boom for the retirement and nursing home sector in the next decade.

Three Shifts, Not One

When someone mentions demographics, investors immediately think baby boomers. Who are these baby boomers anyway? Being a baby boomer myself, I am well equipped to give you the official definition of a baby boomer. Anyone who was born in the United States between 1946 and 1964 is a baby boomer! During that 19-year period there were

76 million children born. In order to put the magnitude of this boom in perspective for you, you have to go back to the 19-year period prior to 1946, that being 1927 to 1945. There were less than 49 million babies; then in the next 19-year period, 1946 to 1964, there are over 76 million babies. Now that's a baby boom. However, to truly understand the impact of demographics in the United States, you cannot simply look at the baby boomers in isolation. The fact is that there are three separate and unprecedented demographic trends that are converging to actually turn the demographics of the United States upside down. These three trends—(1) a senior boom, (2) a birth bust, and (3) the aging of the baby boomers—highlight the virtual boom or bust scenario of U.S. demographics. Make no mistake about it; it is the confluence of these three trends that are changing the way Americans live and the way they work, and ultimately it should also change the way they invest.

Senior Boom

Back in the Stone Age people lived only until the age of 20. By the time the United States was founded in 1776, a child born there could expect to live to be 35. One hundred years later, in 1876, life expectancy had increased to the ripe old age of 40! Did you ever wonder why the United States didn't have individual retirement accounts (IRAs) or 401(k)s back then? You didn't need them. Everyone died before they could even think about retiring. Look what's happening now. A child born in the United States today can expect to live to be at least 76. Now think about this for a minute: It took one hundred years, from 1776 to 1876, for the average life expectancy to be increased by five years. Then all of a sudden, in the next hundred-plus years, life expectancy in the United States almost doubled—from 40 to 76.

This senior boom is not simply occurring in isolation in the United States. Global aging is a phenomenon that is affecting the entire industrialized world. When we use the term *industrialized world*, we are talking about members of the Organization of Economic Cooperation and Development (OECD). Countries that are currently a part of the OECD are Australia, Austria, Belgium, Canada, Denmark, Finland, France, Germany, Greece, Iceland, Ireland, Italy, Japan, Luxembourg, the Netherlands, New Zealand, Norway, Portugal, Spain, Sweden, Switzerland, the United Kingdom, and of course the United States.

In 1960, senior citizens (I am defining a *senior citizen* as anyone 65 years of age and older) accounted for only 9.2 percent of the entire population in the industrialized world. Thirty years later, in 1990, senior citizens accounted for 13.3 percent of the population in the industrialized world. And 30 years after that, senior citizens will account for more than one-fifth of the entire population in the industrialized world. Yes, by 2020, senior citizens will account for an astonishing 20.2 percent of the industrialized world's population!

Consider this: Two-thirds of all of the men and women who have lived to celebrate their 65th birthday in the entire history of time are still alive today. Think about this for a minute. Throughout the entire history of recorded time, two thirds of all people who have celebrated a sixty-fifth birthday are still alive somewhere today. I'm guessing Phoenix. If you haven't been there in a while, be careful; those buzzing golf carts are more dangerous than any New York cabbie!

Again, throughout all of recorded time, only one in ten people could expect to live to the age of 65. Today, eight out of every ten Americans will celebrate their 65th birthday.

The United States actually hit its reflection point in 1983. In 1983 the number of Americans over the age of 65 surpassed the number of teenagers for the first time in U.S. history. You can say that in 1983 the United States hit the demographic crossroads. Oh, and by the way, that trend of having more Americans aged 65 and over than teenagers will not reverse itself during the lifetime of anyone who reads this book.

Here is something else very, very interesting to ponder. Once you reach the age of 65, your life expectancy is now a whopping 86 years in the United States. Not only will the United States have senior citizens, but it will have some very old senior citizens as well. I refer to this demographic phenomenon as the "Canes to Diapers Ratio." The canes represent the most "senior" senior citizens, those that are age 80 and over, while the diapers represent the youngest youths, those age 5 and under.

In 1970 there were 17.2 million diapers to only 3.7 million canes. In other words, there were only 3.7 million people aged 80 and over, while there were 17.2 million children age 5 and younger. By the year 2040 this ratio will also hit the crossroads. The United States will finally have more canes than diapers. In the year 2040 there will be 25 million youths aged 5 and younger, while there will be an almost unheard of 26.2 million "senior" senior citizens. The United States is no longer a nation of youths. There have been demographic baby booms before, but there has never ever been a senior boom.

One of the best barometers of how important any social issue will become is the number of people who study it. In the United States they got real serious about senior citizens for the first time in 1935, the year they adopted Social Security. In the five years after the passage of Social Security, only 10 scholars in the United States chose aging as their subject for a doctoral dissertation. On the contrary, in the past five years alone, there have been over 3,000 such studies. In the next decade, aging will become one of the fastest growing areas of study, maybe even surpassing technology. You need to understand that when you reach the age of 65, you really don't care anymore that the VCR clock is still flashing 12:00; you can't see the little thing anyway. What you want is a few more years to live. There is hope for all of us that can't figure out the VCR clock; technology is moving so fast that the VCR will be outdated in the next decade anyway and no one will have to worry about the dumb clocks, whether you're a senior citizen or not! If it weren't for our younger daughter, our VCR clock would never have the right time.

By now you are probably thinking to yourself, Okay, this is great, the United States has a lot of old people running around. But what in the world does that have to do with investing? You're searching for investment ideas. Well, remember that some of the very best investment ideas are the ones that are usually right in front of your face. Consider these two facts regarding the senior boom. First, the average age of the buyer of an American made luxury car is over 65. Remember, that's the average age. Second, grandparents buy over 40 percent of all of the toys sold (and that number will definitely go up when my daughters have children, and my wife and I go toy shopping as grandparents). So you are still searching for some investment idea? What about all of those people with gray hair driving around in brand new Cadillacs with all of the Wal-Mart toys in the back? Maybe, just maybe, they are trying to send you an investment idea.

Birth Bust

A little over a decade ago, the fertility ratio in the United States plummeted to its lowest point in history. This ratio, which has continued to hover right around its historic lows, is not likely to change anytime soon. The reason is that the senior boom I just discussed is not being offset by an explosion of children. In fact, 20 percent of the baby boomers' families will have no children in them at all, while another 25 percent of the baby boomers' families will be made up with just one child. I refer to this phenomenon as the birth bust. Now there are probably a hundred different theories as to why this birth bust is happening in the United States.

Some say it was the Vietnam War. They say it scared people away from having large families with the prospects of a major war on the horizon. And they point to the shrinkage of births during the Vietnam War years as their proof. Others point to the "women's movement" as the key. They theorized that once the women's movement took off, women no longer wanted to stay home and raise children, so the real cause of the birth bust is the women's movement.

I do not believe that the birth bust in the United States has anything to do with either of these. The U.S. birth bust is not about Vietnam, nor is it about the "women's movement." The birth bust is all about the economy—or I should more appropriately say the evolution of the U.S. economy. Think about how the economy has evolved. When the United States was founded back in 1776, it had an agricultural economy driven by the farm. That agricultural economy then evolved into an industrial-based economy driven by factories, production, and productivity. That industrial-based economy has finally evolved into a service-and-information-based economy driven by technology and the explosion of the Internet. So over the years, the United States evolved from an agricultural to an industrial to a service-and-information-based economy.

Think about what this evolution means to birthrates. In an

agricultural-based economy driven by the farm, the single most important asset is cheap, unskilled labor. Can you think of a better source for
cheap unskilled labor than one's own children? Listen to me—in an agricultural economy driven by the farm, having a large number of healthy
children was not simply an advantage, it was an economic necessity. You
could not survive in an agricultural-based economy without a lot of
children. The farm would not survive, the economy would not survive,
and maybe even the nation would have had trouble surviving.

Look what happens, however, when a nation evolves from an agri-
cultural- and industrial-based economy to where it is today, a service-
and-information-based economy. You need to understand that I have
two grown daughters, and I love them dearly; however, they didn't add
to the economy, they subtracted from it. In a service-and-information-
based economy, children become an increasing economic hardship. A
child today represents tremendous long-term cost with no economic
return. Thus, I contend that it is the cost of raising children that is at
the heart of this birth bust. I don't see it getting any cheaper in the future to raise children; thus I think this birth bust trend will be with us
for a while. The era of the United States as a youth-focused nation is
coming to an end, and it will not be seen again in our lifetimes. Do not
forget that when women moved quickly into the mainstream of the
workforce, a new and additional cost was added to raising children.
The newly working mother would now have to spend a major part of
her newfound earnings on childcare.

And remember, divorce rates are also exploding. The ripple effect
of higher divorce rates means that more and more adults find themselves in unstable relationships. Adults in unstable relationships do not
tend to bring children into the world. And even though Vietnam is
behind them, the real threat was never Vietnam, the real threat was and
continues to be nuclear war. People living in the fear or threat of nuclear
war tend to have a lot of questions about having children.

This birth bust also brings with it tremendous ramifications for the
workforce, especially when you overlay it with the senior boom going
on around the globe. I call this the new "work shift." We used to think
of work shifts as working the 8 A.M. to 4 P.M. shift, or the 4 P.M. to midnight shift, or the midnight to 8:00 A.M. shift. My work shift focuses on

the shift on workers. By the year 2030 there will be an unprecedented global shift in the workforce in the industrialized world. For purposes of my "work shift" I consider working age to be age 15 to age 64 and retirement age to be 65. In the industrialized world in the year 2030, there will be 34 million fewer working-age people. Meanwhile the retirement population in the industrialized world will have 89 million more retirement-age citizens. This work shift may be the single greatest challenge we face as a result of the birth bust trend.

Aging of the Baby Boomers

The most dramatic and influential demographic trend in the history of the United States has been the baby boomers. And as the baby boomers are aging, they are prepared to write their final and most dramatic chapter yet influencing the social, the business, and the political fibers of that nation for the next quarter-century.

Now I know that there continue to be a lot of doubters out there that feel that the baby boomers are not going to have any impact. It's just something everyone's talking about, similar to the Y2K millennium bug; but at the end of the day, it will have little, if any, impact. Well, doubters, I would remind you that unlike the Y2K millennium bug, there is not one but 76 million baby boomers in the United States. They were born between 1946 and 1964. The generation prior to the baby boomers, those born between 1927 and 1945, numbered only 49 million. And you wonder why it's called it a baby boom? Looked at another way, over one-third of all living Americans today are baby boomers. When one-third of a country's population can be categorized or classified into any one group, not only will that group have a great influence, but every single thing it touches will be changed forever. The baby boomers have redefined every stage of their life. You see, when a few hundred people share an idea it is interesting, when a few thousand people share an idea, it may even amount to a trend; when a few million people share an idea, it's a movement. However, when 76 million people share an idea, it's a revolution.

To clearly understand what this revolution is going to mean going forward, maybe we should start by looking backward. At every single stage of their lives, the needs and desires of the baby boomers have become the dominant concerns of American business and political leaders. The only thing is we just didn't give the baby boomers credit for all of those changes. Let's take a quick look at what these baby boomers did on a decade-by-decade basis since they first arrived in the 1950s.

The Baby-Focused Decade of the 1950s

In the 1950s when the baby boomers first arrived on the scene, something happened that had never before occurred in the history of the United States. There was a diaper industry. Not only was there a new sector, but it was a profitable sector as well. Think about it for a minute: With 76 million children, a diaper industry all of a sudden makes all the sense in the world.

And their influence didn't stop there, it was just beginning. As these young baby boomers began to walk, their parents had to put shoes on them. The baby shoe sector began an explosive growth rate that it had never seen before, nor has it seen since.

Don't forget that when these baby boomers took their first steps, they also had to record this moment for prosperity. Thanks also to some technological advancements, the photo sector took off as well. After all, they had 76 million first steps to capture, and 76 million first days at school, and 76 million first lost tooths and so on and so on. It's no wonder that cameras were popping up everywhere. In fact, the turning point for the camera industry was this explosive growth spurt in the 1950s.

Now that they have shoes on them and have taken pictures of them, do not forget that they still have to nourish them. Yes, you guessed it; the canned baby food industry was also born. It exploded on to the scene with rapid growth as this sector struggled to keep up with the changing demands of different flavors and varieties that these young baby boomers were demanding. Continuing on this food theme, by the late 1950s the newest food invention was sugarcoated cereals. Why do you think these young baby boomers were so hyper and energetic? They were the first generation to be sugar charged every morning with a vast variety of sugarcoated cereals. If you turned on your black-and-white television set in the middle to late 1950s, almost every single commercial on Saturday morning was for some brand of sugarcoated cereal!

The final sea change that occurred in the 1950s was in the practice of medicine. Not only did parents need to clothe and feed these baby boomers, but they also had to care for their health and well-being. Created just in time to serve this newfound need of 76 million children was the practice of pediatric medicine. When you have 76 million children with a cold and a runny nose, creating a medical practice exclusively for children is a no-brainer.

The Child-and-Teen-Focused Decade of the 1960s

No more diapers, no more baby food. These baby boomers were setting their sights on new things to change in the 1960s. Elementary school buildings sprang up all across the United States. It was the biggest elementary school building binge ever in the United States. It is unlikely that there will ever be one like it again. After all, how many times in a country's history do you think they are confronted with having to find enough classrooms for 76 million students? Also don't forget that when you are a child, you love to be entertained. With that in mind, the 1960s saw a new wave of toys that not only dominated but overwhelmed the marketplace. It started out with hula hoops, and before the boomers knew it, this craze took over the entire country. Well, what did you expect? With 76 million children wanting hula hoops, this new toy was immediately destined to become a landmark of American culture. Quickly following the hula hoop craze came the Barbie Doll and skateboards. Each one in its own special way was more successful than the one preceding it.

Finally don't forget what these baby boomers did as they were becoming teenagers. Do you know the one thing that every teenager loves to eat? They love to eat whatever is not good for them (french fries, greasy hamburgers, fried chicken, pizza), and they want it fast. Think about this. From the 1960s on almost every street corner, up popped another fast-food restaurant. You don't think that this fast-food explosion had anything to do with the quality of the food do you? Absolutely not—the quality of the food was terrible then, and it is still terrible today, although it is improving. This fast-food sector explosion had everything to do with 76 million teenagers wanting to eat their french fries and wanting to eat them fast! Yes, indeed, it was the baby boomers who made millionaires out of the founders of McDonald's and Kentucky Fried Chicken.

The Young-Adult-Focused Decade of the 1970s

These baby boomers were no longer teenagers; they were now young adults. And when you are a young adult, you want to settle down, get married, and raise a family. With this being your new focus, your new number-one priority becomes buying a house. The real estate explosion the country witnessed in the 1970s was all about the baby boomers. It had absolutely nothing to do with the economy in the 1970s. And there was no special way to close real estate deals in the 1970s that fueled this explosive growth. Real estate agents were there to benefit from this housing boom, but they certainly didn't cause it. In fact, they didn't have anything to do with it!

The real estate explosion in the 1970s had everything to do with 76 million baby boomers wanting to buy a home and wanting to buy it now! With 76 million people wanting to buy a home, real estate prices had nowhere to go but up. Want proof that the baby boomers caused the real estate explosion of the 1970s? In the 1970s the value of real estate increased in every single state in the United States, and that includes West Virginia. Who else other than a boomer would want real estate in West Virginia (besides maybe my baby boomer wife, Cheryl, who was born in the lovely state of West Virginia)?

Now many of you may be wondering when the real estate market will be coming back and booming like the 1970s. I can help you with that answer—never. That's right, never, because the United States never again will have 76 million baby boomers wanting to buy a house and wanting it now!

The Adult-Focused Decade of the 1980s

Now that these baby boomers had their homes and started to raise their families, they were focusing their attention on how to get ahead in the business world. They were suddenly being transformed from the "hippies" of the 1960s to the "yuppies" of the 1980s.

The 76 million baby boomers were now focusing on their careers and trying to figure out how to advance them. Seemingly out of nowhere comes financial news networks like CNBC and CNN. Why? Well, because you had 76 million people trying to figure out how to get ahead in the business world. In addition, the *Wall Street Journal* hit all-time subscription highs as it entered a period of record growth. *Forbes* magazine also hit all-time subscription highs, as it too entered a decade of record growth in subscription levels. All because 76 million people wanted to get ahead in the business world.

Another trend evolved in the 1980s—many of these baby boomer families were two-income families. Thus, for the first time a majority of families found themselves with both the husband and the wife working outside the home. Popping up to fill this newfound need were child care centers and day care centers. It was the baby boomers' focus on their two-income lives that created the day care sector.

The Mature-Adult-Focused Decade of the 1990s

As the baby boomers approach the magical half-century mark, they get serious and focus on one thing . . . retirement. And when you worry about retirement, you are really worrying about having enough money for retirement, so you really begin to focus on investments and the markets. The great bull market of the 1990s was driven only partly by low inflation or low interest rates of the new global economy. The great bull market of the 1990s was the result of one simple fact: 76 million baby boomers worrying about their retirement and realizing that the only way they can accumulate enough money is to be in the stock market.

And, boy, were they in the stock market in a big way in the 1990s. Just look at what the Dow Jones Industrial Average accomplished in the 1990s. In 1991 it crossed 3,000. Four years later in 1995 it crossed both 4,000 and 5,000. In 1996 it crossed 6,000. The very next year, 1997, it crossed both 7,000 and 8,000. In 1998 it crossed 9,000; and as the decade closed in 1999, it crossed the seemingly insurmountable landmark of 10,000 on the Dow!

Don't worry, the baby boomers are nowhere near being done yet. They haven't stopped driving the stock market to all-time highs—they have just started.

You see, beginning January 1, 1996, every single minute of every single day for the next 10 years, seven more baby boomers turn 50 years of age. Think about it: Since you started reading this chapter, more than a hundred more baby boomers are over the hill at age 50.

And guess what! When the baby boomers cross that magical half-century mark, they get even more worried about retirement, and they will be putting even more money into the stock market. And do not forget that these over-50 baby boomers have more money than ever before in their lifetime to plow into the stock market. The reason is the confluence of factors that due to demographics are now playing in their favor.

First of all, the kids are gone. When you reach the age of 50, your children tend to be almost grown up and ready to move out of the house and be on their own. While this "empty nest" saga can be a tremendous emotional strain (my wife and I simply can't imagine our two girls finally being gone from the house), there is a financial strain that goes away as well. Raising children is a costly endeavor. When they finally grow up and are on their own, that frees up a significant source of cash flow that now can make its way to the stock market.

Second, when you reach 50, your home is usually paid for or close to being paid off. There was a time when this mortgage payment was the single greatest financial burden that you had to face every single month. Now you wake up one day, and it's gone. Picking up the void once again is—you guessed it—the stock market.

Third and finally, at age 50, you are at your peak earning years. You see, something magical happens at age 50. Your employer finally pays you what you thought you were worth at age 22. It only took them an additional 28 years to realize how much talent you really had brought to the table.

Also, never lose focus of the fact that it's not just the overall market. Think about this specific sector impact for a moment. Baby boomers are probably going to be the most active 50-year-olds who ever lived. One thing that they are absolutely intent on is feeling youthful and not looking anything like their parents. Did you ever think of this: Perhaps the four-wheel-drive sports utility vehicle craze became so popular because baby boomers were apprehensive about driving the same station wagons their parents drove!

The Senior-Citizen-Focused Decades Ahead

As these baby boomers become card-carrying senior citizens, they will be unlike any group of senior citizens before. First, this group is not going to stand for gray hair and wrinkles. Instead of "working" in the traditional workplace, think of these senior citizens as focusing on working at playing. And finally, they are going to be around a whole lot longer than previous demographic waves of senior citizens. Thus, unlike previous senior citizen groups, not only will these baby boomer seniors be focused on spending, they will still be focused on saving and investing as well. However, they will need help.

Travel and Entertainment

One thing is for certain; this group of baby boomer senior citizens will be turning the travel and entertainment sector upside down. They have always wanted to be entertained all throughout their lives. Now, along with entertainment, they will be traveling more than ever before.

It's a confluence of three factors that cause a likely boom in travel. First is the mobility of families today. Remember, these baby boomer parents never settled far from their birthplace. Family reunions and visits to kin were relatively easy—all you had to do was simply drive across town, and you could see probably everyone. That's not the case anymore. These baby boomers taught their children to be totally independent and to follow their dreams no matter where they lead them. Thus the United States now has a group of senior citizens whose children and grandchildren are spread out all across the country and maybe even around the globe. It's a whole lot easier for the retired grandparents to travel to see the family than it is for the family to come to them. This very well could be the first generation of "grannies on the go." Unlike their parents, who expected all family visits to occur back at their house, these seniors will be happy to hit the road making the tour of all family and extended-family stops.

Second, the globalization of the world's economies has opened up new avenues to travel and explore around the world. As capitalism and, more important, tourism are embraced as a way of life, these seniors will want to see it all and experience it all in their lifetime. Instead of the travel-worn, weary-eyed grandparent getting off the Greyhound bus after a long trip, maybe these seniors will be flying a new airline called "Grandparents 'R Us," exclusively catering to senior citizens flying around the country visiting family. Who knows—maybe instead of in-flight movies, it will be in-flight slide shows of everyone's families.

Third and finally, these baby boomer seniors are affluent, and thus they have the disposable income both to be entertained and to travel. If ever there was a generation that would pay to have a vacation week-end "on the moon," this generation is it. After all, the baby boomers grew up living the dream that President John F. Kennedy planted in their minds regarding space travel. This generation will not stand for letting any other generation beat it to trips in outer space.

Health and Fitness

One thing that money cannot buy (well, there are actually two; however, I do not have the time to talk about love here) is your health. Make no mistake about it; these baby boomers didn't lead a healthy life just so that they could sit around playing checkers when they retire. They intend to continue to be extremely active, and the only way that can happen is to keep up their health focus.

This was not a passing fad. These baby boomer senior citizens will force every senior citizen center to have state-of-the-art workout equipment and health club facilities. They also know that one of the keys to a healthy lifestyle lies in what you eat. These baby boomer seniors will continue to eat right and eat healthy, changing the focus of the food sector forever.

Financial Advice

Historically when someone reaches the age of 65, they are not too worried about investing and saving; they are more worried about making sure that their last will and testament is in order. Not anymore. When these boomers reach the young age of 65, that means that their life expectancy is now 86. In other words, they have 21 more years to live, so they better continue to save and invest some. The only problem is that these seniors want to travel and be entertained. They don't want to worry about every nuance of the market. Enter the stockbroker turned financial advisor. This dinosaur is back from the possible extinction list and will be one of the best possible sectors to be involved with. Remember, when you are busy ruling the world, you convince yourself that the future will always look like the past. You see, that is why the dinosaurs never saw it coming! The stockbrokers however are not dinosaurs. They did see it coming and they evolved from a transaction-oriented stockbroker to a value-added financial advisor. The baby boomer seniors will have more financial and market information at their fingertips than any generation ever. The only problem is that they don't have the time to process it. Look for these senior citizens to turn their financial well-being over to a financial advisor, and the brokerage industry will witness an unbelievable growth spurt. In addition, don't forget that this baby boom senior citizen generation is the first generation in U.S. history that will accumulate more wealth than the generation that follows it. Looked at another way, "transfer of wealth" is more important to this generation than any generation in history. To transfer your wealth in the most efficient and effective way possible, you need the help of a financial advisor. Maybe the biggest legacy that the baby boomers will leave is that they will make the stockbroker-turned-financial-advisor into one of the most important and respected sectors in the world . . . certainly a rightful place for a professional caring for the "financial health" of 76 million people.

Another reason for the financial advisor boom is the complexity in the baby boomers' life. Think about it: These baby boomer senior citizens have an extremely complex life, and they want it simplified, especially from a financial investment perspective. Every minute of every single day, somewhere, some market is open and something is happening that will impact their investments. They need someone to simplify their life that everywhere they turn gets more and more complex.

When these boomers grew up, the choice of coffee was pretty simple—do you want it black or do you use cream or sugar? There was no decaf coffee. And there was no sweetener substitute. Think of all the decisions this baby boomer senior citizen will have to make to get a simple cup of coffee at Starbucks. Who knows, but by the time they are through, they will have probably ordered a double decaf, grande latte, double skim mocha with raspberry syrup, and whipped cream with a touch of nutmeg cinnamon.

Then they go to the greeting card store to pick up a simple card for a "friend." Suddenly they are frozen like reindeer in the headlights of a car—they can't move. You see, they have to decide whether that card is for a "friend," an "old friend," a "good friend," "a best friend," "like family friend," "used to be a friend/friend again friend." So they do nothing—after all you wouldn't want to send a "good friend" card to someone who thought he or she was your "best friend." These baby boomers senior citizens are tired of life's complexity. They want someone to order their coffee for them, pick up their greeting cards, and, most important, take responsibility for their financial assets and financial well-being for the rest of their life!

The European Demographic Landscape

Across the Atlantic Ocean in Europe, something else was going on. Economics, markets, and demographics have changed dramatically over the 50-plus years since the end of World War II. Remember that in the very early days of the post–World War II era, the focus was pretty simple and very, very parochial. You may remember it as, "To the victor belong the spoils." Thus while the United States was basking in the new industrial renaissance unchallenged at home and abroad, a demographic baby boom occurred in the United States. In war-ravaged Europe, however, there was an obvious and urgent focus on reconstruction aimed at restoring the countries' economies so that once again there could be income generation and wealth creation. Their postwar baby boom would have to wait. And to further complicate things in Europe, most countries embraced elaborate subsidy and regulatory schemes in order to pull their sagging economies up by their bootstraps. However, what these countries also did was limit the impact of market forces on European companies and European economies.

Introducing Generation X

The teenage generation in Europe will be one of the key driving demographic forces there in the next decade.

A majority of the teens in Europe work at part-time jobs in addition to going to school. In addition to their employment income, most teens receive a weekly allowance. When you combine these two sources of income, together you can begin to realize the potential economic and market impact of generation X in Europe.

This potential economic and market influence increases in magnitude when you realize that they do not have to pay a mortgage bill or a heating bill or a telephone bill. Teenagers spend their entire rising income levels on discretionary items like clothes, cosmetics, fast food, and entertainment. But most important, unlike their parents, teenagers are not jaded, time-pressed consumers for whom shopping is a chore. On the contrary, shopping is actually considered a form of entertainment.

It is also important to understand how they shop. If they do happen to save money on one item, they immediately spend the potential savings on something else. For any of you who don't have teenagers, you might not be grasping this concept as well as I have. This is one area on which I consider myself a resident expert because, you see, I have not one but two grown daughters (who were once teenagers) that were very well trained by my wife on this concept.

Let me explain the teenage shopping logic to you this way. When my older daughter was a sophomore, she went to her first high school prom. Now before she went shopping for her dress (which I have since come to find out is a real ritual), I explained to her that she was not getting married, she was just going to a prom. I gave her the gold Mastercard to buy a nice new dress and explicitly told her that she didn't need to buy shoes and a purse, and so on, and so on, that she has plenty of shoes and purses at home already. I thought that everyone understood this simple teenage shopping pep talk, and so then my wife and both of my then-teenage daughters went off to the mall. The younger teenage daughter went along for moral support and also used it as a hands-on training session.

Hours later, when they finally returned, my daughter not only had a formal gown, but shoes, a new purse, and a brand new rhinestone necklace to boot! Needless to say, I was in shock. However, before I could say anything, my daughter said, "Dad, you will be so proud of me. You will never guess what happened. I found this awesome dress that was reduced by $80. So with the $80 I saved you, I was able to buy the shoes and purse that you didn't want me to buy and even had enough left over for this rhinestone necklace that I didn't even know I wanted . . . so we're even!" Now that's what the teenage shopping concept is all about.

However, it doesn't stop with just the potential economic impact in Europe. Think of what this might mean to certain segments of the market. You see, you have to remember that when teenagers are deciding what to buy, they are shaping their personal appearance and personal identity during a very formative period in their lives as well. Because they are shaping their personal identity, one of the most important things to teenage shoppers is brand—not price. Brands matter a lot to teenagers.

For a peek at how this could impact the market, simply consider what brands mean the most to teenagers. When teenagers were asked to name the specifics that are considered "cool," the teens' top-five responses in order of importance were: Nike, Guess, Levi's, Gap, and Sega. And you are still wondering what is on the minds of most teenagers? I don't know—let's think that four of the five "coolest" brands are clothing labels. Could they be developing their personal identity by the clothes they wear?

Now don't read this the wrong way. I am not suggesting that you invest in these companies. Heck, I don't even know their price/earnings ratio or the stock's beta or even the capitalization level.

All I know is that teenagers spend money on what they think is cool. And if they think Nike, Guess, Levi's, Gap, and Sega is cool, I think as investors we should all take notice.

Color Europe Gray as Well

Like the United States, Europe has a growing senior citizen population that, going forward, will have a greater and greater impact because Europe has also witnessed a slowdown in birth rates. This demographic problem in Europe was caused by much different factors than those that caused the senior boom in the United States.

In Europe most of the government laws and policies were crafted in such a way as to protect European workers whenever there is a downturn in the European economy. As a result Europe, too, will have more retired people than it has children.

Today a majority of European countries have already hit the crossroads where there are currently more deaths than births. This problem becomes especially tricky in Europe because of some of their misguided government policies. The reason is that most European countries actually prohibit immigration. They do this solely to protect their workers' jobs. However, when you combine this with the fact that there is a void in natural population increases, suddenly you have more European senior citizens than you know what to do with.

Here are some facts to give you some perspective of how this demographic shift in Europe compares to the United States. As we entered the 1990s, the median ages in the United States and Europe were separated by only two years—in Europe the median age was 36, whereas in the United States it was 34. By the year 2020 the median age in the United States will have increased slightly to age 37. Meanwhile in Europe the median age will have exploded to 45. What that means is that over half of the people in Europe will be over 45 years of age. And with Europe, consider the case of one country, Italy. By 2020 its median population will be 50 years of age. So half of the population of Italy will be a half-century old.

One of the reasons why these demographic issues paint a much bleaker picture in Europe than in the United States is because the United States continues to embrace immigration. And the lack of new immigrants in Europe makes the graying of Europe even a more serious problem.

Retirement Savings Boom Ahead!
The landscape of the demographics of Europe bodes very well for a retirement savings boom, especially when you consider the global retirement trends.

Globally, defined contribution plans are the fastest growing pool of retirement assets around the globe. In the United States when you think of defined contribution plans, you think of a 401(k), named after the section in the Internal Revenue Service code that addresses defined contribution plans.

Let me explain the defined benefit plan versus defined contribution system in another way. Instead of trying to figure out the difference between a defined benefit plan and a defined contribution plan, I want to substitute terms for you. The new term for a defined benefit system is "I don't care about the stock market." The reason is that under a defined benefit system, you simply went to work and did your job, and your employer would tell you ("define" for you, if you will) what your retirement benefits were going to be. On your lunch hour you read the sports pages or looked to see what great movies were playing. You never looked at the mutual fund table to see about your retirement funds because they were defined for you, which meant that your attitude was, "I don't care about the stock market."

My new name for the defined contribution system is "I am a stock market junkie." You see, with a defined contribution plan, your employer is saying to you, "I have no idea what you are going to have at retirement." Instead your employer is going to give you money every payday of every month or every quarter along with the message, "Good luck investing this money, it's your retirement." You see, you can no longer say "I don't care about the stock market" because the defined contribution system is actually forcing people to invest. This shift from defined benefit to defined contribution is the greatest Ponzi scheme ever invented. Currently less than 20 percent of the companies around the globe have shifted from defined benefit to defined contribution. I know when the shift will end . . . when it reaches 100 percent. For your frame of reference, the United States is the world leader in this shift; the United States has crossed the threshold where there are now more defined contribution plans than defined benefit plans.

You need to understand that this global trend will never, ever reverse itself. Can you imagine any company saying, "Wait a minute . . . we changed our mind, we will now be responsible for all of our employees' retirement"? It's never going to happen—this global shift is here to stay.

This really hit home to me a couple of years ago in Chicago. My office is at 222 South Riverside Plaza in downtown Chicago, which is connected to the Union Train Station. I frequently give market and economic speeches over the lunch hour to financial advisors. On this particular day I was going to give an economic overview at noon. I calmly walked into our meeting room at 11:55 A.M., and much to my surprise the room was empty. I frantically ran over to our meeting planner and asked; "What is going on? I am supposed to give a speech at noon and there is no one here." To which she calmly responded, "Did you read your agenda?" First of all, you need to understand that I hate people that answer a question with a question. Obviously I didn't read the agenda. She went on to inform me that because of the successful response to the meeting, we had to move it to a larger location—the meeting was now being held at the Westin Hotel—and by the way, I had to start speaking in two minutes.

I immediately ran downstairs and out of the building; the beauty of our location being connected to Union Station is that there are always taxi cabs everywhere. So I ran out of the building and jumped in a taxi. I told the driver that I was late for an important meeting and that he needed to get me to the Westin Hotel as quick as possible. He told me to relax, that he could get me there right away. As we pulled away he said, "I notice you came running out of the Kemper Funds [now Scudder Investments] building. Do you work there?" I quickly said yes. The driver went on to say, "If you don't mind, I have two questions that I would like to ask you. One is regarding a Kemper Fund that I own, and the other is regarding where I think the Nasdaq is headed!"

It wasn't until later that evening when I was telling my wife and daughters about my very hectic day that the significance of that cab ride actually sunk in. Think about what has happened. Ten to fifteen years ago if you were fortunate enough to belong to a country club, maybe someone would come up to you to chat about the stock market. Today, hop in the back of a cab in downtown Chicago, and the taxi driver wants to debate the direction of the stock market.

This retirement shift is creating a New World order of stock market junkies. And once you get into the market and watch your money grow, you really become a junkie.

In the defined contribution area, Europe is expected to have an annual growth rate of 14 percent, while both the United States and the

Pacific Rim slightly top that at 15 percent. The fascinating thing, however, is not just in the growth rates alone. Over the next decade, Europe eventually will have the largest pool of defined contribution assets. Britain is leading the way, where a majority of small and medium-size companies now have defined contribution plans.

But there are other reasons for this explosion in Europe. You see Europe not only has aging populations, it also has governments worried about the need to cut back social security programs. Thus, these European governments are now providing incentives for private retirement savings programs involving employer and employee contributions. Furthermore, dramatic plans to completely overhaul and privatize social security systems are being both developed and debated in Germany, France, Italy, and Great Britain.

The Asian Miracle: Size and Talent

Remember those commercials for the ill-fated remake of Godzilla that declared, "Size does matter"? Well, that sentiment didn't help the Godzilla movie, but it will help Asia. There are over 3 billion people in Asia today. However, the most influential aspects of this demographic bubble are not just the underlying size but also the dynamics of this population bubble. Asia has a comparatively young population, which in turn will tend to drive consumer demand higher than pure economic numbers would suggest.

And it isn't just size, it's talent as well. The basis for this talent is derived from the Asian culture that supports a work ethic that is one of the highest in the world. Overlay on top of that the wide range of complex products that are manufactured in the region, and you will quickly see why the Asian workforce has moved far beyond traditional menial labor tasks. In addition, because of the vastness of technology companies in the region, Asia has also created one of the largest and most technically adept workforces anywhere in the world. When you combine the high penetration and use of technology with the sheer size of the Asian population trends, you will quickly realize that not only is the Asian workforce one of the biggest, it is one of the brightest as well.

One Piece of the Asian Puzzle: China

Almost two hundred years ago, Napoleon said, "When China awakes, it will shake the world." Napoleon was right—the world is shaking.

China is in the process of constructing the largest wealth-creation engine in history. Let me put this wealth-creation engine in perspective for you using the country's poverty level as a foundation. Remarkably, in the past 20 years alone, over 170 million Chinese have escaped from or risen above the poverty level. What's especially impressive about that is that the number who have recently escaped the poverty level in the past 20 years (170 million) is larger than the entire population of Japan.

And now that they are above the poverty level, they become candidates for saving. Saving is one of the keys to China's economic engine. Over the past 20 years, China's economy has averaged a whopping 10 percent growth rate. This explosive economic growth rate is fueled by an unbelievable 35 percent personal savings rate. China has done a remarkable job of using this pool of capital to finance productive capital investment. (By the way, for your frame of reference, the savings rate in the United States is under 3 percent.)

This rate of savings is one of the reasons that China's economy continues to explode. Currently the number-three global economy, China will overtake number two, Japan, and number one, the United States, within the first quarter of this century.

Think about this for a minute: With a population five times larger than that of the United States, China only needs to achieve per capita production levels of just one-fifth of each American worker to outpace the United States. If, however, instead of working at one-fifth the per capita production levels of United States workers, Chinese workers match their major economic and political competitors in Taiwan regarding output per worker (which by the way I think they will), look what will happen. China's gross domestic product (GDP, the broadest measure of the economy) would pass not only those of the United States and Japan, but it would actually exceed that of all the rest of the industrialized world combined within the next 25 years.

The Asian Roller Blade Generation

The single most powerful economic force ever to move through any society in the history of time has yet to begin to make its true impact on economies and markets around the world. This most influential demographic trend that is looming on the global horizon is what I call Asia's "roller blade" generation.

You see, you can classify roller bladers into two groups. The first group is all of the roller-bladers from the age of 10 to 24. The second group of roller bladers is comprised of everyone else who still acts like they are aged 10 to 24. The Asian roller blade generation is about the first group.

There is a population bubble about to burst in Asia. There will be one billion Asians aged 10 to 24—the Asian roller blade generation—as we enter the new millennium. The desires, tastes, and spending habits of this generation will radically reshape the business climate, social fabric, and political institutions of Asia.

In order to understand the potential impact of this population bulge in Asia you must focus on the crucial point that Asia's roller blade generation was born into a world radically different from the one their parents entered.

You see, their parents for the most part were left largely scarred and desolated by World War II. For most of the postwar era, rebuilding societies and countries was the primary Asian goal. This in turn required hard work, dedication, individual sacrifice, high savings, production, and conformity. It was these exact attributes that have underpinned the industrial rise of Asia over the past half-century and have dramatically reshaped the world that the region's teeming population of youths currently live in.

By contrast, Asia's roller blade generation is growing up in an era of prosperity, not poverty, and this roller blade generation has within its grasp opportunities and wealth that its parents did not have. Shopping is more characteristic of this group than savings. Their parents drank tea, wore sandals, ate rice, and bought things with cash, and their life centered around Buddhism.

Not the roller blade generation—think about what they prefer. While their parents drank tea, they drink Coca-Cola. Their parents wore sandals, they wear Nike running shoes. Their parents ate rice, they eat Chicken McNuggets at McDonald's. Their parents purchased everything with cash, they purchase everything with a credit card.

A by-product of Asia's economic success is the fact that this generation is better educated and more willing and able to travel abroad than their parents were. Leisure time, convenience, individualism, indulgence, spending, and other Western habits (or vices) permeate this group. This is a radical change in the mind-set and actions from previous generations.

Let me put things in some perspective for you. Even if an unbelievable 25 percent of this population bracket never buys a single thing their entire life, it's still the greatest consumption bubble of all time. So for argument's sake, I'm going to concede that 25 percent will never see a Coke sign flashing and buy a Coca-Cola, nor will they ever see a Nike swish and want a new pair of running shoes. That would mean that all I have left is the remaining 75 percent, or 750 million Asian roller bladers. Remember earlier in this chapter I talked about how the baby boomers here in the United States will change the world because, after all, they are 76 million strong. Well, 750 million Asian consumers are 10 times greater than the United States baby boom demographic explosion. When they get through with us, the world will never be the same.

The question to investors is clear: Do you own consumer-related companies positioned to satisfy the wants and needs of Asia's roller blade generation—the most powerful demographic trend in the world?

Think back for a minute to when you were aged 10 to 24. You bought beverages, you bought cosmetics, you bought cigarettes, and you saved nothing. This is a consumption bubble. What products will be hot? The Asian roller bladers will cause an explosion in cigarettes, cars, jeans, fast food, shampoo, beverages, and cosmetic products.

In order to truly understand the market influence of Asia's roller blade generation, which is one billion strong, you need to understand that with the United States aging baby boomers, we are talking about millions, while with Asia's roller blade generation, we are talking a billion. Let me try to give you a better frame of reference regarding "a billion."

If I were to give you one billion inches and you were to line them up next to one another starting in New York City, how far do you think that you would make it across the vast United States? Well, with one billion inches, you would make it from New York all the way across the entire United States to Los Angeles, California—you would have enough inches left over, by the way, to go all the way back to New York, back to California (we have now crossed the United States three times), then back to New York, and finally back to California again. We could cross the entire United States five times with a billion inches and still have enough inches left over to make it from Los Angeles to Salt Lake City, Utah.

Here's something to ponder about those one billion inches that represented the Asian roller blade generation. Imagine a burning cigarette in every single one of those inches that crisscrossed the United States five times, and you will realize that in the long run it doesn't matter what Washington, D.C., does or does not do regarding the tobacco industry settlement. Washington, D.C., will not determine the future of the tobacco sector. The future of the tobacco sector will be determined by the Asian roller blade generation.

Japan Is Over the Hill

Not all of Asia is focused on youth. If you are looking for a long life, look no further than Japan. The most recent life expectancy figures are staggering. The average life expectancy for women in Japan is 84 years of age. Meanwhile the average life expectancy for men is 77 years of age. That means that Japan has the highest life expectancy anywhere in the world. It doesn't stop there, however; on the flip side, the average number of children a Japanese woman will bear has reached an all-time record low. That record low is one child. Because of these two trends, Japan has the most rapidly aging population of any leading industrial country.

As a result, Japan will soon find itself dropping out of the Top 10 Most Populous Nations. In 1950 Japan proudly held the number-five position, following China, India, the United States, and Russia. Following Japan were Indonesia, Germany, Brazil, England, and Italy. One century later we will witness a dramatic shift in the Top 10 Most Populous Nations. By 2050 not only will Japan drop out of the top 10, but so will Russia, Germany, England, and Italy. In 2050 the new Top 10 Most Populous Nations will look like this: India, China, the United States, Pakistan, Indonesia, Nigeria, Brazil, Bangladesh, Ethiopia, and the Congo. The most shocking shift of all, however, is no Japan in the Top 10!

The fallout from having the fastest aging population is that you have a shrinking pool of workers on which to support the social security and pensions of these senior citizens. Even in the best of market times, this demographic trend would be a problem. However, the Japanese equity markets in the 1990s have been anything but the best of times; thus this combination is causing a real crisis in Japan.

401(k) Japan-Style

This retirement crisis can only be solved a couple of ways. First, the Japanese government can raise taxes. Not a very likely choice as the Japanese economic recovery remains extremely fragile. Second, companies could increase their retirement contribution levels. This is not a very likely choice either as very few if any Japanese companies have the free cash flow to absorb this additional burden. Third and finally, they could shift more of the burden onto the employees themselves. This is exactly what will happen.

Japan has to look no further than the United States or England for two primary examples of what to do with your pension system. Both the United States and England have moved from a defined benefit system to a defined contribution system. As companies in both England and the United States made this shift, it placed more of the burden on the individual employee. For Japanese business to embrace this model, Japanese employees must be given some incentive to become more responsible for their retirement. The most likely incentive will be a series of tax breaks and tax incentives for individuals to participate in defined contribution systems.

Finally, this system must be adapted to fit the profile of Japanese employees. In the United States, for example, the 401(k) defined contribution model provides the employee with an almost unlimited choice of investment options. In addition the employee assumes complete and total responsibility. On the other hand, in England there is considerably less choice. Also in England the individual companies are still actively involved in deciding employees' appropriate asset allocation levels. Japan will most likely embrace England's model as opposed to the U.S. model. The reason is quite simple—individual Japanese investors are less experienced than individual investors in the United States; thus there will be a reluctance to let the Japanese investors go off completely on their own.

Emerging Markets

Possibly one of the biggest misconceptions in investing today is the thought that emerging markets are off on their own as well. There are many investors that want nothing to do with any emerging market investment, mainly because it's perceived to be too risky and they do not understand what emerging markets are all about.

Let me begin with a definition of *emerging market* so that we all have the same frame of reference. The World Bank defines emerging markets as those countries with per capita income less than $9,655. By comparison, in the United States, per capita income is $23,208. Looking at it on a state-by-state basis, Mississippi has the lowest per capita income at $16,531, which is almost two times greater than the emerging market level. Thus it is easy to see why people in the United States, using this economic backdrop, would want to have nothing to do with emerging markets.

This may be a mistake. Let me give you another way to look at emerging markets that will give you a peek of what's to come.

Using the World Bank definition for emerging markets, currently only 6 percent of the world's global stock market capitalization is comprised by emerging markets. This is despite the fact that, right now, over 85 percent of the world's population lives in emerging markets, over 70 percent of the world's land area is an emerging market, 65 percent of all of the world's natural resources comes from emerging markets, and finally 45 percent of all global output comes from emerging markets. You can't get away from emerging markets even if you want to!

Because Latin America is a key part of this emerging-market phenomenon, let's close this chapter by taking a closer look at Latin America's demographic trends.

Latin American Fever

Sometimes when one looks at global demographic trends, it's easy to overlook some of the smaller regions of the world, like Latin America. It is important to remember, however, that every country, no matter how big or how small, will have some demographic trends and issues that will impact on their markets and their economies. One of the reasons I think it is important not to forget about Latin America is that the countries in Latin America are all considered emerging markets. And it is these emerging markets that will have a great deal to say about what happens long-term to markets and economies all around the world.

Birth and Death Latin America–Style

Regional population growth is gradually slowing down as a result of fewer children being born and people dying later due to longer life expectancy levels.

If you include the Caribbean, population in Latin America is currently around 520 million and falling. The growth rate in the 1980s was 2.0 percent annually. By 2010 that will drop to 1.0 percent, and by 2020 it will be a staggering 0.5 percent.

Birth rates actually began their fall in the late 1960s and early 1970s. Back then women had an average of five children. Over the next decade, that average will drop to two and below.

Meanwhile, life expectancy is climbing. Life expectancy is expected to reach 70 years of age over the next decade. In addition, anyone who reaches the ripe old age of 60 can now expect to live another 20 years and be around to celebrate their 80th birthday.

As the fall in birth rates continues, so does the population of school-age children. Thus the focus on maternal and infant healthcare will fade, as will the focus on primary and secondary education.

As people live longer, there becomes a much greater burden on the national healthcare systems. These systems will now have to learn to cope with the new demands of an aging population. Thus the focus will shift from worrying about childhood diseases to figuring out how to care for an aging population.

 DR. BOB'S NOTES . . . TOP 10 THINGS TO REMEMBER!
Chapter 1

10 Latin American children are living longer due to fewer childhood diseases and there is a senior citizen explosion due to longer life expectancy.

9 The mature-adult-focused decade of the 1990s in the United States created a focus on retirement, which caused a boom in investing and the market.

8 European demographics tend to lag U.S. demographics by about 20 years.

7 Japan has the most rapidly aging population of any industrialized country.

6 In the United States, senior-citizen-focused decades ahead will bode well for travel and entertainment, health and fitness, and financial advice sectors.

5 The consumption in Asia will dominate every single economy in the world. It will be the greatest consumption bubble ever.

4 Generation X will drive Europe, when you combine their income generated from part-time jobs and allowance from parents.

3 U.S. baby boomers are the most influential demographic trend in U.S. history, influencing the social, business, and political fiber forever.

2 Emerging markets represent 85 percent of the population, 70 percent of the land mass, 65 percent of the natural resources, and 45 percent of the world's global output.

1 Age characteristics determine what you buy, save, and invest; the number of households; and even future government policies.

Chapter 2

The Globalization of Economies and Markets

The new electronic interdependence recreates the world in the image of a global village.

Marshall McLuhan
Visionary Educator of Mass Media (1967)

The economies of the world and their markets have been evolving into what Marshall McLuhan dubbed a "global village" back in 1967. This has occurred through a major transformation over the past decade. Investors around the globe used to look at issues in isolation . . . us versus them, if you will. Today it's not "us versus them" but rather "we." We are truly all connected. Two landmark events have provided the one-two punch to changing the way we look at the global markets. First was the fall of communism and the embracing of capitalism as nations around the globe began focusing on improving the quality of living for their citizens. Second was the technology revolution, which gave us the tools to make sure that all of the economies and all of the markets could have the free flow of timely information so that we all could be wired to one another. Want some proof that we've gone global? Back in 1850 there were only five global nongovernmental organizations. By 1900 that number had grown to almost 150 organizations. Today there are over 18,000 global organizations . . . globalization has truly arrived.

Globalization Trends

As an investor, however, in order to understand how to benefit from this rapid globalization of economies and markets, we must first understand the trends, issues, developments, and opportunities within each of the major components of the global markets. What appears on the surface to be extremely obvious—simply invest globally—might lead us to miss things right before our eyes. In other words, don't disregard the obvious.

Think of the U.S. immigration border guard on patrol at the U.S./ Mexican border in southern California. A brand new pickup truck drives up filled with fresh topsoil. The guard is convinced that the driver is smuggling something in the dirt, so he sifts through it by hand looking for drugs, jewelry, or liquor, only to find nothing but dirt. The next day the exact same driver drives up to the border gate with another truck full of topsoil. And again the guard meticulously looks through the dirt and finds absolutely nothing. This time, however, he even has the K-9 sniffing dog help him. This goes on everyday for almost two weeks. The poor border guard is so exasperated that he finally says to the driver, "Look, I know you're smuggling something into the United States. Just tell me what it is, and I will let you go free." The driver replies, "Isn't it obvious? While you're focusing on the dirt, I'm smuggling pickup trucks."

Likewise don't forget the obvious in global markets. These markets are made up of very unique and distinct pieces. You must understand how each of the pieces works before you can benefit from the global opportunities.

In our New World order there are four spheres of influence on global economies and markets: the United States, Euroland, Japan, and emerging markets. Let's get a better understanding of just what's driving these four major economies and markets beginning with the largest, the United States.

UNITED STATES

Workforce and Employment Shifts

One of the major concerns facing the United States is, with record low unemployment and the birth-bust demographic trend we discussed in Chapter 1, will there be enough workers to keep the U.S. economy going? And if there are, won't wages skyrocket because of the low unemployment numbers (meaning those who are employed can demand higher wages)?

Let's start with the second point. Will record-low unemployment cause wage inflation in the United States? No! And here is why. There is a common belief in economic circles that low unemployment will cause higher inflation. This concept is commonly referred to as the Phillips curve or the NAIRU concept. The foundation of the Phillips curve theory is this: Low employment causes high inflation. NAIRU, which stands for non-accelerating inflation rate of unemployment, is simply another way of saying exactly the same thing. In other words, these concepts have convinced the market that too many people working causes wage inflation!

Economists, however, can't explain how we can have record-low unemployment levels with virtually no inflation. Thus, they are attempting to convince the market that inflation is right around the corner. Well, I for one am not convinced. Most of the problem is rooted in the way economists and the Federal government calculate the unemployment rate.

The 1990 census tracked 6.8 million Americans unemployed, while 133.1 million were employed. However, consider this: Another 50 million (actually 49.9 million) healthy, able-to-work, but unemployed adults were omitted from both the employment category and the unemployment category. They weren't counted as part of the 133.1 million employed because they didn't have a job (I can understand that). However, get this—they weren't counted as unemployed either because the Labor Department doesn't count them as unemployed unless they are actually seeking a job. I guess we should consider these people invisible. So the 1990 census should actually read 133.1 million employed, 6.8 million unemployed, and 49.9 million invisible. Give me a break. It's the so-called invisible workforce that is helping keep a lid on wage inflation.

In my way of thinking, you're either employed or unemployed. Maybe the 1990 census should have read 133.1 million employed and 56.7 unemployed, some of which are invisible. Thus, maybe the U.S. labor markets aren't so tight after all. And maybe—just maybe—the record-low unemployment rate will not cause inflation.

In addition, most economists fail to grasp what is truly driving wage inflation today. You see, in theory, wage inflation is when you get paid more money to do the same job. That is not what is happening. People are getting paid more money to do enhanced jobs; they are simply called the same job. Just think of the case of the stockroom clerk.

It is the stockroom clerk's job to take boxes from the loading dock and put them on the shelves in the warehouse. That clerk used to make $6.50 an hour; now the clerk makes $8.50 an hour, and every economist screams wage inflation. It's not wage inflation; in fact, it's wage deflation.

Here's what that same stockroom clerk does today for that $8.50 an hour. He is still responsible for taking boxes from the loading dock and putting them on the shelves of the warehouse. However, now after he does that, he takes a hand-held computer that is clipped to his belt and scans the bar code on the boxes to take inventory. Later in the day he downloads the inventory data in his hand-held computer and then gets the shipping schedules for the next day. Finally, shipping schedules are cross checked against inventory lists, and new orders are processed at the end of the shift.

Where's the wage inflation? We give this person an extra $2.00 an hour, and not only is he the stockroom clerk, but he is also the inventory clerk, the shipping clerk, and the order clerk. An additional $2.00 an hour to do the job of four people! That is not wage inflation, that's wage deflation.

Let's shift gears now and address the first concern of global investors: Will there even be enough workers in the United States? I believe there will be as we start to see an influx of older workers back into the workforce. This influx of older workers is happening for two reasons. First, workers want to continue doing something (working) when they retire. They want to work part-time instead of full-time, and they may even want to try out a different occupation. They want to stay busy.

Many of these potential workers, however, have stayed on the sidelines because of the Social Security "earnings limit." The Social Security earnings limit worked like this: All workers aged 65 to 69 would be required to defer $1 of Social Security benefits for every $3 of wage-and-salary income exceeding a set "earnings limit," which was $17,000 in 2000. Workers would then begin receiving their deferred benefits after age 70.

Not any more—look for an explosion of senior workers aged 65 to 69 as the earnings limit has been completely eliminated. That means that for the first time in the history of the U.S. Social Security system, all retirement-age beneficiaries aged 65 to 69 can make as much money in salary and wages as they want and still be eligible to receive their full Social Security benefits. Don't forget about some of the intangible benefits to having an influx of senior workers in the workforce. Who knows—they might even be able to teach those radical generation Xers to show up on time with their shirts tucked in.

Compensation Changes

Not only is the workforce evolving in the United States, but the compensation structure as well. It is really different this time.

In the United States the military used to draft people when they needed them for services. Look what one branch of the military, the U.S. Navy, is doing today. In order to entice recruits, the Navy is giving them a $5,000 signing bonus. Think about it—20 years ago people were simply drafted into the army; signing bonuses were reserved for prima donna athletes. Today the United States is offering a $5,000 signing bonus to anyone who will join the military. And you still don't think things aren't different?

And the compensation changes don't stop here. A few years ago if you worked in the evening and on a weekend at home, very few companies actually provided personal computers for their employees to work on at home. Think of what's happening currently at Ford Motor Company and Delta Airlines. Not only do they compensate their people with salaries and bonuses, but both Ford and Delta are also giving every single employee a personal computer so that, for a small monthly fee, they can surf the Web and be on the Internet. Do you still think it's not different?

Here's one final example. There's a technology company that's traded on the Nasdaq; the company's called Interwoven. Interwoven has a unique approach to recruitment. It's giving BMWs to its new employees. Remember how companies would maybe give a car to their senior, senior executives after 20 years of loyal service? Now Interwoven comes along and gives a brand new BMW to the first 20 engineers that it hires.

These are truly different times, and these compensation shifts have an impact on the markets as well. Over the past decade the U.S. economy has completed its shift from a manufacturing economy to a service economy.

Consider what this means for compensation. In a manufacturing economy if you work for 40 hours in a week, you are paid for 40 hours. If you work 50 hours, you are paid for 50; and if you work 60, you are paid for 60; and so on. In a service economy, however, things are a little different. If you work 40 hours, you are paid for 40 hours. If you work 50 hours, you are still paid for 40 hours and if you work 60 hours, you are still paid for 40 hours. You see, in a service economy you get paid for your "overtime" in the form of a bonus. Think of the old manufacturing economy as a pay-as-you-go system. Thus you get paid for all of your work incrementally, every payday. And when you get paid in that fashion, you usually spend it. It's tough to get excited about the five hours of overtime pay helping to fund your stock market investments for your retirement. On the other hand, in a service economy when you are paid in one lump sum instead of every payday, deferred overtime if you will, that money makes its way into the market, because it is a large enough amount that it can and will have an influence on your stock market investments for your retirement.

And what really makes this shift from a manufacturing economy to a service economy exciting is that even the old-line manufacturing companies get it. Probably the oldest of the old-line manufacturing companies in the United States is the auto sector. Look what they are doing today. Back 20 years ago the only employees to receive profit-sharing checks were the most senior white-collar executives. That system evolved, and the sector figured out that they could be even more profitable if they rewarded their middle-management employees as well.

Look where it has evolved to today—past the white-collar senior executives, past middle management, all the way to every single rank-and-file, blue-collar, factory-line employee.

In 1999 Ford Motor Company announced that every single one of its 106,000 blue-collar, factory-line employees would receive profit-sharing checks averaging $8,000. Meanwhile, Daimler Chrysler's 81,000 blue-collar, factory-line employees received profit-sharing checks averaging $8,100.

Just think about these investment ramifications. Because of these two old-line auto manufacturing companies alone, we have almost a quarter of a million blue-collar, factory-line employees with more than $1.5 billion dollars, when 20 years ago they had nothing. First of all from an investment strategy standpoint, it might make sense to go "long" on all of the beer stocks. Second, think of the ramifications for the overall U.S. market. While I can't quantify it, nor can anyone disprove it, I'm convinced that a majority of this money made its way into the U.S. stock market. And even with the current downturn in the economy, these two companies are still paying bonuses. In 2001 (year 2000 bonuses), Daimler Chrysler paid $379, while Ford paid $6,700. That's still close to $1 billion!

Trade Deficit Hoax

If one concern is that the United States has too few workers, then the other concern has to be that the trade deficit is too high and will eventually spell trouble for the U.S. economy and markets. I do not necessarily agree. I think that this is one of the most misunderstood economic indicators in the market today.

Think about this for a minute: There is really only one way a country can accumulate a trade deficit; that is, the country is buying (importing) more than it is selling (exporting). And, there is only one way that can happen. The country's economy must be stronger than a majority of the economies of the world. In other words, the country has more buying power and is using it. The only way a country gets a trade surplus is when the rest of the world is stronger and is buying more than it is. You see, not being an economist by training, I always thought that it would be a good thing that my country's economy was stronger than a majority of the other economies around the world.

Furthermore, there are two distinctly unique aspects to the U.S. trade deficit that virtually ensure that the United States has a trade deficit for a rather long term.

The first aspect is who the United States is actually trading with. The headlines read "U.S. Trade with Japan Explodes" or "U.S. Trade with China Skyrockets." That is not who the United States is trading with. The United States is actually trading with itself. You see, over 40 percent of the trade in the United States is actually intracompany shipments by the U.S. multinationals. Think about this: This is not the United States trading with Japan. This is Ford Motor Company trading with Ford Motor Company Japan, and this is Coca-Cola trading with Coca-Cola China. And what's more important than the deficit is the money. When companies are trading with themselves, the money—or profit— comes right back to the home country.

The second unique aspect of the U.S. trade deficit is how it is made up. Like every other country that has a trade deficit, the United States is buying (importing) more than it is selling (exporting). However, the real story behind the story is what it is buying and selling. The United States is the world's number-one importer of commodities and commodity-type products. There is little if any pricing flexibility to boost the price of commodities (other than a temporary price shock, like oil). No price flexibility means that the profit margins on these products are almost nonexistent.

Meanwhile the United States is the world's number-one exporter of value-added goods and services like software and movies and all the things that still have pricing flexibility; and when you have pricing flexibility, you have improving profit margins.

Think about it: The United States is the number-one importer of commodities, whose prices are going down, and the number-one exporter of value-added goods and services, whose prices continue to go up. This makeup alone will keep the United States in a trade deficit for many, many years.

Something else bothers me about this trade deficit scare. Does it really matter as long as the United States continues to have foreign investors invest in the United States? The simple answer is no. As long as the foreign money keeps flowing to the United States, maybe the focus should be not on just the trade deficit but rather on why foreign investors continue to flock to and send their money to the United States.

Certainly the United States has strong equity markets. However, the case can also be made for other equity markets around the globe, and they are not the recipients of the same capital flow.

I think the reason is because the United States has become the technological leader of the world. And the reason for this is because of the flexibility in labor standards and laws. In other words, it's extremely easy to get rid of unwanted and unproductive employees in the United States. If you can find a piece of technology to replace a person, that worker is removed in a heartbeat. The same cannot be said for the rest of the world, where stringent labor laws continue to protect employees.

Thus, even though everyone around the world can use the same new technology, the greatest productivity gains are in the United States due to the flexible labor laws. I think the U.S. productivity number is far more important than the trade deficit.

Dollar Weakness

One of the concerns with a trade deficit is what will happen if global investors are no longer willing to support your currency. Well, the answer is pretty obvious—the currency, in this case the U.S. dollar, would go down. Let's explore why this will not happen for any extended period; and if it does weaken, let's look at some of the positive aspects of a weaker U.S. dollar.

One of the reasons that I do not believe that the U.S. dollar will have a protracted period of weakness is because I don't believe that the U.S. economy will have a protracted period of weakness.

You don't need to be a currency trader to figure out how the currency markets actually work. Just consider a country's currency as no more than a reflection of that country's underlying economy. Eventually a country's currency will trade based on the underlying strength or weakness of its domestic economy. Now that doesn't mean that people don't try to fool the currency markets. In fact, Central Banks do it all the time. All you hear about are Central Banks buying the euro and selling the dollar or buying the dollar and selling the yen. This is nothing more than an ill-advised attempt to influence the currency markets. In the end it doesn't work, and the currency will go back to trading based on the underlying strengths and weaknesses in the economy. Because the United States has evolved into an efficient service-driven economy, the business cycle isn't dead; it has just greatly collapsed. No more boom-bust economic cycles. Thus, when the economy stays strong, which it will, so will the currency.

Now that doesn't mean that the U.S. dollar won't have several months or even several quarters where it weakens. However, a weaker dollar is not the end of the world. Quite the contrary. A weaker dollar has some extremely positive investment ramifications. Thus, a temporary decline in the dollar value has five positive investment ramifications that ripple all across the globe.

First, a weaker dollar actually strengthens the Japanese yen. A stronger Japanese yen limits the risk of another round of the Asia currency meltdown like we witnessed in the late 1990s.

Second, a weaker dollar is good for Latin America and Brazil, which are the leading trade partners with the United States south of the border. The sale of their products in the United States is not hurt by currency exchanges. In other words, they can charge more for the exact same product.

Third, a weaker dollar is also good for the price of commodities. Remember that 90 percent of the commodities are traded in dollar-denominated terms. A weaker dollar will generally lower the price of commodities.

Fourth, a weaker dollar is good for global consumers, who now will be able to buy more American products, which by the way is good for the U.S. equity market.

Fifth, and finally, a weaker dollar eases the debt burden of countries trying to finance their dollar-denominated debt.

Consumer Credit Explosion

One group that appears to have a never-ending supply of dollars is the U.S. consumers; and if they run out of dollars, they simply use credit. Outside of the United States as well as inside, economists and strategists continue to scratch their heads wondering why an explosion in consumer credit has not slowed down the U.S. economy or markets.

In order to understand why, we first need to understand how it evolved. Numerous economists have suggested that the proliferation of credit cards plus the convenience of increasing personal debt are the major reasons that the United States savings rate is so low. Available credit and personal debt are at all-time highs. Consumer credit as a percent of disposable income is at the highest level in decades.

On the surface this all appears quite bad. But is it? Think for a minute about how easy it is to go into personal debt. You can drive into the gas station with no money in your pocket and simply use your credit card to finance the purchase of gas. You can do the same thing at the grocery store, the drug store, the doctor's office, and so forth. And this doesn't even take into account the explosion of the new economy and the Internet. It's pretty tough to buy anything online without a credit card.

Even if by chance you are fiscally conservative and don't want to increase your personal debt, you'll be given incentives to go into personal debt with discount programs. Why, the United States even has frequent flyer programs that give you points for going into debt. I don't know about you, but I'm as guilty as everyone else is.

A few years ago, when both of my daughters were still teenagers, my younger daughter called me from the mall half out of breath and said, "Dad, Mom said that if we can shop for another half hour, she is sure we will earn enough frequent flyer points to get the final airline ticket we need for vacation." I got so excited I screamed, "Go for it!"

Just because credit card debt as a percentage of an individual's net worth is at an all-time high doesn't mean there is a credit card crisis. You have to look beyond the simple usage numbers.

In the United States over 40 percent of all credit card holders pay their credit card debt down to a zero balance every month. Think about this for a minute: If 40 percent of all credit card holders are paying their credit card debt each month to a balance of zero, how can that be a crisis? The answer is, it's not. The crisis is that economists need to come down out of their ivory towers and realize people don't use credit cards to go into debt; they use them for the points. Depending on the type of card that you have, you can get points for frequent flyer miles, points toward the purchase of a new car, points toward free long distance calls, . . .

In addition, if any of these Wall Street economists would ever go into a store to return some merchandise, they would quickly realize why everyone uses a credit card. If you find yourself returning to a store something that you bought with cash, you are about to begin the great negotiating return process that probably will end up with you receiving a store credit, not cash. Not so when you return something that you purchased with a credit card. You simply walk into the store, say I am not paying for this, I don't want it, and if by chance the store clerk is dumb enough to cause you a problem, all you have to do is call 1-800-MasterCard or 1-800-Visa or whatever, and they will credit your account and fight with the store clerk on your behalf. Credit cards aren't about going into debt; they are about shifting the balance of power away from store clerks to the consumer. It will not stop. Trust me, I am an expert on this. My wife and two grown daughters have educated me well on this shopping return phenomenon. Never, ever buy with cash; you never know when you might want to return your purchase.

Now along these same lines there is also a great concern with the recent explosion in personal bankruptcies. Well, I have a different take on this. I don't believe that the increase in personal bankruptcies has anything to do with the financial health of consumers. Instead, I think it has everything to do with an erosion of the ethical standards in the United States.

Think about this: Ten years ago if you couldn't make payments on something, you would call a family member for help. Or you would call a friend or an old college or high school buddy for help. If that didn't work, you would try the neighbors. In other words, you did everything possible to find some source of money to pay your debts because the last thing in the world you wanted to do was to be embarrassed by having to file for personal bankruptcy. Today it's the first thing they do. Simply open up the Yellow Pages, and call 1-800-bankrupt me! Instead of being an outcast, people are giving you high fives because you beat the system by filing for personal bankruptcy protection.

The uptick in personal bankruptcy is not about a change on the consumer's balance sheet; rather it's a change in attitude toward personal bankruptcy caused by too many lawyers with nothing better to do than to fuel an explosion in personal bankruptcy filings.

Poor Savings Rate Problem

It's easy to see why everyone accepts as a fact that the United States has a poor savings rate. After all, if consumer debt is skyrocketing, U.S. consumers have little left to save. Or do they?

The first problem with the savings rate in the United States is how it is calculated. In my opinion, the single greatest reason why the United States has such a low savings rate is the way in which economists calculate the number.

They begin by estimating personal income. Then actual taxes paid are subtracted from that number. The actual consumption expenditures are subtracted from that number, and what's left is what's called the savings rate.

Now think about this for a minute. In the past few years of this unbelievably strong U.S. bull market, capital gains (as a result of stock price appreciation) have been rapidly and dramatically rising along with a sharp increase in capital gains taxes. Now get this. While the capital gains taxes are subtracted from current income, the actual capital gains as a result of rising stock values are not counted as income. And to make matters worse, if people spend some of their capital gains, it makes the consumption figure go up, which in turn lowers the U.S. savings rate.

Without that tax distortion, I believe that the actual U.S. savings rate would be twice what it is. While I will be the first to admit that the United States still has a long way to go, I also strongly believe that it's not nearly as bad in the United States as the number leads you to believe.

Speaking of taxes, the U.S. tax code actually encourages consumption and discourages investment. Let me explain it this way. The majority of taxpayers in the United States fall in the 28 percent tax bracket. Let's say that one of those taxpayers at the end of last year had an opportunity to earn an additional $1,000. Now they didn't plan on earning this money, nor did they need it to meet their ordinary living expenses. So they now have to decide whether they want to work a little extra for an additional $1,000. Let's assume that they decide to go for it and earn the extra $1,000. Now they have to decide what they are going to do with the additional $1,000. Well, it isn't exactly $1,000; it's actually $720 because they are in the 28 percent federal tax bracket. The taxpayers could either spend the $720 or save it. Let's see what the current U.S. tax policy encourages them to do. If they spend the money, all of the money, by going to Disney World, they can ride all of the rides; eat all of the food; drink the drinks; buy the T-shirts, Mickey hats, and other souvenirs; and their additional federal tax liability for spending all of their money is zero! Think about it: If they spend all of the money, the federal government gets nothing. The taxpayers pay no additional federal taxes to the government. Look what happens if instead of spending the money they invest it. Their additional federal tax liability for deciding to save means that they will have to pay the federal government additional taxes on any interest generated from their investment; they will have to pay the federal government additional taxes on any dividends received as a result of their investment. They will have to pay the federal government additional taxes on any short-term capital gains as a result of their investment. They will have to pay the federal government additional taxes on any long-term capital gains as a result of their investments; and finally, when they die, their investment becomes part of their estate and an additional federal tax has to be paid on that as well. The U.S. tax policy actually encourages people to consume, not to save. Changing this misguided tax policy will go a long way toward improving savings rates. Even if the policies are not changed, the overriding forces of demographics are finally coming into play on this important topic. Furthermore, it is important to remember that some of the key demographic trends we discussed in Chapter 1 will begin to have a positive influence on increasing the U.S. savings rate.

Remember, as more and more U.S. baby boomers cross the half-century mark, they will suddenly find themselves with more disposable income to save as a result of a confluence of three factors. First, most of the kids are moved out of the house by the time you reach 50. Raising a family is a costly endeavor; and when the kids are grown and on their own, it frees up significant cash flow to improve the savings rate. Second, either your mortgage is paid off, or it has worked its way down so low that it is a very small part of your monthly budget items. What once took so much cash flow now takes so little that the extra flow can also drive the savings rate upward. Third and finally, when you cross the half-century mark, you find yourself in your peak earnings years. Your employer is finally paying you for all of the education, experience, hard work, skill, wisdom, and maturity that you bring to the job. At age 50 these demographic forces bring your costs down and your income up, which provides a great fundamental backdrop to move a nation's savings rate higher.

EUROLAND

New Economy and Monetary Union

Let's shift gears now and move to our second sphere of influence, Euroland, which many investors now see as a United States of Europe. Soon after the end of World War II, Winston Churchill proposed in 1946 what he called "a United States of Europe." His innovative idea was met with skepticism. Critics pointed out that Europe, unlike the United States, didn't have a single language or a single currency. So how in the world could there ever be such a thing as the United States of Europe?

Well, I am sure that Churchill is smiling somewhere today, more than 50 years later, now that 11 European countries (Austria, Belgium, Finland, France, Germany, Ireland, Italy, Luxembourg, the Netherlands, Portugal, and Spain) have joined together to create a European Economic and Monetary Union (EMU), which gives the authority of monetary policy to the European Central Bank and launches a new currency called the "euro." Even the countries that are not a part of the EMU are adopting the euro. Europe's oldest currency, the Greek drachma, which has been around since 650 B.C., was phased out as the country adopted the euro. And in case you still don't believe in the euro and are looking for some sign from above, even the Vatican has decided that it will adopt the euro as its official currency.

The euro serves to solidify what had been a segmented European market into a major super power from an economic perspective. No longer will investors simply look to the two historic super economic powers, the United States and Japan. The new kid on the map, Euroland, is certainly a force to be reckoned with. From a sheer population perspective Euroland with its 292 million people is larger than the United States with its 268 million and is more than twice as large as Japan with its 125 million population base. From an economic perspective as measured by gross domestic product (GDP), the broadest measure of a nation's economic health, Euroland is right between the other two powers. Euroland's $6.26 trillion economy still trails the U.S. $8.11 trillion economy but finds itself well ahead of Japan's $4.19 trillion economy.

From an investment perspective there are three themes that are developing from the creation of Euroland. First, European equities stand to benefit. To prepare for the launch of the euro, interest rates throughout Europe were cut. Lower interest rates are a tremendous foundation for the equity market. Also, look for the major deregulation across several sectors, which will also fuel the equity market.

Second, multinational companies in the United States could be winners, especially those with major operations in Europe. The creation of the euro should cause European currencies to stabilize and eventually to strengthen versus the U.S. dollar. Thus, instead of a strong dollar eating into the profits of U.S. multinational companies because of currency-exchange-rate transactions, a weaker U.S. dollar can actually help create profits, given the positive currency exchange rate. For example, if the U.S. dollar were 10 percent higher than the German mark, a U.S. multinational company's profits would decrease 10 percent, given the exchange rate to dollars. Conversely, if the dollar were 10 percent lower than the German mark, a U.S. multinational company's profits could increase 10 percent after exchanging to U.S. dollars. Why isn't anyone talking about this in the long run?

Third, from a longer-term perspective, the bonds from Euroland could eventually rival the U.S. Treasury market in terms of perceived safety and security. Just look at the three underlying criteria with which each country had to comply in order to become a member of the EMU. First, inflation could not exceed 1.5 percent of the three best-performing member countries. And remember the biggest enemy of the bond market investor is inflation, and the EMU is taming inflation. Second, budget deficits couldn't exceed 3 percent of GDP. Remember the number-two enemy of the bond market is high government deficits (i.e., too many bonds tilt the supply/demand equation the wrong way), and now the EMU is also getting government deficits under control. Third and most important, if governments couldn't meet the fiscal criteria, they were left out. Greece very badly wanted in, but it could not meet the fiscal criteria and was left out.

For investors the long-term landscape in Europe couldn't look better, no matter whether they are looking to invest in stocks or bonds.

Shareholder Focus

If you are looking at stocks, maybe the single most exciting concept to come out of Euroland, from an equity investor's standpoint, is the emergence of a "shareholder focus." Historically European companies have focused on the needs of customers and employees and paid little, if any, attention to shareholders. That is all changing, as with the birth of Euroland comes the birth of shareholder focus. This newfound shareholder focus can be traced back to four independent facts.

First, stock options are included in the pay packages with which more and more European firms are compensating their employees. All of a sudden an employee's compensation (stock options) is now linked to the performance of the company's stock price. When all employees are focused on doing whatever they can to support the stock price (and to increase the value of their options), it's amazing what can happen.

Second, merger mania hit Europe. And with this merger explosion came a clear warning to all employees. Weak and inefficient companies as reflected by lagging or low stock prices will be quickly absorbed by competitors. And when that happens, everyone's job security is in jeopardy. The best tool for job security is a high and rising stock price.

Third, the government has helped a little as well. Until recently most European countries prohibited firms from repurchasing shares directly from stockholders. Thus as U.S. companies continued to use stock buybacks as a way to return earnings and excess cash to shareholders, European companies sat on the sidelines. Not anymore—stock buybacks are now legal in France, Sweden, and the United Kingdom.

Fourth and finally, with the globalization of economies came an influx of U.S. managers on European companies. These U.S. managers were born and raised in U.S. equity markets, which always have a shareholder focus. These managers have been slowly imbedding that new culture into their European colleagues.

Stock Ownership Boom

Well, Euroland is appropriately focusing on the shareholder—and none too soon, I may add, as stock ownership is about to boom to record levels.

In some very subtle ways the launching of the euro and the creation of Euroland is also creating an explosion in European equity investments. Three changes are leading to this newfound favor for equity investments in Europe.

First, all of the national boundaries have less and less significance, which means that companies within those borders are no longer protected by them. Looked at another way, competition is heating up; and to prepare for this increased competition, companies are cutting costs and figuring out how to become more productive. In reality, each company is also making itself a better investment for investors.

Second, the currency risk is disappearing. You see, by pricing stocks in euros, the single currency, the risk of currency fluctuations is eliminated when an Italian investor buys stock in a German company. Also, don't forget about the fees for investing that are about to go down as well. Just think about how much less expensive it is now without all of the back office overhead needed to deal with all of the complicated currency transactions with all of the various local currencies.

Third and finally, don't forget that to be a part of Euroland, a government has to pledge to keep debt levels in line. That means ongoing budget cutting. At risk for the first time in decades are some of the extremely generous pension programs in Europe. As Europeans now must wonder how secure these benefits actually are, they are now taking on more responsibility for their own retirement. As the pension benefit potentially gets smaller, individuals tend to become more focused investors. And their focus is usually on the equity market.

Retirement Savings Explosion

As the continued focus and debate regarding pensions heats up to a fever pitch, European governments are discovering the harsh reality that state pension plans are inadequate and that the only real solution is to encourage the formation of private retirement accounts used to offset the shortfall. France, Germany, Italy, and Switzerland are moving toward the privatization of state-run plans, and they are considering providing inducements for defined benefit plans similar to individual retirement accounts (IRA)–type accounts in the United States.

The public pension liability for Europe as a percentage of their economy (GDP) is staggering. Pension liability, as a percent of GDP, is 114 percent for France, 111 percent for Germany, and 76 percent for Italy. To give you some frame of reference, pension liability to GDP in the United States, a place that many investors feel has a serious state pension (Social Security) problem, is only 26 percent.

The lone exception in Europe is Great Britain, which has been a leader in U.S.–style private pension plans to complement its public plans. Great Britain has one of the healthiest pension systems anywhere in the world, as evidenced by its pension liability-to-GDP ratio of only 5 percent.

As governments all throughout Europe begin to develop privatization of retirement accounts, the real winner will be the European equity market.

German Tax Reform

Once the reform movement starts, it's hard to stop. After one begins to fix the public pension system, why not go straight to the root of all evil, the tax structure, which is exactly what they have already done in Germany.

While people in Germany and around the world have certainly witnessed their share of economic miracles—first the Berlin Wall comes tumbling down, next Germany discards its proud currency and embraces the euro currency by becoming an initial member of the European Economic and Monetary Union—these landmark events will pale in comparison to the latest economic miracle, major tax reform. The real miracle of tax reform is that its impact is measured not in days or years, but rather in decades and quarter centuries. Germany, which was already a good place to invest, just got a whole lot better. As with any major tax-reform program, it addresses a wide range of issues. German tax reform has created a confluence of three issues that should fuel and boost economic growth and prosperity for decades to come.

First and foremost is the impact that tax reform will have on the common person in Germany, the "rank and file" if you will. Well, this tax-reform plan has something for everyone who pays individual income taxes. Even though people complain in the United States about their highest individual income tax rate of 39.6 percent, in Germany the highest individual tax bracket is 51 percent. That rate will be lowered to 42 percent by 2005. That 42 percent highest tax rate will put German tax rates below every major European economy in the EMU. Meanwhile, at the other end of the spectrum, Germany's lowest tax rate will also fall. The lowest tax rate, which currently stands at 22.9 percent, will fall to 15 percent by 2005. Although it will be a while until we can fully assess the economic impact of those individual income tax cuts, we do know one thing for sure: When you cut individual income taxes, you put more money into the pockets of consumers. And when you do that, it tends to boost economic demands. In other words, people have more money and they buy more stuff. One important wild card in what happens to German economic growth is the psychological impact that this may have on German consumers as well. Tax reform has been debated for decades; now it has finally happened. Consumer confidence in Germany could hit record highs, all because of tax reform.

Second, the corporate tax rate dramatically fell from 40 percent to 25 percent tax on retained earnings, effective January 1, 2001. And the corporate tax rate on distributed earnings fell from 40 percent to 30 percent, also effective January 1, 2001. Now you don't have to be a stock analyst to figure out the potential positive impact that this can have on a company's bottom line. If a company does absolutely positively nothing better next year than this year—everything is the same, sales, revenues, expenses—where do you think profits are headed when that 10 percent or 15 percent corporate tax cut falls directly to the bottom line? The year 2001 is gearing up to be a great year for German companies.

Third and without a doubt the most dramatic and most far-reaching aspect of Germany's tax reform is the elimination of capital gains taxes on cross-holdings (one German company owning shares in another German company). The actual numbers are staggering and range anywhere from $250 billion to $300 billion in cross-holdings. This unique structure developed as Germany was rebuilding after World War II and banks and insurance companies took equity in exchange for loans. After Germany was ravaged following World War II, it was extremely difficult for businesses to get any loans. As banks and insurance companies looked out over war-torn Germany, the prospects for when there would be enough cash flow to pay back any loans appeared dim at best. However, the future of Germany was at stake. So to enable businesses to rebuild, banks and insurance companies took equity in return for loans because they knew it would be years, maybe even decades, until there would be enough cash flow to pay back the loans.

Currently, if a company sells shares in another company, it is subject to a 50 percent capital gains tax. Effective 2002, that capital gains tax will be eliminated. This landmark change will create an explosion of corporate spin-offs, mergers, and acquisitions unlike anything ever seen in the history of the German economy. Think about it: Companies can now shed their ownership in other companies, making both companies more attractive for future mergers and acquisitions. The elimination of this tax may be more dramatic than any economic event in Germany in the twentieth century.

Don't forget that not only is Germany one of the world's largest economies it is also part of the EMU. Thus, when the biggest member (Germany) of the EMU does something dramatic, it puts political, social, and economic pressure on other members of the EMU to soon follow in order to stay competitive. Italy and France are already seriously looking at alternatives to cut taxes to keep up with Germany's tax reform.

Up Next, Labor Reform

The final battleground of the reform movement will be on the labor front. From an employee perspective, Europe remains a wonderful place to work. From an employer perspective, its very rigid labor regulations make it very difficult if not impossible to terminate employees. Add on top of this the nonwage cost of lucrative health and retirement benefits and you can quickly see how European companies will have trouble competing globally.

As the European economies continue to move forward, expect companies to begin to address these very sensitive issues in order to level the playing field so that European companies can truly compete globally without the drag of rigid labor regulations.

Internet Danger

As reforms all through Europe improve the investment landscape, there is one investment in Europe that reform cannot help or fix, and that is the Internet. Now that the dot.com bubble has burst in the United States, everyone is searching for the next Internet runup. And the consensus appears to be Europe. And while I remain very bullish on Europe, I am not quite so bullish on the Internet changing the business-to-consumer model quite as rapidly as it did in the United States.

First of all, in order to reach three-quarters of the population in Europe, your Internet site would need to be translated into five different languages. Second, to purchase an item on the Internet, you need a credit card. In the United States, most consumers possess multiple credit cards. In Germany, which is the largest economy in all of Europe, less than 15 percent of the entire population even has one credit card. Also, don't forget that the population of Europe is far more concentrated than that of the United States; and most Europeans live within easy reach of shops. While I continue to believe that Europe is a great investment, I'm not so sure about the business-to-consumer websites being the next great investment mania. And don't forget cost for Internet access has something to do with it as well. The average monthly price for Internet access in the United States is a little over $30. In Europe's largest economy, Germany, monthly Internet access is over $80. That's a huge monthly difference.

JAPAN

How Did We Get Here?

Now, let's focus on the third of four spheres of influence, Japan. In order to have a better understanding of where Japan is going, one must first begin by clearly understanding where Japan came from.

The modern-day history of Japan really began after World War II, which crippled Japan's economy. Almost half of Japan's infrastructure and industrial and manufacturing capacity was destroyed. It was against this negative backdrop that a positive new Japan emerged.

As Japan rushed to rebuild its factories after losing the war, it was doing so with the latest and greatest state-of-the-art equipment. In a very short time, because of all its modern technology Japan was better positioned to compete than were the nations that actually were victorious in the war. You see, the nations that were victorious were still strapped with all of the old machinery in their aging factories.

Japan made some very key and strategic decisions to invest heavily in the electric utility, steel, auto, and shipping sectors. And it was these investments, along with the evolving electronics sector, that formed Japan's early economic base.

Japan fast became the envy of the world, with its highly efficient and productive manufacturing base. Add to this a highly skilled and disciplined workforce with an extremely high savings rate, and one can quickly see how in a few decades Japan evolved from the economic ashes to become one of the world's economic leaders.

Keeps Getting Older

The real story of Japan today is not about its economy but about its demographics. The simple bottom line is that Japan is getting older and older. Now it's not that Japan is unique with this aging problem.

When Japan rebuilt itself after World War II, its senior citizens population was pretty steady. In fact during the entire decade of the 1950s the Japanese population aged 65 years old and over (senior citizens) remained remarkably constant at 5 percent. The decades that followed, however, witnessed an explosion in this group. It doubled by the mid-1980s. As we began the new millennium, 17 percent of the Japanese population was 65 or older. And by the year 2025, over a quarter of their population will be classified as senior citizens. The most unique feature of this senior boom is in the quickness of its occurrence. In the United States, for instance, it took 75 years to expand the senior citizen group from 7 percent of the population to double that, at 14 percent. In Japan it took one-third of the time for the exact same expansion. So not only will this shift make Japan one of the world's oldest societies, but also the shift will have taken place in a span of time shorter than that in any other country anywhere in the world, ever before.

There was really nothing magical about how or why this happened. The Japanese were having fewer children at the same time that life expectancy was dramatically improving. A confluence of three trends came together to form the foundation of fewer children and much smaller families. First, Japanese couples were getting married later and later. As marriage boomed in later years, couples had much less time on their biological clock to establish a family; and when those families were established, they were much smaller because of their late start. Second, Japan is one of the world's most crowded places. When you have a relatively small island with a lot of people, it tends to dampen the desire to bring even more young ones into this already overcrowded environment. Third and finally, women began taking their place in the working world outside the home. Women in the workforce changed the dynamics of raising a family and tended to influence those sitting on the fence deciding whether to have children, to wait, or not to have children at all.

Now at the same time that birthrates were dramatically dropping, life expectancy was at all-time highs. In fact, Japan has one of the highest life expectancies anywhere in the world today. Again, looking back to the years after World War II, life expectancy in Japan for both males and females was 50 years of age. Today life expectancy for males is approaching 80 years of age and for females is almost an amazing 85 years of age.

This aging population has a very dramatic and direct impact on the workforce. In 1990, 20 percent of the Japanese workforce was made up of workers 55 and older. In the 1960s and 1970s most Japanese companies had mandatory retirement at age 55. As we started the new millennium, that group accounted for over one-quarter of the entire workforce in Japan. Think about this, in the years following World War II, there was virtually no one 55 and older working in Japanese companies. Now that age group accounts for over one-quarter of the entire workforce.

Well, you don't have to have an analyst to figure out that this shift will put great pressures on your pension system. The even bigger pressure however could be on corporate profits. Corporate profits will come under pressure from rapidly rising personnel costs. These costs will continue to spike up because in a majority of Japanese companies a worker's compensation increases along with age. Thus an explosion in age in the workforce will also cause an explosion in salary and payroll costs for most Japanese companies.

It also causes a strain for these senior workers. You see, back in 1986 the Japanese government reformed the public pension plan by cutting the benefits and, more important, by moving the age at which benefits begin from 60 years of age to 65 years of age. The problem is a lack of jobs for this age group. First, there are only so many senior positions; and because of their knowledge and experience, most workers would be in these limited senior (not entry-level) positions. Added to that is the fact that it is more financially rewarding for Japanese companies to have younger workers because these younger workers are actually paid less and thus have a much smaller negative impact on the company's bottom line.

Any aging population presents unique problems for companies as well as for individuals trying to supplement inadequate public pension incomes.

Too Close for Comfort

One part of the aging phenomenon in Japan is due to the decline in birth rates, and one part of the decline in birth rates is due to how crowded it is in Japan. The technical term for how crowded a country is, is *population density*—the number of people for every square mile of land. Looking at the economic engines of Asia, namely Japan and China, you can get some idea of just how crowded it actually is in Japan.

In China today there are 308 Chinese for every square mile. In Japan, on the other hand, it is almost three times as crowded—there are

847 Japanese for every square mile. To give you some perspective, outside of Asia, currently the world's largest economy, the United States, has but 70 Americans for every square mile; and the largest economy in Europe, Germany, has 608 people per square mile. Oh, and by the way, Japan is not the worst country in Asia from a population density standpoint. South Korea has that dubious distinction—1,119 South Koreans per square mile. What's important to understand about this population density issue is that its impact goes far beyond just birth rates and an aging population.

Population density can do strange things to demographic patterns. If the population density of the United States equaled that of Germany, it would place the total U.S. population at a little over 2.2 billion, or almost twice as large as China. On the flip side, if Germany had a population density as low as the United States does, its total population would be barely 10 million people, roughly the size of Hungary.

It was, in fact, this population density that caused real estate values to skyrocket. Remember that inflation is caused by too much money chasing too few goods. Well, too many people chasing too few houses causes real estate inflation. Owning a home in the central city was simply out of reach for most Japanese. And while demographic trends evolve and change over time, one trend that will remain constant is the geographic size of Japan. It's this small size that will tend to keep population density figures extremely high, which would always tend to inflate real estate even though some years and decades will not be as inflated as others.

Wanna Trade?

Because of its relatively small size geographically, Japan has always looked beyond its borders to do business. It wasn't always easy. After World War II Japanese products had a very poor reputation for quality. This led to very low trading. After all, who wants to buy products of poor quality? This trend began to change in the mid-1960s; and by the late 1960s and early 1970s, it had reversed itself completely. Japanese companies have adopted the strictest quality control measures around the globe. These high standards led to a turnaround in manufacturing. All of a sudden, automobiles, televisions, and semiconductors made in Japan have the highest quality standard anywhere. Japan had become the quality leader and trade exploded as a result. In the 1960s exports grew at an annual rate of 17 percent; and in the decade of the 1970s trade grew annually at an astounding 21 percent. Japan had one of the largest trade surpluses anywhere in the world.

However, as I said earlier in this chapter, when talking about the United States . . . trade deficits aren't so bad; and on the flip side, trade surpluses aren't so good.

One has to go all the way back to the "historical roots" of why nations wanted to trade in the first place. The simple answer was gold. The strategy was simple—export a lot (sell things for gold) and import very little (so you don't have to use your gold to buy things). That strategy will ensure that your kingdom will have plenty of gold. And if you have plenty of gold, you can develop a great army, and the royal family will become extremely wealthy as well.

The problem with this misguided strategy is that while it was great to have lots of gold in the castles, poverty was spreading outside the royal castle. In fact, a case can be made that this misguided strategy of all exports and no imports lead to the beginning of the end of royalty ruling the world.

A trade surplus that promotes exports while constantly letting the importing consumer lag behind is a formula for disaster today just as it was in medieval times. The future of Japan depends on developing some balance, with the importing consumer emerging as equally important as the exporting business trading boom that historically has fueled Japan's growth.

"Big Bang"

The quickest way to jump-start the consumer is to instill consumer confidence. And there is no better way to establish consumer confidence than to strengthen your banking system. In 1998 the Financial System Reform Law was enacted. This reform will deregulate and energize the banking, insurance, and brokerage sectors by opening them up to foreign investment and ownership while implementing a series of regulatory reforms.

This so called "Big Bang" reform of the financial markets in Japan allowed individual Japanese investors to invest in "non-yen" denominated investments that would provide higher returns. The name was derived from the explosion of Japanese assets that would start flowing into other countries, especially the United States, in search of higher-yielding investments.

One of the foundations of this reform package was the bank bailouts that were put in place to fix Japan's ailing banking system. Called the "Bank Revitalization Law," this legislation called for the infusion of taxpayers' public money into the failing and beleaguered banks as well as for the nationalization of insolvent banks. There has been close to $75 billion of taxpayers' money used to prop up the failing banking system. The banks that did not want to accept the strings attached to the public money looked for other sources of capital infusion in the form of bank mergers. When the Japanese government opened the financial and banking sector to foreign investment and ownership, the Japanese government was actually encouraging the merger of weak banks as well as the outright purchase of the nationalized insolvent banks. The reason was quite simple. It wanted to limit the taxpayers' cost of this bank revitalization program.

Long Term Credit Bank of Japan was one of the first banks to be nationalized. A U.S. investment firm ultimately purchased it. After the Long Term Credit Bank of Japan deal, the floodgates opened, and a series of major and strategic mergers rapidly changed the structure of the banking system forever. Fuji Bank, Dai-Ichi Kangyo Bank, and the Industrial Bank of Japan decided to join forces to create the world's largest bank with over 140 trillion yen in assets. Sumitomo and Sakura merged as well, making them the second-largest bank in the world with 99 trillion yen in assets.

The historical significance of all of this is mind-boggling. Japan is a very proud business community, which does not take failure lightly. Japanese bank reform was a public admission that the entire banking system failed. By setting its proud tradition to the side, Japan addressed its most serious problem in a most compelling way. They let the bad banks that were poorly managed fail. The banks that could be saved, the government helped bail out. And finally, they encouraged mergers and acquisitions to create even stronger banks. Their bank reform strategy almost mirrors a similar strategy that the United States adopted in the early 1980s as it bailed out its savings and loan institutions in one of the biggest financial crises ever. Back then no one wanted to invest in a U.S. financial services company. Today U.S. financial services companies are the envy of the world. I expect a similar fate for Japan. Its financial system has already risen from the ashes, and 20 years from now it will regain its place as one of the soundest financial services industries anywhere in the world.

Post Offices

Well, after you restore the consumers' confidence by fixing the ailing banking system, you still have to make sure that the consumers have money to save and invest. Enter the Japanese Post Office. Not all post offices around the world are the same. In the United States the post office is used solely for delivering mail. In Japan the post office is used for investments as well as delivering mail. That's because Japanese post offices have an investment product called postal savings accounts. These are, in essence, time deposits, which pay guaranteed rates of return of 6 percent or more. So in addition to delivering the mail, the Japanese post office lets you invest in its postal savings account. A decade ago when the Japanese stock market was crashing and interest rates were soaring, investors flocked to the post office not to mail letters but to get in on the best investment deal around—a time deposit with guaranteed returns of 6 percent or more. These time deposit accounts had a duration of 10 years.

Therefore, because this rush started a decade ago, we are about to witness an explosion in cash as these time deposits come due. In fact, over the next two years hundreds of thousands of postal savings accounts will mature with a value of more than $1 trillion yen. When these postal savings accounts mature, investors can simply decide either to put the money in another time deposit at the post office or to look for higher investment returns on their money, especially because the Japanese stock market was up 37 percent in 1999. Or they could decide to spend some of the money. The answer is probably a little bit of each. This newfound pot of gold at the post office should provide strong fundamental support for both the Japanese stock market and the Japanese economy. What a great post office!

EMERGING MARKETS

What Is It?

Looking beyond Japan, Let's focus on our final global sphere of influence . . . emerging markets. To many savvy investors the term *emerging markets* is as common as the Dow Jones Industrial Average. Yet the Dow Jones Industrial Average has been around for over a century, and the term emerging markets is not even a quarter-century old yet. An employee of the World Bank, Antoine van Agtmael, coined the term emerging markets back in 1981, and it has been with us ever since.

In the simplest of terms an emerging market is one that is trying to "emerge" to become a more developed market. Think of an emerging market as an economy trying to improve itself and move on to the next level. The World Bank classifies economies with the gross national product (GNP) per capita of $9,655 and below as emerging markets. Using that World Bank definition, let me put emerging markets into some global perspective for you. Emerging markets account for 6 percent of the total stock market capitalization around the world. This is despite the fact that emerging markets account for over 45 percent of global economic output, 70 percent of the world's land area, and an amazing 85 percent of the world's population.

Investors sometimes mistakenly think that all emerging markets must be poor. They hear alarming stories about Russia, an emerging market, and the fact that one in ten Russian hospitals were built prior to 1914 and that one in five still has no running water. Investors also mistakenly think that all emerging markets must be small. That is certainly not the case. By World Bank definition, China is an emerging market as well. It certainly isn't small, with a population of over one billion people. And it's not exactly poor, with its vast natural resources as well as its highly sophisticated military and technology advancements in both the public and private sectors.

The one thing that categorizes all emerging markets is that they are extremely volatile. And for an investor, volatility presents opportunity. The reason for this extreme volatility is that these economies are "emerging," or are in transition. As such, they are much more prone to boom-or-bust prospects regarding political, labor, currency, and market issues. In many respects, emerging markets are like a box of chocolates . . .

thinking back to the movie *Forrest Gump*. If you recall, Forrest Gump's mother believed that "life is like a box of chocolates: you never know what you are going to get." Well guess what? Emerging markets are like a box of chocolates, too. No one knows for sure what will happen. Because of this extreme volatility, emerging markets are the recipients of a variety of international funding programs that provide financial resources in a time of need, the most popular of which is the International Monetary Fund (IMF).

The Lone (Loan) Ranger

Just like yesterday, when *The Lone Ranger* raced faster than his silver bullet to rescue victims from danger in the Wild West, today's "Loan" Ranger races equally as fast—only this time we are rescuing entire nations on the brink of financial disaster all around the globe. While yesterday's Lone Ranger used a silver bullet, today's Loan Ranger uses cash.

This modern-day Loan Ranger is actually the International Monetary Fund. The IMF provides both money and structural financial policy advice to help ailing nations get back on the right track. Although many investors may have first heard of the IMF as a result of the recent economic and currency meltdown in Southeast Asia, the IMF has actually been around for over 50 years.

As the global economies languished in the 1930s, confidence for "paper" currency plummeted, while the demand for gold skyrocketed. This demand for gold was far beyond what the various national treasuries around the globe could supply. One by one, nations were ultimately forced to abandon what is known as the gold standard. The gold standard had defined a country's currency in terms of a specific amount of gold, which in turn gave this paper currency a known and rather stable exchange value. Now, when a country's paper currency no longer has a fixed value relationship to gold, exchanging paper currencies with those countries that did remain on the gold standard becomes extremely difficult, if not impossible.

These exchange-rate issues began a snowballing effect worldwide that began with a deterioration of currency exchanges between nations, which in turn led to unemployment pressures within the various nations, which in turn began to actually reduce their standard of living.

All of this added up to the near disappearance of international trade between nations in the 1930s.

It was obvious that a system was needed that would encourage nations to exchange currencies with each other and to establish a clear value for each currency. After great debate in the early 1940s, finally in July 1944, delegates of 44 nations gathered in the United States at Bretton Woods, New Hampshire, and created the IMF.

In May 1946, the IMF opened for business in Washington, D.C., with 39 members. Over the years, IMF membership has consistently grown, and today it stands at 182 countries. Any country can become a member as long as that country conducts its own foreign policy and will comply with the charter of the IMF. Even though the primary reason for its creation and existence was to focus on international exchange rates and payments, its actual focus is a whole lot wider than that. With a staff of over 2,600 employees from 110 different nations, the IMF has a three-pronged purpose. The first is surveillance. The IMF is responsible for monitoring the economic and currency-exchange policies and practices of all member nations. Second is the high-profile financial assistance given to member nations in the form of both loans and credit. Over the past decade this financial-assistance function has exploded, and now most of the focus is on the financial-assistance aspect of the organization. The third function is technical assistance in helping create both financial and monetary policies for member nations.

While the original Lone Ranger received his name because he worked alone to wipe out crime in the Wild West, the modern-day Loan Ranger rarely, if ever, works alone. While much of the attention is usually on how much money the IMF is committing to bailing out a troubled country, it's important to keep in perspective that the IMF is not working alone. The IMF works very hard at putting together a comprehensive financing package; and although the IMF may be the single largest contributor, its share rarely exceeds 50 percent of the total financing package. Think back to the beginning of our most recent economic and currency crisis in Southeast Asia, which began in Thailand. The bailout plan for Thailand was $17.2 billion. Of that amount, only $4 billion came from the IMF.

Unlike the original Lone Ranger who would rescue his victims and leave a silver bullet behind with no strings attached, the modern-day Loan Ranger rescues its victims by leaving hoards of cash behind with numerous strings attached.

Understanding this concept is critical to realizing that once the IMF becomes involved, a country's problems do not go away overnight. When the IMF lends money, it insists that countries fix their banking systems by writing off bad loans, letting insolvent banks fail, and opening markets to foreign business ownership. While all of these steps are like motherhood and apple pie in the long run, in the short run, an IMF bailout can cause unemployment to rise, which in turn causes savings to fall and both political and social tensions to explode. To understand the impact of the IMF bailing out a nation, do not think of that as the "end" of anything; instead think of it as the "beginning." Winston Churchill's historic comments regarding the end of World War II may even more appropriately describe IMF bailouts: "We are not at the beginning of the end, we are only at the end of the beginning." While in the long run the IMF bailout packages that were put together for Thailand, Indonesia, and South Korea will assure those countries' economic posterity in the future, the present will still be filled with both ups and downs. The strings attached to the cash from the IMF virtually ensure that things always get worse before they get better when the Loan Ranger is involved. Hi ho, Silver!

Show Me the Money

If emerging markets don't have to tap the International Monetary Fund or other public and quasi-public agencies for financial help, it is usually a sign that they are able to access their needed capital elsewhere. Thus the flow of capital (money) is without a doubt one of the most critical issues facing emerging markets.

What is more important than the actual capital flow is what is causing the capital flow to happen. It is useful to think of this concept in terms of inside issues (due to events or developments in emerging markets) and outside issues (due to events or developments in industrialized countries).

Let's first look at the inside issues affecting the flow of capital. There have been three developments that have supported the flow of capital.

First, the pure economic fundamentals of emerging market economies have improved. For third-party proof, look no further than the upgrading of emerging market debt by the independent credit rating agencies. Second, the overall fiscal position in most emerging markets is also improving. When your fiscal policies are headed in the right direction, they tend to serve as a catalyst to bring down interest rates as well, which is also happening. Third, the commodity price picture is improving. When commodity prices collapsed in the late 1990s it took many emerging market economies right with it. The rebound in commodity prices has served as a valuable support for emerging market economies.

Now let's look at the outside issues driving capital flow. There are really two critical issues to watch. The first is what the monetary policy of the industrialized world is. Wow, that sounds like a mouthful; however, it is really rather easy. The issue really is whether Central Banks around the world are raising interest rates or lowering them. And an easy way to find this out is to simply watch what the Federal Reserve Board (the Central Bank of the United States) is doing. You see, the Federal Reserve Board with Alan Greenspan at the helm has become the de facto Central Bank of the world. Mr. Greenspan is the most influential financial leader in the world, and where he goes most other Central Banks soon follow.

The second is that stock market trends around the world are also a major influence on capital flows to emerging markets. Because emerging markets are considered to be at the risky end of the investment spectrum, any downturn in the industrialized markets of the world places an additional pressure on capital flows to emerging markets.

Tea for Two

No discussion of emerging markets would be complete without a brief look at the issues facing China, the largest and most important of all emerging markets. The story of China today is not just about China; it's about Hong Kong as well.

International investors around the globe are still holding their collective breath, hoping that the return of Hong Kong to China will not disrupt the global financial emerging markets. Its importance transcends all markets, as Hong Kong has become the benchmark of what every economy and every market around the world would like to become. And while many have tried to mirror Hong Kong's success, no one has been able to do it.

It was nearly 20 years ago that Britain and China agreed that all of Hong Kong would revert back to Chinese rule. At that time (1984) the Hong Kong stock market was valued at $30 billion. Today the Hong Kong stock market is capitalized at over $500 billion. One reason that no one will ever duplicate Hong Kong's success is that the Hong Kong story is so unique. It was the confluence of three factors that fueled Hong Kong's success, and no country on earth can duplicate those three factors.

First, there's that age-old real estate key—location, location, location. Hong Kong is right next door to both the largest source of labor in the world and the largest consumer market on the face of the earth (China). Hong Kong is able to tap into both of these unbelievable benefits without paying any of the costs. You see, Hong Kong does not have to pay any of the social costs of sustaining the world's largest labor and consumption market. That problem and all of the costs associated with it are China's problem to bear.

Second, Hong Kong found itself in the unique position of not expending any of its precious financial or economic resources on national defense. Because Hong Kong was a British colony, national defense was Britain's problem to worry about and Britain's problem to fund, not Hong Kong's.

Third, as a result of the first two factors, Hong Kong's tax burden is among the lowest anywhere around the globe. Think about it for a minute. If as a country you don't have to worry about huge social problems and you don't have to worry about national defense, you don't need higher taxes.

Do not worry about this unique and truly unbelievable economic miracle that Hong Kong has put together. It will be just fine under Chinese rule. China will not destroy the golden economic goose.

Now that does not mean that there will not be major bumps in the road regarding the free and honest flow of financial and political information. And it doesn't mean that there will not be potential pitfalls as the civil service system evolves and changes. And the "human rights" issue will be with us for a long time to come, as will the fear that the next demonstration will turn into another Tiananmen Square affair. While all of these may be legitimate short-term issues, none will stop the successful transformation of Hong Kong and China into "one country, two systems."

Nervous investors around the globe are still searching for clues about what the future will hold for the Hong Kong market now that China has regained control of Hong Kong, ending 156 years of colonial rule by Britain. Perhaps the biggest clue to the future of the reunification of Hong Kong with China can be found in the past, in the title of the 1950s Doris Day movie *Tea for Two*.

You see, the real reason that the reunification of Hong Kong will be successful is because it is not just about Hong Kong, it's about Taiwan as well. Hong Kong is only the first step in getting what China really wants, and that is reunion with Taiwan. Unless the Hong Kong reunification is a rousing success, China can never hope to get Taiwan to the table to talk about reunification with China. While the celebration over the reunification with Hong Kong fulfills a dream of every patriotic Chinese, that dream is only halfway complete. Taiwan is what they are really dreaming about.

Once investors realize that China's ultimate goal never was just the reunification with Hong Kong, they will quickly realize that despite potential problems in the short run, in the long run China will not allow this reunification with Hong Kong to fail. After all, who wants to have a tea party with only one guest (Hong Kong)? It's much more fun having "tea for two" (Hong Kong and Taiwan).

A Modern-Day Mexican Revolution

Well, if China is the most influential of all emerging markets, then Mexico comes in a close second. After all, everyone remembers that when Mexico devalued it currency, the peso, back in 1994, it caused an emerging markets crash all over the world. So I was wondering, if you lead other emerging markets down, could you lead them up as well? After all, there is revolution going on in Mexico that could change emerging markets everywhere.

When you hear the phrase "Mexican Revolution," you probably think back to the years between 1910 and 1920, when Pancho Villa rode his horse through the streets of Mexico during this turbulent time in the country's history. But a decade from now when someone talks about the Mexican Revolution, you may think more about Vicente Fox.

You see, with his election as president of Mexico, Fox just pulled off a modern-day Mexican Revolution, the impact of which could be felt for decades to come. His stunning presidential victory abruptly ended the Institutional Revolutionary Party's 71 years of control, and it gives Fox an opportunity to create his own Mexican Revolution.

The Fox revolution will have little to do with political and military power, however. Instead, it will focus on the power of Mexico's economy and markets. I'm looking for three foundations to emerge from this modern-day Mexican Revolution.

Fox supports the deregulation of the electricity, energy, and tele-communications sectors, which is likely to lead to increased competition, lower costs, increased production, and higher profits. He wants to privatize Mexico's petrochemical plants. He wants to allow foreign investors to own shares of oil companies, which traditionally have been government owned. Eventually, he would like to end all price controls. This major move to privatization and deregulation will set the stage for highly productive and profitable sectors—and will create abundant opportunities for international companies looking to invest in Mexico.

Fox's support came from Mexico's middle class and its energized younger voters. Both of these constituents favor tax reform, which is much needed in Mexico. Oil taxes currently account for a third of Mexico's tax revenues, and this nondiversified tax-revenue stream leads to a volatile economy. Fox plans to eliminate tax exemptions, thereby broadening the tax base without increasing taxes. This will increase total tax revenues and thereby lower Mexico's dependence on oil for tax revenue. Once this transition is complete, I expect to see a variety of other tax-reform and tax-reduction programs. And as we learned all too well in the United States, when you lower tax rates, the economy actually expands.

Fox has repeatedly stated that Mexico needs a better relationship with its most important partner—the United States. With Fox in office, I expect Mexico to shift its foreign policies to better align itself with the United States. This will likely lead to landmark agreements on trade and immigration issues that have haunted the two nations for decades. Under Fox's leadership, we could see the highest Mexican cooperation ever on the war on drugs. When the cooperation starts, it will be hard to stop, and eventually we will realize that what's good for Mexico is also good for the United States and vice versa. With the United States and Mexico on the same page, the whole world will take notice when the two countries flex their collective economic muscle. To give you a peek of where this is headed, let me share this frame of reference with you. Back in 1920 the three largest groups of immigrants to the United States were Germans, Italians, and Russians. Together they accounted for one-third of the United States population. Today almost one-third of the immigrants in the United States are of Mexican origin, and the cooperation hasn't even started. As this border disappears, you will not be able to tell if you are in the southern United States or northern Mexico.

Special Risk . . . HIV/AIDS

While there clearly are more financial risks associated with emerging market investments than with almost any other asset class, there is a nonfinancial risk to emerging markets that may transcend all other risks—and that is HIV/AIDS.

Historically we think of HIV/AIDS as a medical and health risk, not as an economic or financial one. HIV/AIDS is an out-of-control epidemic in the emerging markets of Africa. Let me quantify the magnitude of this problem.

As the new millennium began, there were a little over 30 million people living around the world with HIV/AIDS. Of those 30-plus million people, more than 25 million are in Africa. The most serious problems are in Southern Africa. Currently 36 percent of the adult population in Botswana, 25 percent in Zimbabwe and Swaziland, and 20 percent in South Africa and Zambia are infected. This compares to 1.1

percent for the world as a whole. As a result life expectancy will plunge from 60 years to 30 years for most African nations, and some nations will see their population growth turn negative. What makes this issue even more complex is that HIV/AIDS has a long incubation period. As a result of this long incubation period, the actual impact of the disease will be gradual, and its full effect has yet to be felt.

From a purely economic perspective this HIV/AIDS epidemic will create four economic pressure points for emerging markets in Africa:

First and most obvious will be the explosion in costs of health care to deal with this problem. Health care will continue to take a larger and larger portion of gross domestic product.

Second, the skilled labor force will dry up. It will be extremely difficult to try to replace the highly skilled and highly trained doctors, nurses, engineers, and teachers who fall victim to HIV/AIDS.

Third, productivity will collapse. This productivity collapse will be the result of constant labor turnover, a shrinking labor force supply, and an explosion in absenteeism. In some countries, government employees may take up to one year of sick leave if they are diagnosed HIV/AIDS positive.

Fourth and finally, income disparity will expand to even greater extremes. HIV/AIDS creates a vicious economic cycle. HIV/AIDS reduces economic growth. This reduction in economic growth leads to increased poverty. Increased poverty means households have less to spend on food and health. A decline in food and health expenditures reduces resistance to infections, which in turn causes HIV/AIDS to spread.

At the other end of the spectrum, the highly skilled members of the workforce who are not affected will become more and more scarce, which in turn will lead to even higher wages for the skilled workforce, which will create an even greater economic disparity among African emerging markets.

The HIV/AIDS epidemic just might be the single greatest nonfinancial and financial risk that emerging markets will face in the next decade.

DR. BOB'S NOTES . . . TOP 10 THINGS TO REMEMBER!

Chapter 2

10 The Internet "boom" in Europe will be more like a "bust" because of language barriers and the low usage of consumer credit (credit cards).

9 Whenever the International Monetary Fund (IMF) gets involved with an emerging market, things always get worse in the short run before they get better because of all of the strings attached to IMF money, which forces economies to get a handle on such things as their budget deficit.

8 Continued record-low unemployment in the United States will not lead to wage inflation.

7 Population density (it's too crowded) will always keep Japanese real estate prices somewhat inflated.

6 The senior citizen boom in Japan is creating an older workforce, which, due to higher wages and salaries, will eat into Japanese corporate profits.

5 Tax reform in Germany will have a ripple effect that will lead to major tax reform all throughout Europe.

4 The United States has a unique trade deficit because of the components it is importing (low-priced commodities) and exporting (high-priced, value-added goods and services). As a result the trade deficit will not be falling anytime soon.

3 The single greatest risk to many emerging markets is the nonfinancial risk of HIV/AIDS because of the negative economic impact on the workforce and ultimately on productivity.

2 The Post Office Savings Account transfers in Japan will fuel both the Japanese economy and the Japanese equity market.

1 The United States savings rate will finally begin to improve as baby boomer demographic forces of the "over-50 crowd" kick in.

Chapter 3

The Technology Revolution Is Creating the "I" (Information Age) Generation

Everything that can be invented has been invented.

Charles H. Duell
Commissioner, U.S. Office of Patents (1899)

Poor Charles Duell is probably rolling over in his grave. Since his proclamation in 1899, we have invented the airplane, the radio, the television, the VCR, the microwave oven, the personal computer, the cellular telephone, and the Internet. And remember, it's that last invention, the Internet, that's the real fuel behind the technology revolution.

Any discussion about the technology revolution and the new information age must both begin and end with a focus on the greatest information invention in our lifetime, namely the Internet. To give you some idea of the order of magnitude of this new information age, simply think back to when the information age began. The age of information really began when Gutenberg invented the printing press. It changed the world forever and unleashed information to anyone who wanted it. Think of the Internet as our modern-day version of the invention of the printing press; only we don't have to wait to print anything before we can read it. Instead, everything is online, in real time, connecting individuals from every corner of the earth in a truly global network of information and communication.

Information Explosion

Let me attempt to quantify this information age explosion for you so you can see why its impact will be even more profound than that of the printing press. If we would add up all of the information since the beginning of time that is recorded on paper today, it would amount to roughly 200 petabytes. Now for you nontechies, remember a byte equals a printed character. One petabyte is one quadrillion characters. A quadrillion isn't millions or billions, it's trillions; a quadrillion is a thousand trillion characters. Thus 200 petabytes is actually 200,000 trillion characters. When I say everything that is recorded on paper since the beginning of time, I mean every piece of paper in every government, business, school, and home everywhere in the world. If we would add that all up, it's estimated to be 200 petabytes. So throughout the entire history of time we have been able to capture 200 petabytes of information on paper. Currently the Internet has over 500 petabytes of information. Thus in the short time since the Internet was invented, we have stored over two and a half times the amount of all the printed information in the world. No wonder that little hourglass pops up when you are looking for information on the Internet.

And this wealth of information and the storing of information also means that we can use our minds in better ways. Henry Ford and Albert Einstein knew this long before the Internet was discovered. The *Chicago Tribune* once called Henry Ford an "ignoramus" in print. He actually then sued the paper and challenged them to prove it. In the heat of the trial, Ford was asked dozens of simple questions in rapid-fire succession, such as, "When was the Civil War?" "Name the presidents of the United States." And so on and so on. Ford, who had very little formal education, could answer very few.

Finally Henry Ford, who was frustrated with the line of questioning, blurted out, "I don't know the answers to those questions, but I could find a man who does in five minutes. I use my brain to think, not to store up a lot of useless facts."

Meanwhile Albert Einstein, when asked how many feet were in a mile, responded "I don't know." Einstein went on to say, "Why should I fill my head with things like that when I could look them up in any reference book in two minutes?"

These two legends of industry knew that it's the ability to get information and to act on it that gets things done. The Internet gives us access to greater amounts of information than ever before. Thanks to the Internet, we have the chance to get more things done than ever before.

Where Did the Internet Come From?

Sometimes the best way to figure where something is going to take us is to start by figuring out where it came from in the first place.

Like the Internet itself with its vast array of information, the history of the Internet is vast, complex, and sometimes even confusing. The reason is because the creation of the Internet involved several different aspects: First there were the technological aspects, then organizational aspects, and finally community aspects.

The first recorded descriptions of the Internet occurred in August 1962 at the Massachusetts Institute of Technology (MIT). Back then however it was called a "Galactic Network." This Galactic Network envisioned a globally interconnected set of computers through which everyone could quickly access both data and programs from any site anywhere. In reality this Galactic Network was very much like the Internet today.

The first public demonstration of this technology did not occur until a decade later in 1972. In October 1972 at the International Computer Communication Conference, electronic mail (e-mail) was introduced. Let the games begin. You've got mail!

Impact of the Internet

The Internet means many different things to many different people. The only common thread is that the Internet is affecting every single one of us, whether we realize it or not. The Internet has quickly become the greatest source for information on every subject that you ever dreamed of researching. And when you are not researching something, you can download a song, or buy an airline ticket, or check the weather, or pay your monthly bills or even your income taxes. This all occurs between checking your e-mail and instant messaging your buddy list.

Think about this: As little as 10 years ago most libraries in the United States still used a manual index-card catalog system (the card catalog). Today almost all libraries are computerized and most are connected to the Internet, where you can look up a book, check it out, and have it mailed to you without ever leaving your family room. I am not sure where we will be ten years from now, but I can guarantee you that it will make today's high-tech library Internet system seem as much in the dark ages as a manual index-card catalog system in a library seems today.

The Internet impact in the United States is staggering. Internet activity is increasing at roughly 200 percent per year. Currently Internet activity accounts for over $300 billion, which is just about the size of the entire automotive sector. Almost one-third of the growth of the gross domestic product (GDP—the economy) in the United States comes from the Internet. Oh, and while it is adding almost one-third of the growth, it is also taking away a full percent on the inflation front.

Today over half of the United States population have access to the Internet. Households in the United States with children aged 2 to 17 had limited access to the Internet just four years ago, when the penetration stood at less than 15 percent. Today over 55 percent of U.S. households with children ages 2 to 17 have Internet access. The United States is the world's leader in ownership of modems, the communication devices that enable personal computers (PCs) to connect to the Internet and other online services. The rest of the world is gaining ground, and in fact the United States is no longer the leader in proportional personal computer ownership; that distinction belongs to Australia.

Over 52 percent of Australians own a personal computer. The Netherlands and the United States are next with 43 percent PC ownership. Both Canada and Hong Kong are right behind with 41 percent. Germany, Sweden, Finland, and Switzerland all have over 33 percent of their population owning computers. This is clearly a global story with global impact. In sheer numbers, however, it's easy to see why the United States is still the center of the technology revolution. The United States currently accounts for less than 5 percent of the world's total population at the same time that the United States has more computers than the rest of the world combined!

When thinking of the impact of the Internet, sometimes you get a better perspective if you think small. In other words, instead of trying to figure out the impact that the Internet is having on some country's economy, instead focus on the impact that the Internet is having on an individual company. Take the case of British Telecom, for example. British Telecom spent $10 million developing its intranet site. It has already saved over $650 million thanks to the efficiency of their new intranet. Now that's what I call impact.

Retail, Front and Center

Since the invention of the Internet, its potential and uses seem to expand almost daily. One of those directions in which the Internet is expanding is the retail sector. Although retailing on the Internet is still in its early developing stages, it offers unbelievable opportunity in both sales (dollar volume) and marketing (brand and promotions).

As more and more households have computers and, more important, access to the Internet, this so called "e-tailing" should have a very bright future. And as the adult population becomes more and more familiar with new technology, they will express a new willingness to shop online. Meanwhile the younger generation also continues to get older, to get a job, and finally to get a credit card. You need that plastic if you are going to drive retail sales.

All is not bright however for the retail sector as a result of the Internet. While I firmly believe that the Internet will increase the overall demand for the merchandise that retailers are trying to sell, I also fear that some of these sales are going to come at the expense of the two traditional channels of retailing—stores and catalogs.

How Do You Buy a Book?

If you want a glimpse of just how technology can change retailing, just think of how technology has changed the way we do a simple task like buying a book. Twenty-five years ago, if you wanted to buy a book you went a small local bookstore. The clerk would know the exact location of every book in the store. And if you wanted a book that the store didn't have, you could order it and stop back in a week or so to see if the store had located a copy for you.

Fast forward to our options regarding how to buy a book today. . . . Instead of the small neighborhood bookstore, we have the mega-bookstores. These stores would never have been possible without technology and the birth of the computer. Whether you find yourself at a Barnes & Noble or a Borders megabookstore, you can browse over 200,000 books under one roof. Not only would it be tough to find a book without the aid of computers, but inventory would take forever if it weren't computerized.

If by chance you don't want to leave your home to go to one of these megabookstores, you can just buy books online. Amazon.com has over 2.5 million titles available for you to purchase on its website without ever leaving your home.

Just think about the choices and options technology has created for us in the simple task of buying a book. We went from a few hundred choices under one roof at your local bookstore to 200,000 choices under one roof at a megabookstore to over 2.5 million choices under your own roof when you stay at home and shop online.

It's Not Just the Book

The Internet has not only changed how we buy a book, but it has also changed how people that sell a book make money. In the traditional business model, profit margins on traditional books ran about 5 percent. Thus when you bought a $25 book, the bookstore profited $1.25. With this profit the bookstore had to pay its employees, rent, taxes, and so forth.

Now in the Internet world, the margin on these books is getting lower and lower. Thus you may now make less than $1/2$ of 1 percent if you are an Internet site such as Amazon.com selling books. In order to make up the difference, you sell something else. And what you sell is information. Information regarding book reviews, information regarding what other readers think, information about other books the author has written, information about authors similar to this author. Amazon.com gets paid for selling this information through vendors that pay Amazon.com to advertise on their website. Thus in this new Internet age, Amazon.com gets paid both for the book (from the ultimate buyer) and for information about the book (from advertisers on their website). You see the rules are changing for everyone.

If you want to be a hunter on the Internet, remember you don't shoot where the rabbit was but rather where it's going.

Technology Is First on the Internet

Whether you run a book store, a clothing store, or a general discount store, successful retailers on the Internet will have three distinct keys to their success: technology, marketing, and implementation.

The technology piece is pretty straightforward and easy to understand. In the most basic of terms, the technology has to work. People are shopping online because it is a convenience to them not to have to drive to the store but rather to shop right at home. If, however, a retailer's Internet site is complicated and hard to get around, where is the convenience? Also, the system needs to be fast and efficient. Remember again that these are time-pressed shoppers. They don't want to waste a lot of time at a site because a retailer does not have the necessary system capacity to do all the things it wants its site to do. And finally, remember that the whole reason that there is a website in the first place is to get people to buy something; thus the ease and simplification of ordering merchandise is paramount to success. You can do your own test on your favorite retailing site. One of the neat unwritten rules of the Internet is the three-click rule: If you have to click on the mouse more than three times to get to an item to buy, chances are that not many of these items will be sold on the Internet, nor will this site be a very viable site.

Marketing, Marketing, and Marketing

Technology will not determine which retailers will be the winners and losers on the Internet. Rather technology will enable retailers to compete on the Internet. This technology will quickly become nothing more than a commodity. Most retailers will be able to pay for the technology that enables them to compete; however, it becomes clear that marketing and not technology will determine the winners on the Internet.

Successful marketing on the Internet will embrace two key principles: information and customization. From the information front the Internet provides the retailer with the possibility to provide potential customers with more information than ever before dreamed possible. Details on how things are manufactured and produced will soon become commonplace on a retailer's website. If a customer—any customer—wants to know about a product, the answer should be able to be found on the website.

The real future of the Internet and the one that will launch the ultimate winners and losers is in the area of customization. In an age where the customer rules, customization becomes the founding principle.

I can't tell you how many times in my life that I have gone shopping and *almost* found the right thing. Like when I tell the salesperson, "This is the perfect shirt. However, do you have it with French cuffs?" No. Or, "I love this striped shirt. Do you have it in white?" No. Or, "I found it, however, do you have any without front pockets?" You guessed it. . . . No.

That frustration will be a thing of the past with the customization on the Internet. Once you log on, you can design your shirt exactly the way you want it with the exact features and styles that you want. A retailer will never, ever again be out of what you want because as soon as you customize it and order it, the retailer makes it for you . . . similar to ordering a whopper at Burger King, where they pride themselves on you having it "your way." Every retailer will have to follow Burger King's lead. If you want to win the retail battle on the Internet, customization is your best weapon.

Implement This

The final piece of the retail Internet puzzle will be implementation. In other words, was your order handled properly and fulfilled, and was it delivered where it was supposed to be delivered? Just like technology, this aspect of retailing on the Internet will be commoditized as well. Customers are not going to do business with you on the Internet just because you handled their order properly and delivered it to the right place. Very soon everyone will have the infrastructure in place to be able to carry out the implementation. Thus there will be very little, if any, way to differentiate your product here. As everyone is able to implement and as this becomes a commodity like the technology, it becomes clearer and clearer that the company that will win the retail battles on the Internet will be a marketing-driven organization.

Beyond Apparel

When most investors think of retailing on the Internet, their thoughts begin and end with the apparel sector. Whether it's Gap or Nordstrom or Guess, when we think retail, we think apparel. And although this will be a key driver of retailing over the Internet, it will not be the only driver. Think of the pharmaceutical and health care sector, for example. Think of how the old fashioned drugstore will now automatically replenish a prescription for you and send you an e-mail telling you it's in the mail, on its way. And just think of the possibilities when you have all of your medical records and information filed on your drugstore Internet site. The drugstore will be able to exactly match its products with your health care needs. The potential is limitless. And it doesn't stop at the pharmaceutical and health care sector.

Think outside the box for a minute to a sector that very few people think about buying online, namely major home furnishings. This forgotten sector, major home furnishings, might just have the most to gain with the birth of the Internet. Consider these possibilities—you go online not just to buy furniture, but to design your room. After you put in the dimensions and add windows, you pick a paint color or wallpaper. Next you choose the type and the color of the sofa to put in your room. You change the sofa fabric, change it again, and then you get to see exactly how it will look. Then you move on to select tables. You choose the wood, and after you see it, you decide the wood selection doesn't go with the wallpaper, so it's back to paint. When you are finished with your high-tech interactive experience, not only are you buying furniture, you are also custom designing your lifestyle. And when you are done, you simply click on any item, and you've just bought it.

European E-tailing Goes Global

What becomes quickly apparent is that no matter what subsector you are in within retail, there can and needs to be an Internet strategy. This is especially true of European retailers who have traditionally thought of themselves as this nice little cottage industry serving only Europe. Well, the Internet has certainly changed all of that. Today all European retailers better be aware of global competition because the Internet is bringing those competitors from around the globe, right to their front door. Like it or not.

In my opinion, European retailers will be some of the big losers when the Internet forces all European retailers to go global. I think that less than 20 percent will be around a decade from now. Two things will cause that 80 percent to fail. First, some products or services will actually become redundant with the Internet. In other words, manufacturers and service providers alike can go straight to the buying public. Second, too many European retailers are ill-equipped to stand the onslaught of global competition. Think about the remaining 20 percent, however. The beauty of the stock market is that there are always winners and losers. The 20 percent that remain will not just be winners; they will be *big* winners representing Europe in the global retail marketplace. And although I may not be able to correctly select all 20 percent of European retailers who will make it, I can correctly identify the one trait that the successful 20 percent must and will have—a strong brand name and identity. Brand is critical in the retail Internet world where you have an abundance of choice—some would say far, far too many choices.

No one has time to visit over 100 websites to buy a shirt online. Instead, consumers will gravitate to the websites of those companies that already have and continue to promote brand identity.

What about TMT?

No discussion regarding Europe and technology would be complete without briefly touching on one of the hottest acronyms in investing today, namely TMTs. The acronym TMT stands for Technology, Media, and Telecommunication. One of the really exciting things about investing in TMT in Europe is that these sectors have evolved in such a way that they are so interrelated and rely so much on each other that they feed off each other's synergies, which tends to support all these components. In some ways it has become a self-reinforcing sector.

You need Technology because without technology you would not have the necessary infrastructure. This technology could be in the form of a personal computer, a mobile handset, and so forth. Now that you have the technology, you need some content. You guessed it; the Media controls the content. So it's easy to see how technology and media support one another; however, without telecommunications, the third and final piece, the consumer, is not able to access any of the content. There needs to be a way for the media to provide transmissions to the consumer. Enter Telecommunication. One really can't grow without the other two, and it's easy to envision how one could find oneself in a very positive loop regarding TMTs in Europe.

Although TMT is commonly viewed as one sector, it is still extremely important to understand the different components that make up TMT.

From the technology perspective, European Internet service providers (ISPs) as well as equipment manufacturers face a huge challenge due to the diversity of the cultures that make up Europe. Think about it this way: The technology that is driving the Internet as well as personal computers is English language based. Any wonder why penetration has been slower in Germany and France and Italy and so on? It's a slam dunk that the United States leads on the Internet; after all it's speaking their language. Also, within Europe a national leader dominates each country, which is the central reason why the market has remained extremely fragmented. And as if things aren't tough enough, technology in Europe is further hampered by costly regulatory and operating license fee issues. The silver lining in Europe is the rapid advancement and the increasing sophistication of multilingual systems. As this aspect of the Internet develops, it will bring all of Europe along with it.

Media companies are facing their own set of challenges. Publishers are scrambling to make their mark online the same way that they have with traditional networks. Meanwhile television stations continue their merger-and-acquisition binge as they realize that consolidation is the only way to fight off the onslaught of U.S. networks. In Europe publishing companies just must be a better player than television networks.

Now for the final leg of the TMT strategy, Telecommunications. It may be the last; however, it certainly is not the least. Telecommunications in Europe is one of the most, if not *the* most, exciting sector. And the reason is quite simple, integration. European cellular telephones operate on one digital standard. To service the entire United States, you would need almost 400 cellular phone licenses. And you guessed it; these licenses operate on multiple digital standards. The United States continues to be light-years behind Europe in telecommunications. Unlike their counterparts in the United States, European telecommunications companies are able to offer the full spectrum of service—fixed telephone, cellular phone, long-distance, Internet service, cable television, network television, and data transmission. With this diversification it's no wonder that they leave the U.S. telecoms in the dust.

European telecoms also have another advantage, and that is related to their geography. You see, nations within what once were considered isolated areas of Europe are now all connected. To them, telecommunications isn't a luxury; it's an economic necessity. If they had to wait for the traditional impractical telecommunications infrastructure, the world would pass them by. However, with mobile phones, we have instant infrastructures.

Where's My Shopping Mall?

From my observations of two daughters who have logged more than their share of time at the malls and a wife who loves shopping as well, all of this Internet discussion at the retail level leads to the question, "Will shopping malls become obsolete?" And what will my wife and daughters do?

I do not believe that malls will become obsolete; however, the Internet will continue to change everything it encounters, including the shopping mall. And the reason is pure economics. Retailers have to figure out how to converge the old economy with the new. I'm sure you've heard of the great one-liner in retail, "It's the clicks versus the bricks." Well the clicks represent the new wave of Internet retailers where you simply click on their websites and the bricks represent the old traditional retailers with their brick (and mortar) buildings.

Well, the pure economics of these clicks versus bricks is causing everyone to take a second look. On the negative side, the costs for the traditional retailer continue to trend only one way, and that way is upward. The cost of bricks and mortar and wood, for that matter, is rising. Real estate and real estate taxes continue to rise. The cost of people and the cost of providing them health care benefits continue to rise. And finally, taxes continue to go up as well.

On the positive side the clicks retailers' basic costs are coming down. The cost to make a phone call is trending down, the cost to fax data is falling. Both hardware and software technology costs are falling as well. Thus everything the clicks retailer needs to conduct business just got cheaper, while everything the bricks retailer needs continues to get more expensive.

What does all of this have to do with shopping malls? Simply that to survive, they need to change. They need to be more than just a place to shop; they need to be an entertainment center. Think of the Mall of America in Minneapolis as leading the way. For any of you that haven't been there, I'm here to tell you your life is not complete without a stop at the Mall of America. It's not just a shopping center; it's an entertainment center. Movies, food, roller coaster, more food, you name it; there is more to do there than at most amusement parks. Believe me, malls are not going away. However, they must reinvent themselves to become entertainment centers, not just shopping centers. If you build it they will come, especially if you entertain them.

Get Smart (Card)

The final frontier, which will push retailing on the Internet to levels never before dreamed possible, is the development of the smart card. These smart cards, which will be the same size if not smaller than today's traditional credit cards, will know everything there is to know about you.

The smart card will have your entire health history in one chip—every surgery, every doctor's visit, every medication you have ever taken, allergies, doctors both past and present. Just think how great it will be never to have to answer those dumb questions when you go to into a hospital. Simply swipe you smart card and the hospital has it all.

It doesn't stop with medical information. Every bit of your financial information is here as well—checking account, savings accounts, investment accounts, credit cards, mortgages, loans, insurance, anything that has anything to do with your money.

In addition, the smart card will contain all of your travel information—airlines and your frequent flyer numbers; an inventory of every car you have ever rented, listing the ones you loved and hated; every hotel you've ever stayed in; restaurants in every city you've traveled to; and the list goes on and on.

Let your imagination wander for a minute on how this smart card will change retailing forever. Swipe the card at any computer, and instantly it will get your travel options. Hit "Yes," and everything is loaded on your card—airline travel, hotel, rental car. And on each step of your trip, your smart card will pay for whatever portion you want. The paperless society is coming.

The single greatest addiction in the world today is not alcohol or tobacco or heroin. It's technology. You see, just like heroin or tobacco or alcohol, once you get it you need more. No matter whether it is a new gadget or an old gadget with a new bell and whistle placed on it, technology junkies will line up in droves to buy it. Because of this, the smart card will be a huge success.

I don't know about you but I can't wait to get my smart card. The opportunities are endless. I had the misfortune last year of having a kidney stone attack; and for any of you that haven't had one, the pain ranks right up there with childbirth (my lovely wife, Cheryl, still holds out that childbirth is number one and reminds me that I'll never know). Anyhow, I had the misfortune of being hospitalized while I was traveling away from home. Now you have to picture this—I'm in extreme pain, I'm convinced I'm dying, and all the paramedics in the ambulance want to know is my Social Security number. Once I get to the hospital, I have to go over all this information again regarding insurance, employment, allergies, . . . because the people in the ambulance obviously kept it for themselves and didn't share it with anyone at the hospital. Finally to get out of the hospital, I had to answer these same questions another time. While I don't wish any of you a visit to the hospital anytime soon, I for one can't wait to make the visit with my smart card.

Global Infrastructure

No matter how many smart cards are or are not developed or no matter how "smart" you think you are, you aren't going anywhere in technology until the global technology infrastructure is firmly in place.

The global infrastructure needs are not merely billions of dollars but rather trillions of dollars. This global infrastructure buildout is going to occur in all countries, both developed and underdeveloped, which is typically not the case when you are talking about the infrastructure for anything. Normally your basic infrastructure needs are required only in the underdeveloped or emerging nations, not the developed ones. Here's why technology is different and why it will impact both. In the emerging economies—the underdeveloped nations, if you will—the global infrastructure needs that are being addressed are pretty simple and basic telecommunications needs and services. On the flip side the developed nations face an equally daunting task as they attempt to wire their nation with fiber optic networks and integrated satellite systems in order to stay on top of the information superhighway. Both of these buildouts will require trillions of dollars of investment to complete. The future should indeed be bright for those companies that provide the services to create this global infrastructure. If you think about it, the whole world is virtually their client, both the developed nations as well as the underdeveloped nations. And while investing in underdeveloped nations or emerging markets sometimes can be risky, that risk too is somewhat mitigated when dealing with infrastructure projects. You see there is very little debate or disagreement about whether these basic infrastructure telecommunication needs should be met. In addition, many of these projects in underdeveloped nations actually receive a guarantee from the government to ensure payment for the various infrastructure projects.

One of the reasons that this global infrastructure buildout is so misunderstood is that there really is no clear or accepted definition of exactly what global technology infrastructure is. Very few, if any, of you would consider a simple television set as global technology infrastructure. Not so fast, though. What if your television set happens to be high-definition television? Would that be technology? Or let's take it one step further. Suppose your television has web-TV and is your interface to the World Wide Web; and every day before you turn on your favorite sitcom, you first turn on your TV to check your e-mail. Now would your television be considered technology infrastructure? Now let's not stop with your television. What about your automobile? No matter what make or model you happen to drive, more and more vehicles are becoming more and more computerized and high-tech gadgets. Should an automobile be considered technology infrastructure? Probably not, but somehow we have to account for all of the technology that is embedded in these new high-technology computers that happen to have wheels.

Maybe the best way to think about the global technology infrastructure buildout that is needed is to think of it as the train that you see on the horizon heading toward you. First, you can't tell exactly how far away it is. Second, you can't tell how fast it's traveling. But third and finally, you do know that the train is coming. Well, that's the same with the global technology infrastructure. We really don't know exactly how far away it is, nor can we quantify exactly how fast it is coming. The only thing that we know for sure is that it is indeed coming. And it is bringing along with it a great long-term-investment opportunity. All aboard!

PRODUCTIVITY

Once the global technology infrastructure is in place, we will begin to reap the real benefits of technology, namely productivity. Just about all of the enhancements and improvements in technology over the past decade have led to improved productivity in some capacity or another. Consider the fact that the actual price of computing power has fallen in half each year over the past decade, while at the same time the speed of computers has doubled. Think about this for a minute: The price of computing is falling by half while at the same time the speed at which your computer can process information is more than doubling. That means that every new chip that's added in a new computer is adding value to all of those computer chips that are already in existence. This unprecedented trend has caused Wall Street economists to quip that if the same phenomenon were applied to the automobile sector, for example, a new car today would cost less than $10 and would run thousands of miles without refueling; and when it got old, there would be no need to trade it in on a new one—you'd simply throw it away! Now that's what I call productivity.

Productivity Defined

Let's step back for a minute and clearly define exactly what *productivity* is. From a purely economic perspective, productivity has been defined simply as "output divided by input." In other words, how much did it take (input) to create a finished product (output)? Thus, if you wanted more productivity, you simply increased the input hoping for even more increased output. And the input has traditionally been labor and capital. So if you want more of something, simply have more people and more material. This will not only give you more, but it will be more productive as well. Consider the case of building a car. If our input is 3 people and the metal to build a car, it takes a certain time to produce the output, in this case the car. Thus, if you want to improve the productivity, increase the input. In this case, instead of using 3 people, you use 10 people. With 10 people and metal material, you can build a car a lot faster than three people and metal material. Want to increase productivity even more? Change some of the metal input to plastic, which is easier to work with and lighter to move around. Thus, it's easy to see under this definition of productivity that when you tinker with the input, productivity will improve.

The problem with this definition of productivity is that eventually simply increasing the input (labor or capital) would have less and less impact on the output. In economic circles this is called the theory of diminishing returns.

Back to the automobile example. Let me show you what is meant when I say that eventually increasing input will have little if any impact on output. When you double the number of people to make a car from 3 to 6, productivity rises. When you move from 6 to 10, productivity rises again. When you move from 10 to 20, productivity still continues to rise. However at some point adding more labor will not enable you to make cars any faster. That point is called the point of diminishing returns. In the automobile example, maybe that point is when you get to 100 people. With this many people working on a single car, they are falling all over each other. In addition one worker has to wait for another to finish something so they are not getting in each other's way. In this case adding 10 more people to make it 110 would not get the automobile produced any faster because the point of diminishing returns has been reached. The problem with this definition of productivity is that it doesn't account for technology. You see, this model always considered input as only labor and capital. But technology is input as well; and unlike labor and capital, technology doesn't have a point of diminishing returns. The reason is that technology creates more new ideas, which creates more efficiency, which again improves productivity. While everyone has pretty much accepted the economic miracle of productivity as being driven by our technology revolution, no one has come up with a good methodology of how to capture this productivity boom.

It's Different This Time

I know that you are probably sick of hearing someone on Wall Street arguing about whether it's different this time. Well as it relates to productivity, this technology revolution is really different. If you think of it in terms of the most recent major revolutions being the agriculture revolution, the industrial revolution, and the technology revolution, watch what happens. The agricultural revolution changed the farm and the way we do farming around the world forever. It's impact however was limited to the farm and had very little, if any, impact beyond the agricultural sector. Next came the industrial revolution. In simplistic terms, this revolution modernized the manufacturing process. Thus every sector or industry with a manufacturing process was touched by the industrial revolution; thus it had a much greater impact than the agricultural revolution did. Now comes the technology revolution. This revolution will have a greater and more far-reaching impact than all of the other prior revolutions combined. The reason is that it touches everyone's life everywhere around the globe. The way we work and the way we live have been and are continuing to be changed by technology. Technology is everywhere, from controlling the heat and air conditioning in most buildings to controlling traffic signals to telling you when your food is done. Technology touches almost every aspect of everyone's life. There has never been a more far-reaching revolution in the history of time. Like I said, it really *is* different this time.

Want more proof of how it's different this time? Consider the aspects of prior revolutions. Both of the most recent prior revolutions, agriculture and industrial, were very capital intensive. The technology revolution uses less capital, not more. Both the agricultural and the industrial revolutions were very labor intensive. The technology revolution is less labor intensive. And finally, and most important, the prior revolutions were heavy users of raw materials like steel, water, chemicals, and iron. Meanwhile the raw material that the technology revolution utilizes is free and it is limitless. Knowledge is the raw material of the technology revolution.

Knowledge Based

Recall that in the Introduction of this book I stated that the Internet couldn't be constrained by the economic laws and principles of scarcity. Well guess what—knowledge is the same way. Remember that scarcity was one of the key economic principles that formulated the concept that the population will always increase faster than the food supply. But unlike food or water, which are physical resources to which the principles of scarcity apply, knowledge is not a physical resource but rather an intellectual resource that defies the laws of scarcity. The more physical resources you use, the less there is—the resources become depleted. Knowledge, on the other hand, cannot be depleted. And the most amazing thing about knowledge is that using it actually creates more. So unlike a physical resource, when once you use it there is less, with the intellectual resource of knowledge, the more you use the more there is. This is because if you use your knowledge in a certain field and pass it on to someone else, then that person has a level of knowledge in this field. That person in turn passes that knowledge on to two more people, and so on and so on and so on. Thus with knowledge, the more of it you use, the more of it there is to use.

Furthermore, think of how we access knowledge. Physical resources become very complex to access, whether it's steel or water or some other physical resource; whereas the intellectual resource of knowledge is very simple to access—you need one basic principle, education. Education is the key to knowledge, which is the key to productivity, which is the key to technology, which just may hold the key to everything else. Do you remember when your mother told you to get a good education? Well, guess what, she was right.

Drives Competition

Watch how productivity will drive competition to levels that we never dreamed possible. Remember, productivity is driven by knowledge; or looked at another way, the resource that productivity uses the most of is knowledge. What does this mean for the typical technology company? The answer is pretty simple. The way you use knowledge is through extensive research-and-development (R&D) efforts; so we can expect to see R&D budgets continue to soar to the moon. Now think about the entire product cycle for a minute. You spend a boatload of money on research and development; you bring your product to market and as sales rise, your cost of this product falls and you in turn drop the price of your product. The key technology company will be the innovator—the first to market—and as other companies scramble to compete with your new product, you are attempting to maintain your competitive edge by inventing or in some cases reinventing different products. There is a deadly one-two punch going on here. First, he who innovates wins; thus this focus on innovation will keep everyone competitive. Second, even if you hit a product "homerun," you cannot rest on your laurels. Technology is moving so fast and product life cycles are so short that obsolescence is no longer thought of in years but rather in months. You are always forced to look for the next new product. This collapsed product life cycle will also keep companies competitive. When technology moved slowly, it was okay to rest on your laurels. After all, it took a while to move from 8-track to cassette tapes. Then it was a little shorter time to move from cassette tapes to compact discs (CDs). Now technology is moving so fast that even if you have the winning product, that product will very soon become another dinosaur of our times.

Mr. Dee Hock, the founder of the VISA card, summed it up best when he said, "The problem is never how to get innovative thoughts into your mind, but how to get the old ones out."

The Results Are Mind-Boggling

When more and more companies continue to compete with one another, productivity continues to soar. A great measure of productivity is to track where costs have gone. When you do this with technology, it is absolutely staggering. Thirty years ago, the cost of one megabit of data storage was $5,252. (A *megabit* is one of those techy terms for one million bits of information.) Put another way, 30 years ago, to store one million bits of information cost $5,252. Today it costs only 17 cents! But the story doesn't simply end with storing information; it transcends to sending information as well. Thirty years ago, if you needed to send one trillion bits of data, your cost was $150,000. Today you can send one trillion bits of data for 12 cents.

If you go back even further in time, these examples become even more dramatic. In 1930 the average airline revenue per mile was 68 cents. Today it's fewer than 10 cents. In 1930 the cost of a three-minute, person-to-person, long-distance telephone call from Chicago to London was over $250. Today it's under $2.50. Remember one of the great measurements of productivity is whether prices are falling.

And it's not just the falling prices but the enhanced capability as well. Remember my example of the automobile earlier in this chapter? Well, to help you quantify how far things have come, consider this: Today's typical automobile contains over 100 microchips to do and control a wide range of functions. The cost of all of these high-tech microchips is less than $150. Now here's where it really gets interesting. There is more computing power in those 100-plus microchips in a typical car today than there was in the Apollo lunar spacecraft in 1968!

The Laws Help

Did you ever stop to wonder just why the productivity rates in the United States always appear to be headed to the moon and off the charts while the rest of the world seems to always lag behind, or why and how it is that the United States is the productivity leader of the world? After all, the United States doesn't have a corner on new technology.

When something is invented, it is available around the globe. So what could it be? If it's not some corner on all the latest and greatest technology, it must be something else. Well, it is, and it's something you don't necessarily think of when you think of technology and productivity. The secret weapon for the United States is its weak labor laws.

You see, looked at another way, labor unions in the United States over the past 25 years have become weaker and weaker. The weaker that those labor unions become, the weaker the labor laws have become. Depending on which side of the fence you're on, this is either a bad thing or a good thing. You see, what is weak to some is simply considered flexible to others.

In the United States, because of the extremely flexible and weak labor laws, if someone invents a piece of technology that can do your job for you today, I'm here to tell you that you will be unemployed tomorrow. In the United States new technology, innovation, and productivity improvements are implemented immediately; and if that implementation results in the loss of jobs, so be it. That's not the case with the rest of the world. Even though they have access to this technology, they don't implement it as rapidly.

Take the case of Europe. What a wonderful place to work. Your first day on the job, and already you've earned a six-week vacation. Lunch hours are typically two hours, and weekend work is virtually nonexistent. Many of these practices were put in place to protect the small mom-and-pop stores from competition, from megastores from elsewhere, typically the United States. Thus in Europe, even if there is a computer that could replace you, chances are you wouldn't be replaced. And Japan is even worse. In Japan once you get a job, you basically have that job for life. No computer is going to replace you. Thus the real story behind U.S. productivity leadership is not about technology, but rather about flexible or weak labor laws that allow for the immediate implementation of new technology at the expense of employees.

EMPLOYMENT MARKET

Shifting Jobs

One of the single greatest concerns around the globe regarding technology is that all this new technology will eventually eliminate all the jobs. And if no one is working, who can afford to buy all of this great stuff that the new technology is producing?

Well, there is nothing new about this argument and concern. Its basis, however, is in innovation, not just technology. You see innovation causes us to change the way we do things, and those changes can and will have a dramatic impact on the employment markets. And because technology is our latest innovation, it is currently the one that is feared the most. However, step back a little to watch the evolution of some prior innovations.

Of course you were not around at the time, but can you just imagine the great debate and the concern about jobs with the advent of electricity and, even more important, the light bulb? I can just hear the discussion now . . . "What are we going to do with all of the poor candlestick makers who will now be without a job?" And what do you think happened when the automobile hit the roads for the first time? If you were a buggy whip manufacturer, you suddenly realized that your product was not going to be needed nearly as much in the future as it had been in the past. After all, you don't need to buggy whip an automobile to get it going.

I don't believe that innovation, and in this case technology, kills jobs. I think it simply forces a shift in our economy regarding the jobs that are needed and those that are not needed. While it is easy to focus on the jobs that technology has clearly made obsolete, like the bank teller, what about all of the new jobs that innovative technology is actually creating? You will get a distorted view if you only look at half of the equation.

In 1908 a Bell Telephone Company engineer forecast that by 1930 every female in the United States between the ages of 17 and 30 would have to become a telephone switchboard operator, based on the explosive growth rates forecasted for the telephone. Two years later, in 1910, automatic switches were invented. Goodbye, switchboard operators!

I like to think of the bankteller or the candlestick maker or the buggy whip manufacturer not as someone whose job was killed but rather as someone who through innovation has had his or her job shifted to fill a new and different need in our economy. Who knows—maybe that's where all of the people came from who are designing all of those Internet pages on the World Wide Web.

Shifting Skills

As technology continues to have a profound impact on the employment market by creating a job shift, it can also have a profound impact on the new skill sets necessary to succeed. In other words, there will be a shifting in the set of work skills as well as in jobs.

Think back 20 to 25 years ago before the technology explosion that caused us to develop a New Age economy, and recall what were the skill sets, or traits, that employers were looking for.

First, they wanted someone with a specific technical skill, whether that skill was in accounting or engineering or assembly line work. Second, they looked for someone who excelled in a structured environment. In other words, the business world was very hierarchical, and employers wanted someone who both respected and understood that structure. Third, employers looked for someone who could potentially be a manager. After all, with the very structured hierarchical organization, there were abundant levels of opportunities for managers. Fourth, they looked for someone who would accept and be comfortable with the status quo, someone who would focus on doing the job, not changing the job. Fifth, employers wanted someone who clearly understood that in business it's labor versus management, it's us versus them . . . this is business war. And finally they wanted someone who, at the end of the day, would be very happy, satisfied, and motivated based on the sole reward that you gave them, namely their wages.

So the ideal skill set of 25 years ago consisted of a technical skill, structure orientation, managerial potential, status quo acceptance, labor versus management, and wage satisfaction. Boy, have we come a long way. Because of technology, which has leveled the playing field in terms of information to all levels of the organization, and because of the speed at which that information now travels, there is a new set of skills in this new economy that are now needed. First, instead of looking for a specific technical skill, employers now look for people who can reinvent themselves over the years. Lifelong learning and the desire for learning different things are now more important than a specific technical skill. Second, the ideal candidate today will excel in a fluid work environment, not a structured one like before. Third, employers aren't looking for managers anymore. Instead, business is looking for entrepreneurs. Fourth, the status quo employee is out; what businesses want and need now are change agents, people who like change, thrive on change, and change quickly. Fifth, the old school of labor versus management is dead. Today you need to be a team player. More and more companies need cross-functional solutions in order to compete. One of the most important traits in this New World order is excelling in a team environment and setting. Sixth and finally, ownership and options are replacing wages. Employers don't want someone who is happy simply taking a paycheck. Instead they want someone who, like them, will have a major stake in the success of the firm. Make no mistake about it; technology is causing a dramatic skill-set shift. It's out with the old skill set and in with the new: lifelong learning, flexibility, entrepreneurs, change agents, team players, and ownership oriented.

The Big Shift

Jobs shift and then skill sets shift, and these two things combine to create dramatic shifts in the overall economy. Every major innovative movement has created a major economic shift that has impacted the employment market. Again, think back to the prior revolutions that we have previously discussed: the agricultural revolution, the industrial revolution, and the technology revolution.

Well, in the 1800s, in the United States over 80 percent of the jobs were agriculture related, 1 to 2 percent were in manufacturing, but not one job was in the area of technology.

In the 1900s, with the industrial revolution came an explosion in manufacturing and industry-based jobs. Over 50 percent of the workforce were in a manufacturing or industry-based job, with 40 percent still in agriculture and 1 percent in technology.

Fast forward to today in the 2000s with the technology revolution. Agricultural jobs now account for a mere 2 percent, dropping from its high of 80 percent. Industry-based and manufacturing jobs have dropped from over 50 percent to a little over 10 percent. Meanwhile technology and service-industry jobs now account for over 70 percent, whereas the 1800s they accounted for zero. Sometimes when you focus on all the little shifts—like "Am I going to lose my job?"—you lose sight of the big shifts.

Work Leisurely

All of these technology-driven changes in the employment market have in turn created a new breed of workers. I'll call them the "leisurely group." Because we have become more productive, we have also been able to reduce the average workweek. In other words, workers have more time to spend at leisure. Over the past 30 years the average workweek in the United States has dropped from 37 hours to 34 hours. In our lifetime it is not beyond the realm of possibility to see it drop to 30 hours a week. This technology-led productivity boom is the reason behind the increase in leisure time. It is also the foundation behind the birth of "flextime" in the workplace. Employers could be more flexible with their schedules because the work was getting done in less time.

You also are able to enjoy some leisure time at work because of technology. You see, because technology has enabled everyone to do his or her job better and faster, employees can chat on the phone with friends and family and still get their jobs done on time. Employees can pay their bills while at work over the phone through automated tellers. And while on the Internet the opportunities of what could be accomplished are limitless, from planning a vacation to doing the weekly shopping.

Remember, innovation is about progress and progress should improve our lives. Well, maybe all the credit can't go to technology, but in many ways it has made us more leisurely workers.

The New Technology Time Line

One of the reasons that our New Age technology is changing everything so much faster than ever before is that the time line for implementing new technology has been dramatically reduced. In just a few short years the Internet has transformed not only the way we communicate, but also the way we think and feel. Whether it's in your personal life or professional life, the Internet has changed the way you look at things or are looked at by other things (business and people).

At the cornerstone of this fast-paced technology revolution is the simple fact that new technology and inventions are spreading much faster than ever before. The Internet spread to a quarter of the entire U.S. population in a shorter time frame than any other invention. This is such a critical point because the number of people who use it will determine the economic impact of any invention. Remember that the first automobiles were produced in the United States in 1886. Yet when the U.S. stock market crashed some 40 years later in 1929, the United States still had more horses than cars on the roads. And the television did not invade our homes until the early 1950s, even though it was invented in 1926.

This technology time line is now dramatically changing, especially when you consider the three most recent inventions: (1) the personal computer, (2) cellular phones, and (3) the Internet. It took the personal computer only 16 years to reach a quarter of our population, whereas it took the cellular phone only 13 years. Amazingly, the Internet has reached a quarter of our population in an astonishing 7 short years. Once or twice in our lifetimes an invention comes along that will change the world completely. That's the potential impact of the Internet. Airbags are a very useful product especially if you're in a car crash; however, they have not had the same impact as the invention of the telephone or the television. The wheel, the steam engine, electricity . . . they have all been landmark inventions that have changed our lives forever, with very far-reaching impact.

The combination of computers and the Internet may be the greatest inventions of all time. It is useful to look at these inventions together. After all, it's impossible to envision the explosion of the Internet without the computer. The Internet will be the greatest invention in history. A new website is launched each minute on the Internet. Its growth will not be constrained by scarcity. Unlike food or clothing or other resources, the Internet is not constrained by scarcity. The Internet is an intellectual resource, not a physical resource, and as such, it can be copied, downloaded, and recopied ad infinitum; its supply of this intellectual information will far exceed the demand. Thus there are no growth constraints on what the Internet or technology can accomplish.

What does all this mean for our markets? Well, consider that the technology revolution's foundation is really the increased capital outlay for more and improved computer hardware (which in turn creates the need for more and improved software). This increased use of the latest and greatest hardware and software eventually increases productivity. When productivity increases, profits tend to rise. When profits rise, the prices of stocks as well as the overall market also rise. Could the real fuel behind this bull market be capital outlays for technology?

Technology can and will continue to have a major influence on our stock markets and our economies for decades to come. One has to look no further than the tremendous commitment that companies have to spending money on new technology. It's an area in which no industry can cut back and still stay competitive. Plus technology product cycles are now often measured in months instead of years.

Capital Spending

The relationship between capital spending and profit growth has been well documented in the stock market. You see, when companies make major capital expenditures, they tend to become more efficient; and when companies become more efficient, they in turn become more profitable. I think that companies are going to continue their spending spree on capital equipment, and here is why: No matter where you look in our stock market today, no sectors have any pricing flexibility. If you have no pricing flexibility, the only way you can maintain and increase profit growth is to rely more on cost cutting. The best way to cut costs is to figure out how to do things better, faster, and cheaper. In other words, sectors need to become more productive. You guessed it. When companies and sectors are forced to boost their productivity, they are being forced to increase capital spending on technology. It doesn't matter what the reason or motivation is. All that matters is that sectors continue spending on technology. And with no pricing flexibility, they have no other choice.

Old Economy

The technology revolution is not just about these new dot.com companies that seem to be launched almost daily. It's really about the old economy sectors embracing the new economy of the Internet. After all, if we can get the old economy sectors hooked on the Internet, just think where the overall technology sector could go. Want some proof that they are hooked already? Maybe the oldest of the old economy sectors is the transportation sector. Let me share with you what they are doing today. First, the Big Three auto makers created a web-based, auto parts supply exchange to transact more than $250 billion of auto parts a year. Demonstrating that this revolution in transportation isn't restricted to the ground, Southwest Airlines hit a new milestone recently—more than one-quarter of its passenger revenues came from bookings over its website. Remember that most Americans still work for old economy companies, and it's these companies that are largely driving the technology revolution. And remember, it's all these old economy companies like the Big Three auto makers that are giving substance to the potential of the Internet. Simply put, you can't have one without the other. Technology will soar because the old economy will take it there.

Technology Influence

Sometimes to get a proper perspective on where things are going, you need to step back and realize where things came from. This could not be more true regarding the influence of technology on our markets. When the decade of the 1990s began, technology stocks accounted for less than 7 percent of the overall value of the entire Standard & Poor's (S&P) 500 index. As recently as five years ago, there wasn't one single technology company among the top 10 of the S&P 500. Five years ago, that list read like this: General Electric, Exxon, AT&T, Coca-Cola, Wal-Mart, Royal Dutch, Philip Morris, Merck, General Motors, and Procter & Gamble. Today four technology companies (Cisco Systems, Microsoft, Intel, and IBM) have made their way to the top 10 of the S&P 500. You don't really think that five years from now tech will have a lesser influence, do you? Four down and six to go! Think about it for a minute. Maybe technology is telling you something. Paper prices have firmed (inflationary), yet paper stocks have declined. Oil prices have soared (inflationary), yet the relative performance of oil stocks continues to lag. Office rents have risen steadily (inflationary), yet real estate investment trusts (REITs) are flat. Meanwhile, technology, which encourages deflationary activities, is soaring!

We've Only Just Begun

I know that you may be concerned that the Internet fuels this tech revolution and that the Internet has to run out of steam soon. Let me give you a perspective on why we have only just begun. There are approximately 100 million homes in the United States. Of those 100 million, 79 million have personal computers. However, only 35 million have access to the Internet. And you think that we don't have room to grow? Think about the rest of the world for a minute. There are approximately 1.1 billion homes in the rest of the world, and both personal computer usage and Internet access is in the single-digit millions! And you still think that there is no room to grow? The Internet allows us to do everything better and faster. Consider zShops, an online shopping mall launched by Amazon.com in September 1999. zShops has more than 500,000 products for sale. For your frame of reference, that's not just one or two or three, but a whopping four times the products of your typical K-mart store. And, finally, don't forget your e-mail. In the United States, we mail 100 billion pieces of first-class mail annually. Meanwhile, on an annual basis we send not 5, 10, 20, or 30 but an unbelievable 34 times as many e-mails as "snail mails" every single year. I'll do the math for you: Each year in the United States, 3.4 trillion e-mails are sent. So for every first-class letter, there are 34 e-mails. Remember, the Pony Express became obsolete, too.

Even in Russia

Would you like some final proof that this technology revolution is real? Look what recently occurred in Russia—Boris Nemtsov, Russia's first deputy Prime Minister, has become that country's first e-politician. He has launched his very own Internet website so that everyone can follow his political views. Several Russian government agencies already have Internet websites; however, Mr. Nemtsov is the first politician to launch his own web page. The Internet can be a wonderful communication tool for a country like Russia that actually spans 11 separate time zones. Today there are over 7,500 Russian-language websites. Like I said, this Internet technology revolution will touch everyone, everywhere!

DR. BOB'S NOTES . . . TOP 10 THINGS TO REMEMBER!
Chapter 3

10 Innovation and technology don't kill jobs; rather they force a shift in which jobs are needed.

9 Marketing, not technology, will determine which retailers will be the winners and the losers on the Internet.

8 European retailers will be one of the big losers when the Internet forces all European retailers to go global.

7 In the United States, Internet activity is increasing at 200 percent per year and accounts for over $300 billion dollars, the same amount as the entire automotive sector.

6 The actual price of computing power has fallen in half each year over the past decade, while at the same time the speed of the computer has doubled.

5 European Internet service providers as well as equipment manufacturers face a huge challenge due to the diversity of the cultures and languages that make up Europe.

4 To service the entire United States, you would need over 400 cellular phone licenses, each of these licenses running on multiple digital standards. In all of Europe, cellular telephones operate on one digital standard.

3 The invention time lines are consolidating. The Internet spread to a quarter of the entire United States population in a shorter time frame than any other invention in the history of time.

2 Education is the key to knowledge, which is the key to productivity, which is the key to technology, which just may hold the key to everything else.

1 The United States currently accounts for less than 5 percent of the world's population, yet it has more computers than the rest of the world combined.

Chapter 4

Government Downsizing and Privatization

I have always thought of government as a kind of organism with an insatiable appetite for money, whose natural state is to grow forever unless you do something to starve it.

Ronald Reagan
Former President of the United States (1990)

There are only two ways to starve government from what former President Ronald Reagan fondly referred to as its insatiable appetite for money. You downsize it, and you privatize it.

Capital Is Key

Government downsizing and privatization around the globe have never, ever had a better chance for success than they have today. And I for one firmly believe that we will be successful in downsizing government around the globe. The significance for the markets cannot be understated. After all, there is only so much capital (money) to go around. Thus, everyone competes for capital. So the more government there is, the less capital that makes its way to businesses around the globe, the same businesses that when successful create even more jobs, which in turn spur more economic growth that can create even more jobs. The key in my belief to why we can be successful in downsizing lies in one simple fact—the Cold War is over.

The Cold War Is Dead

There simply was no way that we could ever hope to achieve any significant government downsizing as long as the threat of the Cold War was on everyone's mind. It was simply too easy for politicians to scare their constituents into begging them to spend more money on big government to protect everyone from the supposed threat of the Cold War. That time however is now over.

It all began to unravel in late 1989. On November 9, 1989, the Berlin Wall came tumbling down, and with it the threat of the Cold War began to disappear. One month later, on December 3, 1989, Soviet Prime Minister Mikhail Gorbachev and United States President George Bush held a summit that concluded with their joint declaration that the Cold War had ended. Two short months later, on February 7, 1990, the Soviet Communist party relinquished exclusive power in Russia. Eight months after that, on October 3, 1990, West Germany and East Germany were united to create a unified Germany. A little over a year later, in December 1991, the Soviet Republics became independent states. Finally, on Christmas Day of 1991, the Soviet flag was removed from the Kremlin. A year later, on January 3, 1993, the United States and Russia entered into the most dramatic nuclear disarmament treaty ever (Start II), and the Cold War was history.

Impact of No Cold War

As with any major change, the end of the Cold War sent shock waves around the global economies and markets. Some of the shock waves were very, very destabilizing, whereas others had the potential to revitalize entire economies and markets.

The Soviet Union and all of Eastern Europe were destabilized as a result of the end of the Cold War. You see, much more fell than simply the Berlin Wall. With it fell the "protectionism" mentality, which was one of the key by-products of the Cold War. The Soviet Empire was effectively shut off from the free world; in other words, it was closed off to world trade. As a result of being shut off from trading with the

West, the Soviet Union fell behind very quickly. Its industrial base was strapped with outdated technologies and "old school" management approaches. This slowdown in industry caused such a collapse economically that the Soviet Union could no longer afford its overgrown and out-of-control military budget. As a result the misguided Soviet Union economic system failed completely when it was forced to compete in a global marketplace.

The basis of this meltdown was centered in the most inefficient businesses and industries that had to deal with more efficient and productive competitors once trade was opened up. Thus the end of the Cold War actually triggered an immediate depression all throughout the former Soviet Union and into the Communist block of Eastern Europe as well.

The German Consequences

The end of the Cold War brought about negative consequences that were much different in Germany than those in the Soviet Union. You see, we sometimes forget that not only did the end of the Cold War open up, or free, global trade, but it also opened up the labor markets as well. Specifically it opened up a new global supply of very cheap labor, especially from East Germany.

As a result, employees in Western Germany were now looked at as a very, very costly component of production. Enter the German government, which made a huge public policy mistake. They decided to adopt a series of laws and regulations that in essence raised the compensation of Eastern German employees to the levels of their counterparts in Western Germany. The only problem was that employees in Western Germany were already overpriced from a global standpoint, which was one of the reasons German businesses had problems competing on price globally. The end result was that everyone lost whether in East Germany or in West Germany. Unemployment ran rampant all throughout Germany, most of it as a result of the Cold War ending.

One Bright Light—China

As I said as this chapter began, the end of the Cold War was destabilizing to some and revitalizing to others. Enough about the destabilizing. Let's look at one economy and market that really became revitalized as a result of the end of the Cold War, a nation that at first you might not think of—China.

Now that the Cold War is dead, where do you want to invest? You could invest in Russia by buying old outdated technology and industrial facilities. Or you could buy raw land in China, the same raw land on which you could build the latest and greatest high-tech, state-of-the-art, innovative industrial factory ever built. Oh, and by the way, with one billion Chinese, there is no shortage of very cheap labor to work in your new state-of-the-art factory. China will emerge as one of the real winners as a result of the end of the Cold War. The biggest winner, however, is not any individual country; the biggest winner is the fact that the end of the Cold War will finally enable governments around the globe to downsize.

Don't Forget Capitalism

No discussion of the end of the Cold War would be complete without tying its significance back to the role of capitalism around the globe.

It was August 13, 1961, when the communist government of East Germany closed its borders to Berlin and started construction of the Berlin Wall. Remember that prior to the Berlin Wall, East Germans were able to actually choose between two radically different economic and political systems; capitalism to the west or communism to the east. The East Germans fled by the thousands to the West, which was one of the central reasons that the Berlin Wall was built in the first place. Left alone to free choice, the East German people voted resoundingly with their feet. They voted for capitalism and democracy and against communism and a social dictatorship.

Twenty years after the construction of the Berlin Wall, there was an amazing contrast between the communist East Germany on the verge of economic collapse and the vibrant West Germany that was looked up to as an economic model of how to do it right around the world. This division of a common people by a wall offered us a rare opportunity to see which economic and political system worked best, capitalism or communism. You simply could not create a better political and economic experiment if you tried. Remember, if you will, the fact that the people of West and East Germany possessed the same history, the same genetic endowment, the same past intellectual achievements in the arts and the sciences. The sole difference was that the system in West Germany proposed a limited role for government and a wider liberty for individuals and business. The East Germans through communism were forced to adopt socialism, central planning, and the idea that political solutions would advance the prospects of all East Germans equally.

Over the years the dramatic differences in living standards and the absence of freedom in East Germany became too glaring and unacceptable. Thus in 1989 the whole world watched the end of an experiment that pitted capitalism against communism. The beginning of the end started when Hungary, a member of the Soviet block, announced that it would no longer monitor its borders and restrict the movement of East Germans. Almost immediately not thousands but tens of thousands of East Germans fled through Czechoslovakia and then crossed the Hungarian border into Austria and ultimately into West Germany. The socialist system in general and specifically communism came to an abrupt end on November 9, 1989, when the Berlin Wall was dismantled by East Germans who were tired and weary of giving in to dictatorship and poverty. It wasn't long afterward that the entire Soviet Union collapsed. Thus after 70 long years, Marxist Communist dictatorship was over and capitalism reigned free.

Do you want proof that capitalism will beat communism every time? To have capitalism embraced around the globe, all we need to do is place a JC Penney catalogue in everyone's hands. When consumers in communist nations see the choices that capitalism brings in one simple catalog and when they then realize that they don't even have to leave their home to buy any of this stuff—they just pick up the phone— they will be hooked on capitalism forever. Whoever thought we'd pick JC Penney catalogs over missiles to win the war over communism?

The United States Leads the Way

Now that the Cold War is over, the United States has taken the lead around the globe in at least making an effort to reduce the size of government. This dramatic first step was accomplished through the balanced budget agreement.

In order to understand the true significance of this landmark deficit-reduction, balanced budget agreement, it is helpful to put it into some historical perspective. Budget deficits in the United States are nothing new. In fact, the federal government generated its first-ever deficit when the country was just a teenager. It had the first budget deficit in 1792, a short 16 years after the country was founded in 1776. Since that first-ever budget deficit, there have been over a hundred occasions when the federal government ended the year in the red. The real ballooning of the federal government deficits did not begin to occur until the late 1930s. Two things were forcing the deficits higher: First of all, the country had to pay for President Franklin D. Roosevelt's "New Deal," and second, the outbreak of World War II mandated enormous expenditures in military spending.

The next ballooning of the federal government deficit did not occur until the 1980s. Again, just like in the 1930s, a tremendous increase in defense spending was part of the reason. However, in addition to increased defense spending, there were major cuts in income tax rates, meaning federal tax revenue was reduced. However, there were no offsetting cuts in federal programs, and thus the deficit skyrocketed. If this wasn't bad enough, the recession in the economy in the early 1980s also reduced tax receipts. In addition, interest rates were rising; so not only did the government have more debt, but it was also paying more in interest cost for the debt that it had.

While keeping track of the U.S. deficit is important, how to measure it has become equally important. It is not enough to just look at the deficit in isolation; the deficit should be looked at as a percentage of gross domestic product (GDP). This is the most important way of looking at the deficit because it reflects the economy's ability to absorb the federal deficits. This is one reason why one of the key economic measurements for a country to become eligible for membership in the European Economic and Monetary Union (EMU) is that its deficit, as a percent of GDP, must be 3 percent or less.

To give you some frame of reference to what that 3 percent level would mean in the United States today, consider this. The current projection of the Congressional Budget Office shows the federal government ending this fiscal year (September 30) with a deficit of approximately $30 billion. With a $7.1 trillion economy, the deficit could balloon by a whopping sevenfold from its current level, and we would still have a $3 billion cushion before we wouldn't meet the deficit criteria for admission to the EMU.

Measuring the deficit as a percent of GDP provides us with an interesting analysis. When we look at the U.S. deficit as a percentage of GDP, the highest level that the deficit has ever reached was in 1943 when it was an unbelievable 31.1 percent of GDP. The highest level that the deficit has reached in the past 50 years was back in 1983 when it stood at the high water mark of 6.3 percent.

While lowering the federal government's deficit is good news for the overall financial markets, it is especially good news for the bond market. The lower the deficit, the less debt (treasury securities) the government has to issue to fund the deficit. The balanced budget agreement means that the United States will be issuing less debt, and this decrease in future supply will increase the current value of the debt that is outstanding. It doesn't matter what you are buying, whether it's luxury cars, coffee, or Treasury securities. If supply is less, the value or the price of what is available goes up. For anyone that was waiting for a sign from outer space to invest in bonds again, your sign has just arrived.

While the United States is clearly in the forefront, before you get too excited you need to realize that the United States has a long, long, long way to go in terms of downsizing its government.

Regulation Overkill

One of the attributes of big government and government spending is that with all of these government employees running around, they will eventually create enough regulations and mandates to strangle a horse. Which is exactly what they have done in the United States.

Listen to what Congressman Hinshaw of the State of California sarcastically read into the *Congressional Record* in an attempt to put some perspective on how regulations in the United States are out of control.

In the beginning, God created heaven and earth. Quickly He was faced with a class action suit for failure to file an environmental impact statement. He was granted a temporary permit for the heavenly part of the project, but was stymied with a cease-and-desist order for the earthly project.

Appearing at the hearing, God was asked why He began the earthly project in the first place? He replied that He just liked to be creative.

Then God said, "let there be light," and immediately the officials demanded to know how the light would be made. Would there be strip mining? What about thermal pollution? God explained that light would come from a huge ball of fire.

God was granted provisional permission to make light, assuming that no smoke would result from the ball of fire, that He would obtain a building permit, and to conserve energy, would have the light out half the time. God agreed and said He would call the light "day" and the darkness "night." Officials replied, they weren't interested in semantics.

God said, "Let the earth bring forth green herb and such as may seed." The EPA agreed as long as native seed was used. Then God said, "Let the waters bring forth creeping creatures having life, and the fowl that may fly over the earth." Officials pointed out that this would require approval of the Game and Fish Commission with the Heavenly Wildlife Federation and Audobongelic Society.

So everything was okay until God said he wanted to complete the project in six days. Officials said it would take at least 180 days to review the application and the impact statement. After that there would be public hearings. Then there would be 10 to 12 months before . . .

God said, "To Hell with it!" If that doesn't say it all, I don't know what does.

Currently in the United States the regulatory burdens placed on both industry and individuals exceed 10 percent of the country's gross national product (GNP). And while in many respects the burden equally discriminates against business and individuals, small businesses especially get the short end of the stick.

Consider the rash of regulations that kick in on small businesses when they reach a certain "threshold." These so-called threshold regulations kick in and mandate employers to take some form of action once their workforce rises above a certain number (threshold) of employees. There are currently a dozen federal laws that impose threshold compliance costs on small businesses including the Civil Rights Act of 1964, the Age Discrimination Employment Act of 1967, the Employee Retirement Income Security Act (ERISA) of 1974, the Occupational Safety and Health Act (OSHA) of 1970, the Americans with Disabilities Act (ADA) of 1990, and the Clean Air Act Amendments of 1990. What makes these regulations especially difficult for small businesses to deal with is the almost incomprehensible bureaucratic maze that a small business faces when attempting to comply with these laws.

Why would any small business want to expand beyond the most commonly used threshold number (15 employees) only to then find itself forced to comply with all of these new regulations? If you think government regulations don't retard economic growth, think again! How many small businesses do you think there are in the United States that refuse to expand and grow because they are afraid of what their compliance costs will be with these new threshold regulations?

State and Local Government Mandates

In addition to the U.S. government placing financial burdens on businesses and individuals, it also has the power to "mandate" that certain things be done by state and local governments. These certain things or services are known in Washington circles as "mandated costs." The beauty of this whole Ponzi scheme is that it does not cost the U.S. government one penny. The cost of compliance and implementation of these federal mandates is borne entirely by state and local governments.

It's important to understand how this all came about. In the early 1980s there was great focus for the United States to curb government spending and to get their deficit under control. It adopted landmark federal budgetary control legislation called the Gramm-Rudman Act, aptly named after the two politicians sponsoring the legislation. This landmark legislation put caps on government spending in an attempt to slow down the growth of government. Not to be denied, these Washington politicians came up with a new plan. They figured if they couldn't spend more or raise taxes to spend more, they would do the next best thing. They would force other governments (state and local), which are not covered by the provisions of the Gramm-Rudman Act, to spend more on their behalf. Over the past 20 years the U.S. Congress has enacted more than 25 landmark laws that were passed on to state and local governments who were required to pay for the provisions. After all, it's the law.

The numbers are staggering. Currently local governments pay close to $40 billion annually simply to comply with the environmental mandates of the Environmental Protection Agency (EPA).

Nothing Taxes Like Taxes

No discussion on regulations and mandates and burdens from the federal government would be complete without a brief look at what is without a doubt the single greatest burden that the U.S. government places on businesses and individuals, the income tax. Think of a "fine" as a tax for doing wrong. A tax then is a fine for doing well.

The U.S. income tax system is one of the most complex tax systems anywhere in the world. But don't take my word for it. Listen to this: "Of all the systems in the entire universe the most complex is the U.S. tax system." While that quote may not be all that enlightening to many of you, the person who said it may interest you—it was none other than Albert Einstein.

If you don't think government needs a massive dose of downsizing, look a little closer at this complex tax system and the unbelievable burden it places on the American people. If you don't think Albert Einstein was correct, consider this. Currently the Internal Revenue Service (IRS) publishes 480 different individual tax forms. It then publishes an additional 280 different individual forms to explain the other 480 forms.

Each and every year the Internal Revenue Service sends out over eight billion pages of forms and instructions. Here's something to think about: If you laid those eight billion pages end to end, they would circle the entire globe not once, not twice, but 28 times! In order to accomplish this task, over 300,000 trees are cut down each and every year simply to produce the paper on which the IRS forms and written instructions are printed.

The bigger cost however is in the time it takes for Americans to comply with this tax system. Each year Americans devote 5.4 billion hours complying with the complex tax code. To give you some perspective, that 5.4 billion hours is more time than it takes to build every car, truck, van, and sports utility vehicle produced in the United States. And it's all a waste of time.

Is It Fair?

In addition to being an extreme waste of time, it is also extremely unfair. You see, at the heart of the complexity of the tax system problems lies the mushrooming proliferation of various deductions, credits, and special tax law preferences that combine to make up the tax laws. Because of these loopholes, taxpayers with the exact same amount of income can end up paying vastly different amounts in taxes.

And the fairness issue goes well beyond taxpayers that earn the same income; it is also creating a class war between the different income classes because of the unfair treatment to various taxpayer classes. You want proof that the system in the United States is unfair? Currently the top 1 percent of taxpayers pay over 50 percent of the entire personal income tax burden. Meanwhile the bottom 50 percent of taxpayers pay less than 2 percent of the burden. The top 1 percent pays over 50 percent, while the bottom 50 percent pays only 2 percent. Is that fair?

Fairness Gets Flattened

Any discussion of fairness and tax codes usually ends up in a debate regarding the flat tax. The flat tax is a tax in which every taxpayer, regardless of income level would pay the same tax rate. Opponents quickly and emotionally point out that it wouldn't be fair if everyone paid the same tax. But wait a minute, not so fast.

While it's true that everyone would pay the same rate, they would not be paying the same tax. The amount they would pay would be different. Don't let these do-gooders use the terms *rate* and *amount* interchangeably. It doesn't matter if you pay the same rate as long as you pay a different amount. Remember that under a flat tax, if you make more, you pay more. Don't worry about the rate, it's the amount that's important. This ill-conceived philosophical political debate regarding whether a tax is progressive or regressive doesn't matter as long as if you make more, you pay more.

The next time someone tells you that a flat tax lets the rich get off the hook too easy, remember this example. Suppose you lived in the United States and it adopted a 10 percent flat tax. If your neighbor earned $10,000, his or her tax burden would be 10 percent of $10,000, or $1,000. Now let's say that you earn $100,000 with a 10 percent flat tax; your tax burden would be 10 percent of $100,000, or $10,000. What's wrong with this picture? $1,000 versus $10,000. You are paying an amount 10 times greater. Would you like to know what you get for paying 10 times more? Well, you don't get any additional Medicare or welfare benefits. And, no, you don't get an express lane just for you on the interstate highway system because you paid 10 times more tax. And, no, you don't get a special pass for the national parks so you never have to stand in line again. And, no, you don't have your home marked with a white "X" on the roof so that your home can be provided additional national defense and security in the event of a war or civil unrest. Well, I guess you figured it out by now—you get absolutely nothing for paying 10 times more. How is this getting off too easy?

In order to understand how crazy this logic can be, suppose you and your neighbor decided to go to the movies on Saturday. Your neighbor, the one who earns $10,000, buys the $7 ticket and goes into the theater. Now you walk up to the ticket window and—remember, you earn $100,000—the ticket clerk immediately informs you that because you make 10 times more than the person that just went in, your ticket will cost 10 times more. That will be $70, please. So you inquire, "What do I get if I pay 10 times more? Do I get a reclining seat? Do I have champagne and hors d'oeuvres delivered to my seat?" The ticket clerk responds, "You get nothing for paying 10 times more." I'm willing to bet that you wouldn't want to see that movie anymore because it's not fair that you pay 10 times more and get nothing for it. It's simply not fair. Think about this the next time you hear someone say that a flat tax would not be fair. Always remember that there are two sides to every fairness issue.

The Big Fix

It is now clearer than ever that government downsizing is the only way to "fix" the problems with big government today.

The explosion in the size of government did not happen because governments or government employees had ill intentions. In fact, it happened for just the opposite reasons. There are a tremendous number of good people in government, and these good people had good intentions, theoretically. They wanted to provide free health care and a comprehensive welfare and food stamp program. They also wanted to create swimming pools and tennis courts and theaters and parking garages and just about anything else that you could imagine.

The basic problem with this is that these government employees are doing all of this with other people's (yours and mine) money. When you are using other people's money, there is simply no end to the potential ways you can come up with to do good. It is a simple financial fact of life; you always spend your own money more carefully than you spend someone else's. Thus when someone is spending someone else's money, waste is virtually guaranteed.

The real catch-22 of the government spending cycle comes with the pure logic that the government can't do anything with (spend) your money until they get it from you. Enter the dreaded tax collector. The role of the tax collector (in the case of the United States, it's the Internal Revenue Service) is to take your hard-earned money away from you. Taking money away from you requires force. The force is that if you don't give them the money, you go to jail. What is lost on most people is that "force" is the most basic and fundamental requirement of establishing a welfare state. If you think of how we got to where we are today in simple terms, the government is doing their so-called good deeds with other people's money, and to make matters worse, they use force to get the money. Is it really a surprise to anyone that under these circumstances government simply doesn't work?

It is pretty simple to see how all of this could evolve in theory. If you have a lot of people paying taxes (a large tax base, if you will) and a small number of people receiving benefits (the social welfare base), the system works like clockwork. After all, you only have to take a little bit of money from a lot of people to make ends meet. Take a little bit from a lot of people and give a lot to a little bit of people. As long as you only take a little bit of money from a lot of people, things work well. This Ponzi scheme breaks down, because eventually everyone wants something free. If more and more people want to be receiving something from government, that means that you will need to tax more and more people to provide that government service. Before you know it, you are taxing 50 percent of the people to help the other 50 percent of the people. Now in the beginning, if you take $1 away from 100 people and give $10 to 10 needy people, hardly anyone notices. But as the "welfare state" (government) grows more and more, people want to be receivers, not payers; and the more people that become receivers, the more the payers have to pay. Now the amounts needed from the individual taxpayers have become so large that they no longer can be hidden. Want a little proof of how all of this spending doesn't work for the purposes intended? The U.S. government has paid out almost $5 trillion in social and welfare spending to fight poverty since 1960, but today the incidence of poverty is just as high as it was in the early 1960s. Government does not work.

Small tinkering changes will have little or no impact. We are in dire need of a major overhaul. The global high-tech economy demands flexibility and agility to act quickly. These are the two traits that the government simply does not possess. Maybe the government could be taking a clue from the private sector. United Airlines found out that they must contract out for their food services to Marriott Corporation. United realized that there just might be someone better equipped and better prepared to deliver food service than an airline. Marriott, on the other hand, contracts out the hotel's parking function. They too realized that there was someone else that was better equipped and staffed and more knowledgeable about parking facilities than a hotel. If this is happening among some of the best-run companies in the world, why do many school districts still have their own food staff and why do numerous municipalities still operate parking garages? Do you really think that school districts and municipalities can do it better than the private sector? I don't.

In addition, this new-age economy is causing every business to think and to act differently. From General Electric to Microsoft to Alcoa to Boeing to IBM to Procter & Gamble to Wal-Mart, corporations are restructuring and downsizing by eliminating layers of management and unnecessary bureaucratic waste, all in order to serve their customers better. Wanna bet that no one at the Food and Drug Administration is doing that? Or at the Environmental Protection Agency or the Department of Commerce?

A recent survey measuring consumer satisfaction tells it all. This survey asked over 50,000 people how they felt about products and services provided by a variety of 200 different companies and government agencies. All aspects of the private sector were included in this survey along with the government agencies. Clothing companies and food companies scored the highest, averaging almost 85 out of 100. And no one was surprised that at the very, very bottom of the list were two government agencies. The Internal Revenue Service and the U.S. Postal Service tied for last with a score of 55 out of 100. I could have saved that survey a lot of time and money. Those results should be obvious to anyone who walks and chews gum.

Government will always remain at the bottom of the list. Governments will never, ever, ever deliver efficient services. And the reason is pure economics. They simply do not have the price signals of profit and loss to tell them how to respond from a business perspective. As long as government employees are not risking any of their own money, they have very, very few, if any, incentives to be efficient or to deliver good service with a smile. If you want some proof, just drive down to any motor vehicle registration office on a Saturday morning, and you will quickly realize exactly what I am saying.

Every day that goes by it becomes clearer and clearer that government is wasting money. I no longer believe that the issue is about trying to make the public sector as efficient as the private sector. Having the firsthand experience of working in both, I do not ever believe it will happen. The central issue needs to be limiting the activities that the government should be performing.

One Solution—Privatization

I believe that most government functions will be privatized out of a job. The private sector never sleeps; it works 24 hours a day 7 days a week to become more efficient and more productive and ultimately more profitable. This efficiency and productivity gap between the public sector of government and the private sector of business will become too wide not to take dramatic action. I believe that most government functions will be privatized because incentivized business people will always be able to do it faster, more efficiently, and eventually cheaper as well.

There is a key fundamental difference between the public sector and the private sector. The public sector uses political means to solve problems, while the private sector uses market means. The market means in the private sector is a highly competitive process highlighted by selective access to goods and services. You see, under a market-driven means, if an individual wishes to have a pair of new shoes, for example, they must provide something in exchange (most likely cash or credit card). This is not the case when we use political means. In this case the government provides goods and services with a guarantee to equal access to all. The direct out-of-pocket cost of using municipal swimming pools, public libraries, and highways is zero. The goods or services are provided free to anyone who wants to use them. The cost is covered by the high taxes charged the taxpayer. What ends up happening is that those who use the service seldom if ever have to pay and those who pay (in taxes) often never ever use the service. The government never makes any attempt to match up the benefits with the costs. This Ponzi scheme eventually comes tumbling down. At some point everyone wants to receive from the government, and no one wants to give to the government. This is one of the flaws of using political means. This never happens using market means. You see, in the market place, the benefits of having new shoes are tied directly to a purchase price; and if you can't meet that cost, you are excluded from the enjoyment of that particular good, in this case a new pair of shoes.

The political means also creates other problems. If you provide something for free, that usually means that somewhere there will be cross-subsidization. Those who use the city swimming pool or the mass transit system are subsidized by those who pay their local taxes but, in turn, financially support and use a private swim club and drive their own automobile to and from work. This mismatch of benefits and costs creates an equity argument in favor of a system in which those who benefit from a service should be those who pay for it. Individuals should be permitted to choose the services they want and therefore to determine the ways they wish to spend their money. The fundamental issue becomes freedom of choice.

One of the sad side effects of providing things for free is that political leaders are usually given false and misleading economic information regarding the great demand and the need to provide certain goods and services. What we are forgetting here is the basic economic principle that one of the key functions of price is to ration goods, services, and resources. I can't imagine anyone who wouldn't prefer to drive a BMW until they see its sticker price. An $85,000 price tag convinces a lot of people that a Chevy or a Ford will do just fine. You see, price not only measures the cost to buy something, it also measures the demand, or more important the intensity of demand. On the flip side, goods and services provided free always encourage wasteful consumption. I simply can't imagine any grocery store that would be amazed to see their shelves emptied quickly if food prices were dropped to zero.

Despite all this, government officials always want more money (taxes) so that they can embark on more projects, whether it's swimming pools or parking garages, citing this intense need and great demand for the good and service in question. Providing things free simply guarantees that people will want more. Remember, however, that government must tax (take) before it can give. Now everyone wants to be a tax receiver not a tax giver. Political means have failed because they are inefficient and unfair. Market solutions will be tried because they work. I don't mean to imply that the market is perfect. Actually it's far from it. The market means in business has created as many problems as the political means in government. But here's the key difference. When business through market means creates a lemon, I don't have to buy it and neither do you. On the other hand when government through political means creates a lemon, whether I want to or not, or like it or not, I *do* have to pay for it and so do you. Remember, if business through market means produces a Yugo car, forget it. But when the government through political means produces the license plate bureau, we're all stuck with it. Our only choice here is we simply pay our money or go to jail.

Privatization—Where Do We Start?

Maybe that's exactly where we should start—with the prison system. Why is the government operating the prison systems? If they were privatized, I would be willing to bet that they would be operated more efficiently than they are today.

And what about schools? Government currently has a stranglehold monopoly on schools that also will be broken with privatization. School choice, vouchers, and competition among schools will break the age-old monopoly of government-run schools. When competition hits schools, how long do you think it will take in this high-tech world for every school to either be "wired" or be vacant?

Airports should all be privatized. Once turned over to the private sector, these one-time cost centers become profit centers. If you want some proof in the United States, look at either coast—out west in Burbank, California, or back east in Westchester County, New York. Or if that doesn't convince you, look at the success that Great Britain has had in privatizing airport operations. And don't stop with the airport; go right on to the air traffic control as well. I know it would be cheaper and I for one would feel safer if private, profit-making business were in charge of air traffic control, not the government. Today the average cost of operating and maintaining a Level I air traffic control tower (Level I is lowest/slowest in terms of volume of air traffic) is almost four times higher for government towers as it is for private ones!

We need less government ownership, not more. All across the United States, cities own airports, hospitals, museums, golf courses, swimming pools, and even parking garages. In addition they subsidize (give our money to) education, real estate, and thousands of different businesses. Yet they still can't keep the streets clean and teach the children how to read and write properly. In many respects government is doing what they shouldn't be doing and not doing what they should be doing. Nothing is a bigger waste of time than trying to improve something that shouldn't even be done in the first place. Don't make government more efficient at something it shouldn't be doing anyway. Make no mistake about it; government has clearly grown beyond its means. And budget cutting simply does not work. As someone who has personally spent 10 years in government, I can help you understand how the government cuts budgets. Let me give you a tennis analogy to explain this, as both of my daughters and my wife are great tennis players. Suppose last year I spent $200 on a new tennis racquet for my wife, and this year I was going to upgrade her to the biggest, baddest tennis bag around, one that cost around $100, which would bring us to a total of $300 in new tennis equipment. But my wife informs me that she doesn't need that big bag, she would instead prefer the smaller one that only costs $50. Thus we were able to drop our tennis budget back to $250. Now to any normal person that is still a $50 increase over what we spent last year. But the way government employees look at it, that's a $50 spending cut, because I am spending $50 less than I thought I would! Simply cutting budgets and streamlining services that governments should not be providing is still a waste of time and money. Privatization, not streamlining, is the answer.

The Global Mandate

One of the key forces pushing toward privatization is our global economy. Globalization of economies reduces the power of government. Politicians don't like to acknowledge the fact that free enterprise requires economic growth as its key foundation and that government requires economic contraction so it can stay in charge and in control as its key foundation. The only problem is that people want growth. Around the globe people are realizing that government has become the major obstacle to them having the best and the cheapest products and services from anywhere in the world. Putting taxes and tariffs on goods crossing borders is like the government supporting "muggers" to wait in line at the Greyhound bus station and rob everyone who steps off the bus. The concept is ridiculous. The thought of imposing tariffs on trade to ensure freedom of competition would be like breaking a kicker's foot to make him kick further.

The global economy is now producing wealth like never before because governments are downsizing and privatizing and lowering taxes. Global trade is not about warfare. When you have mutual gains from voluntary exchange, it is win/win. Simply put, people want higher standards of living, and the government is getting in the way.

Every single minute of every single day it becomes more and more difficult for politicians to try to unscramble the emerging global economy in an attempt to reassert their declining power base. This new global economy is dissolving, reforming, and creating new industries faster than governments can put together lists in a vain attempt to try to regulate them.

And the great thing about this global experience is that you don't need to manufacture something to create wealth. If I sell a business book that has been sitting on a shelf in my study to someone for $20 through e-bay, three things happen. First, I now have extra cash in my pocket (wealth has been created), e-bay has money in their pockets (more wealth has been created), and the buyer has a business book so that he or she can figure out how to create wealth. Everyone wins. Wealth is enhanced; yet absolutely nothing was produced or manufactured except a trade. I love this New World economy.

The United Kingdom—Privatize the Mail

Speaking of global economies and global markets, this push for privatization will not be confined to the United States; rather it will be a global push as well. Consider the current push in the United Kingdom regarding its postal service. Currently there are about 18,000 post offices in the United Kingdom, most of them owned and run privately by local storeowners who are under contract to the government. There are only 1,500 of what is referred to as "Crown" post offices (referring to the royal crown), which are wholly owned, managed, and operated by the government.

The United Kingdom is now faced with the challenge and the political debate that because so many of the customers interface with postal services in private hands already, why not simply completely privatize the entire postal systems. Weak political leadership in the past on this privatization issue had created the half-baked system that they are strapped with today, having left the post office in a halfway house between government and private ownership. This two-headed monster can't get anything done. Because of this structure the postal system doesn't have the ability to raise enough capital to expand into new services. On the other hand it lacks the confidence to make decisions without government officials and politicians second-guessing it and interfering with its plans.

The United Kingdom must take heart in the fact that other countries have completely privatized their mail systems. This privatization has allowed them to expand internationally and to develop new services, such as guaranteed same-day deliveries. In order to survive, post offices must be run like a business. The letter mail load in the United Kingdom is expanding at about 5 percent a year. The communications world is quickly changing, however, and the threat from e-mails, faxes, phone messaging, and other new forms of communication means that post offices need to be both proactive and flexible enough to survive such change. One thing we know for sure is that government-run industries are neither proactive nor flexible.

The traditional argument against mail privatization simply doesn't hold any water, in my opinion. The argument against privatization has always been that private operators would focus only on the extremely lucrative intracity routes and leave the rural routes with no service. That's easy to solve once privatized; it simply becomes a requirement to offer universal service to both rural and urban customers.

Never lose sight of the fact that privatization creates competition and that the more competition you have, the greater the chance of someone coming up with an innovative way of reducing the cost of rural deliveries. While they are at it they may even find a way to drop the cost of the extremely high volume urban mail as well.

By privatizing the United Kingdom postal services, the United Kingdom would be creating more competition. More competition breeds greater customer choice, new and innovative customer services, as well as a cheaper and much more reliable postal system. Post offices in the United Kingdom will be privatized.

Regulation "Lite" from the United Kingdom as Well

While privatization of the post office is a no-brainer in my opinion for the United Kingdom, there is another concept being bantered about the United Kingdom that I think might just be the smartest approach to regulation ever. I'll call it Regulation "Lite," after all the lite beers that have been created.

Here's how and why it would work. Tradition based on British standards makes it impossible to have laws on the books without the intention of enforcing them. You could complete the time-consuming task of analyzing every single regulation there is and rank them with respect to their importance. However, this would all be for naught because regardless of their importance, their status in law is equal. This guarantees that both the essential and the trivial regulations are equally binding and equally enforced.

Regulation "Lite," or indirect regulation, starts out by throwing away all of the regulations (I love this plan already). Thus instead of starting with a list of regulations to deal with, you start with a concept. What needs to be regulated? Well, to start with, we would want all motor vehicles to be safe; we wouldn't want buildings to fall down; nor would we want restaurants that make their clients sick. Are you getting the picture here? We talk about what needs to be done, not how to do it.

The "how" is taken care of by insurance. Under this new indirect regulation, all that government would require is an insurance certificate. Think of my automobile safety example for a minute. Automobiles would be required to display an insurance tag; without it being displayed it would be illegal to drive. The insurance companies would ensure that vehicles met appropriate safety standards before being issued their tag.

And in the case of a building, a new building would not be certified for occupancy and use until it had an insurance certificate. Again it would be the insurance companies, during both the planning and the construction phases, that would be responsible for ensuring that the building met appropriate safety standards with respect to such things as building materials, fire risks, and potential hazards.

On to the restaurant example. Restaurants would not be allowed to serve the public unless they had an insurance tag in their window. And in order to get an insurance tag, they would have to satisfy insurance company conditions and inspectors.

Is this the most logical plan you have ever heard of in your life or what? Now the actual regulation and inspection will be overseen by the insurance companies, not by politicians and their appointed bureaucrats. Government, if you will, sets the goals of regulation; it doesn't implement them. Instead of political bureaucratic cronies who administer the letter of the ill-informed law to a "t," there will actually be regulators that know something about the sector they are trying to regulate. In this way regulations can be applied in a more flexible and sensible way. The insurance companies will make it their business to have detailed knowledge, understanding, and insights on the sector concerned. They will best be able to identify the potential risks, to assess their importance, and to make the necessary requirements accordingly. Instead of the whole process being set up to blame someone, it will be set up to support sensible and rational decision making.

This new concept could be implemented sector by sector to replace the current system of direct regulation by this indirect one. It will phase away from government over time completely. Think of this interesting side benefit. One major advantage of a requirement for insurance is that immediate problem solving is built in. Someone who suffers is eligible for an insurance payoff. Disputes would cease to be a part of the political process; they would now involve insurance companies, as opposed to government agencies. And think of this additional benefit: In the process of moving to indirect regulation, the government now gains access to the services of experts more skilled and experienced in technical details than it could possibly expect its own in-house civil servants to ever achieve.

Finally the insurance company teams would make it their responsibility to achieve the regulatory goals of government. That means that the government will not have to appoint new armies of bureaucrats to implement and monitor compliance with government regulation. This plan could change the world!

The Alarmists

Like anything that proposes something new and different, there will always be a faction that wants to support the old current system and to keep things exactly the way they are. That is certainly the case with government downsizing. Machiavelli provided the classic perspective on this when he said, "It must be remembered that there is nothing more difficult to plan, more doubtful of success, nor more dangerous to manage than the creation of a new system, for the initiator has the enmity of all who would profit by the preservation of the old institution and merely lukewarm defenders in those who would gain by the new one." By the way, Machiavelli said this way back in 1513 A.D., long before anyone thought big government would be a problem.

Anyhow, because there is a highly vocal group (government employees) that will obviously be opposed to any calls for government downsizing, alarmist views will tend to appear in the marketplace.

Alarmists will look at government downsizing in a much different way. They will theorize that if we have a smaller government workforce, there will not be as many government employees to fill the potholes in the streets. More potholes in the streets mean deteriorating driving conditions and safety hazards, which in turn will lead to an increase in traffic accidents and fatalities, all for the want of a pothole. Give me a break! Government downsizing doesn't mean there won't be anyone to fix the potholes. Filling potholes is an essential function. Focus your downsizing on the layers upon layers upon layers of bureaucratic overhead and red tape that are required to do the simplest of tasks, like get a building permit. What we need to do is to downsize the bureaucratic waste right out of a job; or better yet, let's let them fill the potholes. These alarmist views, regardless of how vocal, will not deter government downsizing.

The Big Prize—Public Pension Privatization

Government-run pension systems in the United States (Social Security) and all throughout the world will see privatization as the only way to save these ailing public pension systems that, quite simply put, do not have the financial strength to be able to pay future retirees all of their benefits. Let me give you some perspective on how to quantify this problem.

Most experts would quickly agree that the high-profile Social Security system in the United States has certainly achieved one of its stated goals, namely, reducing the poverty level among senior citizens. What is interesting to note, however, is that the actual financial benefits of the Social Security system are considerably less than the benefits of other major nations around the globe. For instance, in the United States the average level of the minimum old-age benefit (the major component of Social Security) provides less than one-third of the median income for a retiree in the United States. Meanwhile the overall average in every other industrialized nation around the globe accounts for well over 50 percent of retirees' income.

Maybe it goes back to what I call one of my unwritten laws of economics: "You only get what you pay for." The reason that Americans get less is quite simply that they pay less. In the United States a worker must contribute (or should I say, is taxed) 6.2 percent from the first $65,400 that they earn. In Japan, however, workers contribute 8.25 percent. And in Germany workers are forced to contribute a whopping 9.3 percent. Don't forget my unwritten law of economics: "You only get what you pay for."

Because the amount of benefits that are provided varies, it becomes very difficult to compare various countries' public pension liabilities. The most readily used number is a country's unfunded pension liability as a percent of total GDP, which is the broadest, most comprehensive measure of a country's economy. The reason for this is quite simple; after all it is the economy that will ultimately create the resources to pay off these liabilities. While some of these comparisons are pretty easy to analyze, the two largest economies in Europe, Germany and France, have unfunded public pension liability of 110 percent and 114 percent, respectively (the lower the percentage, the sounder the financial condition of your public pension system). Anything approaching 100 percent means that your system is approaching meltdown. When you use this measure to look at the United States, however, its unfunded public pension liability as a percent of its economy is only 25 percent. One of the distortions here is that U.S. benefits are smaller, so that keeps the percentage down. One thing this measure doesn't capture is the number of potential retirees: Remember those aging baby boomers that will be holding their hand out for assistance from the U.S. government. Even though the numbers don't reflect it, the public pension system in the Untied States is in much worse shape than the public pension systems in either Germany or France.

Public Pension Privatization—What Is It?

Most public pension systems (like the Social Security system in the United States) are established as a pay-as-you-go system. The system in essence works like this. Current workers pay a payroll tax that goes into some sort of a trust fund. The trust fund then immediately turns around and pays most of the money out that it just collected in the form of benefits to all of the current retirees. Now in addition to pay-as-you-go, these systems are also defined benefit plans (or as we referred to them in Chapter 1, "I don't care about the stock market" plans). All that means is that the exact amount of your "benefit" is clearly "defined" and spelled out for you. In other words you know exactly what you are getting. Now a pay-as-you-go defined benefit plan can be a great plan as long as two things are happening. First, the workforce is growing faster than the group of retirees. Second, the wages of the workforce grow faster than inflation.

And in the United States, for example, that is exactly the way things used to be. You see, after World War II, the United States had a rapidly growing population, which in turn meant a growing labor force. In addition, wages were growing faster than inflation. Life was good. And there certainly was no problem on the horizon for the U.S. public pension program.

Times change, however. The U.S. population, thanks to the baby boomers, is now aging. Within the next decade the workforce will actually stop growing altogether. And what's more, to make matters even worse, people began living longer. Looked at another way, the longer people live, the more they actually cost the public pension system.

Now remember that the United States is not alone on this issue. The crisis is a global one. Everyone got into this together, and everyone will have to get out of it together. When the nations of the world were adopting their pay-as-you-go defined benefit systems, little did they realize what a cruel trick demographics was going to play on their pension system. As you look out around the globe today, most nations are now facing an aging population. In addition, with a slowing general population growth, there is no growth in the workforce. This crisis gets even worse when you consider that private pension plans are not taking up the slack. In one European country, Italy, for example, of a workforce of over 23 million, only 840,000, or less than 4 percent, are enrolled in private pension plans.

As a result of this impending crisis, we have witnessed countries moving away from their pay-as-you-go defined benefit systems. With

Chile leading the way, Australia and the United Kingdom have made substantial changes to their public pension system as now virtually every country around the globe is being faced with the economic and political challenge of changing its public pension plan.

The changes will look like this. What you do is let your system evolve from a defined benefit plan to a defined contribution plan (recall again from Chapter 1 that another name for this plan is the "I am a stock market junkie" plan). The term *privatization* was latched on to explain what was happening. And while this term can sometimes be intimidating, let me explain exactly what it means in terms of privatizing public pensions. Privatization simply means that you are giving your workers more control over their own retirement funds, so these funds are in essence private or privatized.

And while it is very difficult if not impossible to generalize about privatization because all of the details of the plans will vary greatly, there is still one common thread. The plans let younger workers invest their payroll taxes on their own while older workers are kept on the present system. Having two systems for a period of time will greatly increase the transition costs from one system to another, which is why the reform movement has been slow to catch on.

European Public Pensions

The most logical place to start is Europe. After all European countries have some of the most established public pension funds anywhere in the world. These public pension fund systems are facing the exact same deadly one-two punch that the United States is faced with, namely an aging population and a shrinking workforce.

While all of Europe is facing this daunting public pension crisis, most countries are doing very little about it. The lone exception is the United Kingdom. Over the past 25 years, the United Kingdom has embarked on a series of changes to fix its public pension system.

The current public pension system in the United Kingdom begins with a basic benefit of 15 percent of the average wage for all workers. This portion is still a pay-as-you-go system. In addition to that, however, there is a state earnings-related pension scheme, commonly referred to in the United Kingdom as SERPS. The innovative feature about this system is that workers and companies can opt out of SERPS. And when they opt out, they are in essence privatizing the system. Currently over 50 percent of workers in the United Kingdom have opted out and are now in private company-run pensions. Another 25 percent have opted out and are in personal pensions. While not a perfect system, the United Kingdom stands alone in Europe in addressing this important issue.

The Chile Example

Without a doubt the most dramatic and radical pension fund reforms are not in Europe or in the rest of the industrialized world for that matter. Rather the birthplace of public pension privatization is none other than Chile. Back in 1981 Chile privatized its public pension system from a defined benefit system to a defined contribution system.

Here's how it works. First, the Chilean system has a minimum pension guarantee financed by the government. Second, everyone has an individual retirement account funded by a mandatory contribution (tax) of a whopping 10 percent of his or her salary and wages. Now even though these are individually owned, they must be invested in accounts held by 25 different certified private financial institutions. In addition the Chilean government guarantees that the return on the funds falls within a certain range of the average among all of the certified private financial institutions. The current makeup of those individual accounts in aggregate is 40 percent in bonds and 60 percent in stocks.

Believe me, the rest of the world is taking notice, especially Latin America. Following Chile's lead, Colombia, Argentina, Mexico, Uruguay, and Peru have already implemented public pension privatization programs similar to Chile.

Where's the United States?

On most public policy fronts the rest of the world tends to look to the United States for leadership. However, in terms of privatizing their Social Security system, no one is looking to the United States for leadership. In fact the United States actually lags in pension reform. The reason is that there are several myths regarding the U.S. Social Security system; and until those myths are debunked, pension reform will continue to lag.

Now consider this: With Social Security facing almost certain doom in the twenty-first century, there has been much talk and no action about "privatizing" the system. Privatization of Social Security would divert part of a worker's Social Security tax payments into a personal retirement account that could be invested in U.S. Treasury bonds, stocks, or other securities. Privatization will not be approved until the political myths regarding Social Security are addressed. Here is a quick overview of some of the myths that have crept into that nation's collective consciousness.

Myth #1: *Social Security and its benefits could never be cut.* It's a political myth that Social Security will always be there and an even bigger myth that no politician would dare cut any of its benefits. In fact, the problems of Social Security have been so great that politicians began cutting them more than 20 years ago. In 1977, Congress made its first cut to Social Security, reducing the benefit formula enacted as part of the 20 percent, across-the-board increase passed in 1972. Guess what happened to Congress? Absolutely nothing! This was truly a watershed event that opened the floodgates—Congress has made nine separate cuts since 1977.

Myth #2: *You don't need Social Security anyway because you have a private sector pension that is insured by the federal government.* Did you know that it is actually illegal for companies in the private sector in the United States to put enough money into their pension funds to ensure they'll have sufficient assets to pay promised benefits? This happened with an obscure provision that slipped into legislation with the Omnibus Budget Reconciliation Act of 1987. A company's pension plan contributions are tax deductible. The government determined that it could collect more current corporate taxes by forcing companies to postpone funding their plans until their employees reached retirement age, thus making more of their current income taxable.

And the safety net behind the private pension system, the Pension Benefit Guaranty Corporation (PBGC), is not what most people think it is. Most people assume that this organization is backed by the full faith and credit of the government. What actually stands behind the PBGC—which, by the way, is supposed to insure the pensions of 32 million employees in 65,000 plans—is a law authorizing it to borrow up to $100 million from the U.S. Treasury. That's less than what the PBGC spends in two months! In effect, the desire to raise federal revenues has been delaying the funding of employer-sponsored pension benefits, with no consideration of the long-term impact or cost.

Myth #3: You have a legal right to your Social Security benefits. Contrary to what you might believe, no American has any vested right to Social Security benefits. Social Security is essentially a "social contract" whereby the next generation promises to pay for the retirement of the previous generation. Unlike participants in funded private pension plans, Social Security system participants have no property rights to their benefits. System payouts, as well as eligibility requirements, are entirely in the hands of Congress, which can change the rules to meet current economic problems as it sees fit.

In the 1960 landmark case *Fleming versus Nestor,* the U.S. Supreme Court settled the matter of Social Security property rights once and for all, ruling that workers do not have any accrued property rights associated with the Social Security system and no legal claim to either their accrued contributions or anticipated benefits.

The prevalence of these three myths, among others, must be changed for the American people to wake up to the need to privatize.

The States Are Coming

Even though the United States is lagging in pension reform, the same cannot be said of the individual states that make up the United States.

One of the keys to public pension reform happening at the individual state level is the simple fact that the states are flush with cash due to the 10-year record economic expansion in the United States. And the time to address problems is when you have the money to fix them. All across the United States individual states are looking to make the shift from defined benefit to defined contribution systems. Over half of the 50 states either have adopted pension reform or are in the process of adopting pension reform. The eye-popping facts associated with the state of Michigan's reform are what really jump-started this thing at the state level.

Michigan projected that if it stayed with its current defined benefit plan, a typical 35-year-old worker making $30,000 per year would receive an annual pension of only $4,500. By contrast if they switched to a defined contribution system and that employee's individual investments yielded an 8 percent annual return, that same worker would build up a $200,000 nest egg, which would produce $16,000 per year for living expenses at retirement. Oh, I don't know, what do you think . . . $4,500 or $16,000? You don't have to be an economist to figure this one out.

It doesn't stop there, however, it gets even better. Remember, under the current defined benefit plan, the benefits end when the pensioner dies. Under the defined contribution plan, on the death of the pensioner the investments earned are passed on to any heirs.

But wait, it still gets better. Under the defined contribution plan all pension benefits will now follow the individual employees when they leave public service. Moreover, under the defined contribution plan, employees are vested (eligible) after just four years. Under the defined benefit system, vesting took 10 years; and if you were not vested, you receive no benefits. Over two-thirds of Michigan's public school workers never receive one penny of retirement benefits because they don't work long enough (10 years) to become vested.

The problems that Michigan faced were the same problems that the rest of the states faced. Currently most states use a defined benefit pension program in which annual payments are calculated by the number of years worked and an average of the last few years' salary. These plans are simply a poor deal for most state workers. In California, the largest state, and most other states government workers, for example, who change jobs or retire before working a full 10 years never qualify for a state pension. Currently, more than half of all state employees never "vest" in their state pension systems because they move or shift jobs.

This movement toward government-employee defined contribution plans follows the exact same development in the private sector. In the private sector the number of defined pension plans is falling while defined contribution plans are rising. In fact, in the United States there are now more defined contribution plans than there are defined benefit plans.

Don't underestimate the unbelievable long-term ramifications that these shifts at the state level can have on the overall government. Consider it this way: From a purely economic perspective, the key is that state workers with defined contribution pensions are now property owners. Each and every month they receive a statement informing them of how their investments performed. Watch what happens now. All of a sudden state government employees will care about government regulations. They will care about antigrowth fiscal or monetary policies as well. Believe me, being a property owner is key. It changes the way you think and act. Do you want proof? The next time it's a nice day around your neighborhood, watch how many neighbors wash their car. Do you know why? It's their property; they are property owners. Answer me this—I wonder when the last time was that any of them took the time to wash their Hertz Rental Car. Trust me, it never happens. Being a property owner will change the way state employees think and act forever.

Government and Technology Converge

In closing out this chapter on government downsizing and privatization, I thought it might be interesting to reflect on the previous chapter on technology and to figure out what impact, if any, it will have on governments around the world.

Just as technology has dramatically changed everything it has encountered in business, it will do the same with government. In fact, it will turn government upside down in the way it thinks. You see, historically government policies have focused on macroeconomic stabilization policies, as well as macroeconomic stimulus policies. In addition, government focused on fiscal and monetary policy, as well as government mandates and exhaustive regulations to provide direction.

The technology revolution, however, needs none of that. The technology revolution requires flexibility—freedom for business to innovate, restructure, and reorganize in ways never before even thought about. Thus this new way of governing will really be a "bottom-up" approach, driven by the creativity of entrepreneurs and businesses. The old-school "top down" approach of government policy making simply will not cut it in this New World order. The reason is that traditional government policies and regulations actually represent impediments to the technology revolution. In this New World order government policies need to create a framework that supports and promotes the speed-of-light restructuring and innovation needed to be successful.

This technology revolution that in many respects is the fuel that is creating our new economy will stress governments from two fronts.

First, the technology revolution is creating massive corporate and financial restructuring through mergers and acquisitions, downsizing, spin-offs, and even bankruptcies. Government policies must be relaxed to encourage this restructuring; and in many respects the laws should actually encourage restructuring.

Second, the technology revolution is causing layoffs, job loss, and retraining. Furthermore, a big shift is going on as well. Employees are being shuffled from large, somewhat bureaucratic companies to more responsive, fast-growing innovative firms. So on the one hand we have the need for large corporations to reduce their workforce to increase efficiency by using more technology, while on the other hand smaller firms need experienced and skilled workers to succeed. Government policies and regulations must support labor market flexibility and mobility. In fact, the laws should encourage both companies and individuals to do this, not penalize them.

Who knows—maybe the biggest change to government will come not from the votes that are cast in the voting booth but rather from the computers that count the votes. Just as the technology revolution has forced businesses around the world to innovate and change or be left behind, so too will technology force government to change the way it thinks, acts, and governs.

DR. BOB'S NOTES . . . TOP 10 THINGS TO REMEMBER!
Chapter 4

10 As the welfare state (government) grows more and more, people want to be receivers, not payers.

9 The global economy is now producing wealth like never before because governments are downsizing and privatizing and lowering taxes.

8 The U.S. Internal Revenue Service publishes 480 different tax forms; then it publishes an additional 280 forms to explain the other 480 forms.

7 The move to indirect regulation begins by throwing away all the current regulations.

6 Most public pension systems are established as a pay-as-you-go system.

5 Over half of the 50 states in the United States either have adopted public pension reform or are in the process of doing so.

4 Contrary to popular belief, no American has any "vested" right to any Social Security benefit.

3 Most government functions will be privatized because incentivized business people will always be able to do it faster, more efficiently, and cheaper.

2 One of the biggest winners is the fact that the end of the Cold War will finally enable governments around the globe to downsize.

1 Technology will force governments to change the way they think, act, and govern.

Chapter 5

Corporate Restructuring, Mergers, and Acquisitions Go Global

Change is the law of life. And those who look only to the past or the present are certain to miss the future.

John F. Kennedy
Former President of the United States (1963)

R emember when you had to change jobs in order to work for a different company? That's certainly not the case today. It's the companies that are changing. In fact, at one stretch in my investment career, the company I worked for recreated itself (merger, acquisition, and ownership changes) four separate times over a 10-year period. And while I held basically the same investment position, I ended up working for four dramatically different companies without ever leaving my desk.

Not Just Tires Anymore
And think for a minute how BF Goodrich & Company has dramatically changed itself. It is a 130-year-old company, one of the world's

155

largest manufacturers of rubber products, known around the world for its BF Goodrich tire. In 1985 it decided to get out of the tire business and recreated itself by focusing on aerospace. It then sold its entire tire business to Michelin. At that point in time aerospace accounted for only 7 percent of BF Goodrich revenue. Now BF Goodrich & Company, which has changed its name to Goodrich Corporation, derives 84 percent of its $4.4 billion in revenue from aerospace. In 1984 you might have joined this company expecting to engineer "tires"; and if you are still there today, you might find yourself working on a highly classified, top secret, "Star Wars"–type aerospace project for the future. And just like me, you didn't have to leave your desk. President Kennedy's message regarding change is as timely for businesses today as it was 40 years ago. The only thing that has changed is the reason why businesses are changing.

Fuel behind Merger Boom

Mergers, acquisitions, and the eventual change that occurs in every business as a result of mergers and acquisitions are being driven from several fronts. There are three key ingredients to the fuel that will drive the global merger boom. The first ingredient is global competition. Very few businesses, when they are first looking to sell their services and products to the world, realize the downside to a global economy—the cold reality is that a lot of new competitors have also just been created for your business from around the globe. The second ingredient, in addition to the global competition and in many respects as a result of this intense competition, is the collapse of pricing power. When a business has to operate by looking over both of its shoulders worrying about potential and real competition, you can rest assured that it is probably not going to raise prices and give someone a foot in the door to steal market share. The third ingredient behind this merger boom is the strong desire to build scale. Building scale is happening in one of two ways, either buying up your competition to give you dominant scale in your line of business, or moving and acquiring businesses outside of your traditional line of business. And in many cases both of these strategies are being used simultaneously. I believe it's the confluence of these three factors—increased competition, little if any pricing flexibility, and the need for scale in order to go global—that has been and will continue driving the merger boom around the globe. If anything, going forward, these issues will play an even more dominant role than they do today, which means that we are seeing merely the tip of the iceberg of mergers and acquisitions around the globe. One other thing that will also fuel more mergers is that they are more acceptable and encouraged. Take the mergers in the United States last year, for example—only 1 percent were hostile mergers. A short decade ago in the United States, a quarter of all of the mergers were hostile mergers.

Customer Satisfaction—The Final Straw

In addition to competition, pricing, and scale, something else is going on that is pushing more and more companies to merge, and that is customer satisfaction—or should I more appropriately say deteriorating customer satisfaction. I, for one, believe that this steep decline in customer satisfaction can be tied to the very tight labor markets that we have today. Because of the tight labor markets, particularly in entry-level and lesser skilled positions, businesses find themselves forced down one of two paths. Option one is to make do with fewer employees. In other words, if you need ten employees and can only find seven who are qualified, you simply have to figure out a way to make do with seven. Option two is to lower your hiring standards by hiring less-qualified employees.

No matter what option you choose, it leads you to the same result, lower customer satisfaction. Think about it for a minute, under option one businesses are simply hiring fewer people. That means that the lines for service will probably be longer, which in turn means that the customer will have to wait longer. It also means that the employees will try to move you along through the line faster so that they can get to the next person. All of these activities lead to lower customer satisfaction. Choosing option two, hiring less-qualified people, doesn't put businesses in a much better position because less-qualified typically means some combination of less education and less experience. Oh by the way, those are the exact two ingredients (education and experience) that lead to customer satisfaction. Anyway, watch how hiring less-qualified employees also leads to lower customer satisfaction. I am sure that you have experienced this during the holiday shopping season. You're in a rush, pressed for time in your favorite retail department store, and you ask a clerk for help. Well guess what? You happen to pick one of the clerks hired on to help during this holiday season rush. They know absolutely nothing about the product line of the department they work in; they know little if anything about any of the store's policies and/or promotions. If you had to go to the bathroom, however, they could probably point you toward the restroom. I'm sure you will recall how personally disturbing this is. And it doesn't stop there. Sometimes you are lucky and find the one store clerk that actually knows what he or she is doing and actually helps. Is this satisfying? Think again. Let me tell you what happened to my wife and me recently, something that I'm sure has happened to you, too. We had a very knowledgeable store clerk in women's coats helping us. The problem was that she was not just helping us; she was helping everyone. You see there were two other store clerks that couldn't even walk and chew gum at the same time. Every single time any customer asked either one of them any question about anything, they immediately came over to our clerk, interrupted our conversation, and asked our clerk how they should handle this customer request. Even though we had a very knowledgeable employee helping us, we left the store extremely dissatisfied because of the poor quality of staffing.

And it isn't just department stores. Across the board in banks, insurance companies, airlines, automotive companies, telephone companies, cable companies, you name it . . . customers are dissatisfied. I'm not sure if I can develop a proven investment theory on this. However, isn't it interesting that all of the sectors that I just mentioned as having poor customer satisfaction also happen to be some of the very same sectors that are leading this merger-and-acquisition boom? Who knows, we may have stumbled on a new leading indicator for investment bankers.

Euroland Mergers

The fuel that is driving mergers is not unique to the United States. These issues will impact all businesses no matter where you are located, even Europe, which was at one time thought to be isolated from the rest of the world, at least from a business perspective. In Europe, remember, most companies never dared to cross their national borders. They were not "European" companies; rather they were German companies or French companies or Italian companies. All of that is changing.

Europe is the beneficiary of one other source of fuel to drive mergers and acquisitions that is unique to Europe, namely the launch of their new currency back in 1999, the euro. The euro was to help remove these national borders between European countries. This new currency could help transform German companies and Italian companies into European companies and even global companies. And that is accomplished through mergers and acquisitions. The results so far are staggering, both within countries' borders and across borders as well. Within its country borders Italy witnessed the largest European hostile takeover ever when Olivetti, an Italian company, acquired Italy's Telecom Italia. Then the British mobile phone company Vodafone-Air Touch went outside its borders to Germany to acquire Mannesman, a German conglomerate of a company in engineering, automotive, and Internet communications.

Big blockbuster deals like these change the landscape and force other deals to happen for merger mania to really get going. In Europe, however, European companies will need some assistance from European governments. For example, how in the world could you even consider pulling off a major merger if you were a French company and had to be burdened with the threat of financial penalties from the French government if your company made "abusive" job cuts? Earlier this year (2001), a French judge actually ruled that British retailer Marks & Spencer PLC violated national labor laws when it abruptly informed its 1,700 French employees that they would lose their jobs. Give me a break! Is there anything other than abusive job cuts in a merger or acquisition? After all, if you can't cut the overlap, you lose all the potential cost savings, so why merge at all! France, and the rest of Europe for that matter, must back off on their concern that their citizens will lose jobs: They must focus on nationalism and stop focusing simply on job loss within their own borders.

There are really three important keys to watch for that will support an uptick in European mergers and acquisitions. And all three fronts are with the governments of Europe. First, governments must continue to revamp and overhaul their outdated labor laws so that mergers and acquisitions can be supported and encouraged. Second, reforms in the financial markets must continue to progress so that the necessary infrastructure is in place to support the merger-and-acquisition boom. Third and finally, the laws and regulations on corporate governance must be pulled into the twenty-first century. European companies will never be able to move quickly enough during the merger boom if they remain strapped by the same corporate governance laws and regulations for business that have been on the books for hundreds of years. All you have to do to see if the governments in Europe are making any progress on these reforms is watch the merger-and-acquisition announcements. If governments reform their labor, financial markets, and corporate governance issues, then mergers will skyrocket. If they don't, then European mergers will lag, and European companies will be threatened with the possibility that the rest of the business world just might pass them by.

Why Go Global?

There is a very important issue that we must address in order to get the proper foundation for these mergers and acquisitions. Think of the European example we just discussed, and ask yourself why a company would want to move from a German company to a European company to a global company? There has to be some benefit. Well, besides the obvious issue of providing scale and the ability to sell your products and services to people all around the world, there is an even more important issue at play here. Global companies mean that there will be even more and more trading across borders of more and more countries going forward. In other words, these mergers and acquisitions will be supporting and encouraging even more trade than we have today. And with all of the rhetoric regarding the problem with trade and trade deficits, it might be important to figure out if increased trading is good or bad, not for businesses but rather for individual consumers. After all, if the ultimate consumer benefits from more free trade, then that will create another cycle to support and encourage more mergers in the future. From strictly a consumer's perspective, free trade does two important things—it lowers the cost of goods and services, and it increases the number of available goods and services.

Free Trade—It's Cheaper

It is a simple fact of economics that the ultimate price you pay as a consumer for anything that you buy, whether it's the automobile you drive or the food that you eat or the clothes on your back, will be affected by trade policies.

In order to figure out why products of free trade are cheaper, it's interesting to look at the opposite of free trade, namely protectionism, to see how that can actually add to the costs of goods and services. In the 1980s the U.S. government decided that it would protect its ailing automobile sector from the better-built Japanese imports. Thus it limited Japanese car imports in the early 1980s. During the first half of that decade, car prices rose more than 40 percent—that's twice the average price rise for all other consumer products during this same time period. The reason the U.S. government did this was to save automotive sector jobs; however, just the opposite happened. The 40 percent skyrocketing price hike of new cars was one of the key reasons why millions fewer U.S. cars were sold, which resulted in even more American automotive jobs being lost.

The World Trade Organization has developed some extremely interesting figures on how free trade impacts the cost of the food we eat and the clothes on our back. The World Trade Organization estimates that the protectionist policies surrounding the agriculture sector in Europe have caused the annual cost of food for a typical family of four in Europe to rise over $1,500. Meanwhile the protectionist trade policies for agriculture in Japan have caused food prices to be 50 percent higher than they otherwise would be. Think about how outrageous this is. That's like the Japanese consumers paying a 50 percent tax on food, and they don't even realize it. And in what just might be the most misguided protectionist food policy ever, in 1988 the U.S. trade policies added over $3 billion to U.S. consumers' grocery bills in just one year, just to support one product. That product, in case you forgot, was sugar. There is nothing sweet about protectionism.

Finally, consider the price that you pay for clothing. In the United

States the combination of import restrictions and high customs duties have combined to raise U.S. textile and clothing prices by over 60 percent. But this is not unique to the United States. Canadians pay an extra $780 million dollars annually because of import restrictions. And across the ocean in the United Kingdom, British consumers pay an estimated $500 million dollars more per year because of these import restrictions and high custom duties.

The textile and clothing sector has some of the most stringent import restrictions and high custom duties of any sector. In fact if we were to do one simple thing (well, it's actually not so simple), like eliminate all of the customs duties for clothing and textiles around the world, the results would be staggering. The net effect would be that the world economy would gain $23 billion. More than half of that, $13 billion, would be for the United States, over $2 billion would be for Europe, and $8 billion for emerging markets. Make no mistake about it; protectionism increases costs to consumers, and free trade actually makes things cheaper.

Free Trade—It's All about Choice

While there is no doubt that free trade makes products and services cheaper, maybe equally important to consumers around the globe is the fact that it also gives them access to more products and services than they ever dreamed possible.

Free trade enables consumers to buy things that they typically would not have access to. Living in Chicago as I do, it doesn't really matter what season it is in Chicago. You see, even if something is out of season in Chicago, it's in season somewhere else, and I can simply import it from that somewhere else, whether it's food or fruit or vegetables. And it certainly is not limited to out-of-season produce in Chicago. I have access to household products, books, and electronics from any part of the world I want. And on the flip side, think of all of those people who don't live in Chicago or even the United States, for that matter. Think of all of the things that people in other countries can have because they buy exports from all around the world.

If you want to realize the impact that free trade has on your life, just look around you and consider all of the things and choices that would disappear without free trade. Wow! If you happen to be a U.S. citizen like I am and if you start removing everything imported from Japan and China and Taiwan and Mexico and so on, you would watch the choices that you have become so accustomed to evaporate right before your eyes. And don't lose sight of the impact that free trade has on the products that are not imported. You see, by importing a wide range of products and services, some of which have higher quality than others, it forces the quality of local goods and services to improve because of the competition from imports.

And as consumers, we sometimes only focus on the things we ultimately buy. However, free trade impacts more than just the finished products of things we find imported and placed on a store's shelf. Imports are also used for materials, components, and equipment. So in my case, even though I might pick something up and see "Made in the USA" stamped on the bottom of it, the fact of the matter is that most of the parts and components could have come to me from other parts of the world because of free trade.

The only thing that consumers like better than a great choice or selection is a great price. And guess what? Free trade promotes both of those things to consumers around the globe, greater selection at a lower price. As long as consumers are happy, free trade will thrive; and as free trade thrives, so will a company's desire to become more global. And you guessed it—the formula to become more global quickly is mergers and acquisitions.

Businesses Goin' Global

With the solid foundation of free trade as a cornerstone, the globalization of business should not be looked at as merely a trend but rather as a revolution on how business must evolve to become successful. In many respects globalization is not a recent or unique focus. In fact over the past decade the globalization of business has been the focus of virtually every business, no matter what sector. The real focus on globalization began to explode with the end of World War II. Back then, nations, with prodding from the United States, began supporting the opening up of trading and, more important, the opening up of investment. The motivation for globalization back then was really quite simple. Globalization was looked at as the best way to develop a mature global financial system.

From a business perspective globalization is about far more than simply buying and selling products. Consumers are excited, remember, because globalization allows people from all over the world to buy goods and services from virtually anywhere in the world at a price much cheaper than they could make it. And while this consumption prize is important to business, it is not the real prize that globalization provides business. The real prize comes in the form of what it now allows businesses to do. Businesses around the world now share information. When you begin sharing information, it is simply the first step to gaining and sharing knowledge. The scope of this knowledge and information ranges from management practices to technological advancements. And the real beauty of this is that you get to experience it live—firsthand, if you will. This is because with globalization comes the side benefit of opening up travel to all parts of the world. Now business has the opportunity to gain information, knowledge, and insights from other businesses, other cultures, other governments, even other people. From a business perspective globalization has opened up an almost unlimited new source of business ideas.

Think of the impact, for a minute, that globalization of businesses can have on entire nations. Watch how this ripple effect works. Sometimes businesses underestimate the ripple effect—how something that appears unrelated can impact something else. Consider the most recent, hotly contested, highly controversial presidential election in the United States. In many respects the outcome may have been determined by Elian Gonzalez's mother. Think of how different the events might have been if Elian Gonzalez's mother had decided to stay in Cuba. There would have been no high-profile Elian affair, the same high-profile Elian affair that was so mishandled by the Clinton-Gore Administration that it angered the Cuban community in Florida. They were angered so much that thousands protested by voting for George Bush, the same George Bush that won Florida by a mere 537 votes, the same George Bush that is president today because he won Florida. All because Elian Gonzalez's mother got into a boat . . . talk about a ripple effect!

Now watch how this ripple effect works on business. The globalization of businesses means we will be doing more trading worldwide. Looked at another way, there will be a sharp increase in the amount of goods and services traded worldwide. This increase in the amount of goods and services traded has the effect of increasing competition. With the true globalization of business, everyone is potentially your competitor. This increased competition causes businesses to increase their investment in their own business. After all, whatever it is that they do or provide they better figure out how to do it better and cheaper and faster, and how they do that is to invest more in their business to figure out the hows and whys. So, are you still with me now? The globalization of businesses has led to an increase in the amount of goods and services that are traded worldwide, which in turn has increased business competition, which finally has led to increased business investment. Do you know what increased investment leads to? A better standard of living, all because of globalization of businesses.

How Do You Manage the Globe?

As sector after sector and company after company downsizes, restructures, merges, and gets merged, all with an eye toward becoming global, businesses must suddenly wake up to the fact that someone has to manage this new global business. Maybe the single most important determinant of which businesses will be successful in the next decade will not be found on any company's balance sheet. Rather it will be determined by who has the best global business managers. The company that has the best global managers will win!

Could there be a more daunting task today than developing global managers—finding these managers who will be the champions of touting why the firm's going global and what advantages this globalization will bring for both the company and its clients? Ultimately these global managers will be putting in controls, checks and balances, and various other systems that eventually lead to greater control of all local activities around the globe. How this is accomplished is determined by how the various resources of the global firm are aligned. The people, process, technology, and product will each play a key role that is somewhat interdependent on the others.

This constant struggle between local autonomy and global control will become one of the most important issues that global managers will face. And how they address it could ultimately determine the future not just of their career, but also of their firm. Since globalization has become so popular, I am sure you have come across the business strategy, "Think globally and act locally." This used to be the simplistic battle cry of how a company could become a global powerhouse. Two problems have emerged, however, with this simplistic approach. First, I'm sure that you have heard the phrase, "You are what you eat." When in business, you become how you act. Even if you claim to think globally, if all of your actions are like those of a local company, are you really anything more than just one really, really big local company? Second, this approach assumes that local businesses may not have something that could be applied globally. Who knows, maybe it would be better if the local market drove the global strategy instead of vice versa. Thus companies have come to the realization that managing globally is a complex and challenging job.

Global Management, Anyone?

Well, now that businesses know what they need, they have to figure out how to find it. The traditional school of thought says that a global manager should have over 20 years' experience with the organization. That is how long it will take for the manager to know the company from top to bottom and inside out. After all, it takes time to know all there is to know about a company's people, its corporate culture, the systems that it operates, and the competitive landscape of its sector around the globe. As an investor you have to change the way you have been taught to look at companies in regard to managers. You see, investors like yourself have been taught that you watch out for the company that doesn't have enough management talent internally and always has to go outside of itself to fill key management positions. This theory is based on the concern that there is no "bench strength" at this company. And while this still might have its merits for some positions, it has no merit whatsoever regarding global managers. First, instead of penalizing companies that went outside of their own management ranks, you should reward them because what that company is actually saying is that they have no one that can lead them on the globalization battlefield but they have the resources to find someone who will. Some of the best businesses in the world are the ones that know what they don't know. Second, the world is moving and changing too fast to develop global managers internally. Where do you think your business would be if you decided to wait 20 years to develop good global managers and then take your company global?

Global Traits

It really doesn't matter whether a company hires its global managers from within or from outside its ranks, it still must look for the success-ful personal traits that will lead to a successful global manager. The most important trait is how a candidate handles stress. Global management's very complex to begin with; then when you add in the ambiguity en-countered on the global level, it's easy to see how stress levels go off the charts. Adding to that stress are the physical strain as well as the emotional strain of being a global manager. Add on top of this the pres-sures on family life. If handling stress is number one, adaptability comes in a close second. Remember, global managers are constantly thrown into new living environments with quality of life and quality of living standards that are dramatically different from what they are used to. In addition, they have to give up the things that they like and enjoy the most, whether it's food choices, dress, or even leisure activities, and then adapt. If you know such a person, chances are she or he is already a highly compensated global manager.

A Regional Option

As an investor, you may find it necessary to search out the firms that have a regional approach to their global company. Think about it for a minute: How are you going to develop a global manager over 20 years when to most employees today 20 months is considered long term? Add to that the fact that a global manager's job is burdened with an unbe-lievable travel schedule. The job is grueling, no matter the aspect from which you look at it, physically, mentally, and emotionally. And it most certainly is not conducive to a happy family life. Maybe we should give up trying to find superman or superwoman. Instead maybe it's time to recognize as investors that maybe the firms with a regional approach will evolve as the global winner. So that means that maybe the way you manage the globe is that you don't manage it at all, you simply regionalize it. Once you consider the time needed to develop global managers, and the difficulty of running global companies, and throw on top of that all of the unique customs and systems and idiosyncrasies of people around the globe, what you might come back to is that if you can't manage the entire globe, how about just the Americas and Europe and the Pacific Rim. While as a business you will lose some global coordination, what you may gain by being able to both think and act locally will more than offset your losses.

The Price Is Not Right

No matter how hard it is to manage a global organization, whether it's from a regional or a country level or with real global managers, the only thing that I know for sure is that regardless of the management challenges, globalization will not slow down. The reason is that price pressures won't let it.

Right about now you are probably thinking, "What about this price pressure? I just filled up my gas tank, and prices have almost doubled. Isn't that pricing power?" It most certainly is pricing power. It is also an isolated incident; and even though the price of oil matters to you each and every time you fill up your gas tank, from a bigger-picture economic perspective, the price of oil isn't nearly as important as it once was. Here is why.

Now depending on exactly how many years you go back, the price of oil has either doubled or even tripled over that time. What is more important than the price increase in oil is the fact that oil is not as important to our economy today as it was in years past.

Twenty-five years ago in the United States, the consumption of oil accounted for almost 10 percent of the U.S. economy (as measured by gross domestic product). Back then the price of oil really did matter. That spike-up in oil in the early 1980s ended up putting the United States into an economic recession. Today, even with the recent run up in oil prices, oil consumption's share of the U.S. economy is only 1 percent. There is something else going on here besides the lack of importance in the price of oil today. This highly competitive global market that we find ourselves in today makes it much more difficult to pass on the rising cost of something. Twenty-five years ago if the price of a raw material that you were using (such as oil) in the production of your product rose dramatically, you simply passed that higher cost on to the consumers whenever they bought your final product. This is not so today. Instead businesses are forced to figure out how to cut costs and save money elsewhere so the net effect to the ultimate consumer is nothing.

Because of productivity and technological advancement, we are able to do more with far less oil than ever before. What used to take a gallon of oil in a production process may only take a pint today. And at the end of this decade, what took a pint in the production process when the decade began may only take an ounce. And these dramatic changes in the demand side of oil are only half the story. Remember that when you are trying to figure out the price of something, you need to look at both supply and demand. From the standpoint of the oil supply, I simply have no idea what in the world OPEC (Organization of Petroleum Exporting Countries) will do, but I do know what technology will do to it . . . and that's increase it. You see, our advancement in sonar and state-of-the-art technology has made it easier and easier to locate and develop oil more quickly and more efficiently than ever.

This shouldn't surprise you; after all, technology lets us find everything more easily than before. A few years ago when our family was on a spring break vacation in Florida, I convinced everyone to go out on a boat fishing. This was no small task because both my wife and older daughter get seasick. Anyway the point of my story is not that they got sick, which by the way they did, but how fishing has gone high tech. Now you have to picture this—we were on this crusty, small, old fishing boat that smelled; and as we were headed out to sea, I peeked inside the cabin and thought I was in a *Star Wars* movie. There were more computer screens and digital cameras and high-tech whatever than most businesses had 20 years ago, all under the control of this salty old fisherman and his completely wired high-tech fishing boat. Believe me he found the fish with no problem. In case you're interested, we still didn't catch any. Technology may show you where the fish are but not how you can catch them.

It's Technology, Not Oil

Think about it: If technology can help us find moving objects like fish, what can it do with stationary objects like oil? Here's something else to consider: As oil and the price of it has become less and less important to the U.S. economy, what has become more important? Technology. If we go back 20 years, technology accounted for less than one-half of one percent of the U.S. economy. Today technology accounts for over 2 percent. In fact the impact of technology on the U.S. economy is greater than the impact of all of the consumption of oil.

Consider the pricing ramifications of this shift as well. While the price of oil has been busy doubling and tripling, the price of technology has been in a constant freefall. And what's more, the freefall is in all aspects of technology—computer hardware, computer software, semiconductor chips, you name it. Just look at what this does to pricing. As we use less and less oil, the fact that its price has risen becomes less and less important. On the other hand we find ourselves using more and more technology every day, and the price of that technology continues to fall every single day. It's technology, not oil, that will drive pricing in the decade to come.

Pricing and Technology Converge

Although it may be interesting from a strictly philosophical standpoint to debate whether technology is driving pricing or pricing is driving technology, maybe the most dramatic example of where pricing and technology have truly converged as one, is the bar code.

The technical name for this bar code that you find on every product everywhere is the universal product code (UPC). My wife and I have another name for it when all we want to know is the simple price of something and all we can find is this dumb bar code. Anyway, the UPC is a series of vertical lines with 12 digits. It is these vertical lines that have led consumers to dub it the bar code. Half of these digits identify the producer of these various products, and the other half tell you exactly what this product is.

If you were the producer or manufacturer of a product, you would actually purchase or own a series of UPCs. You would then assign a

different UPC to each and every product that you produce or manufacture. You would have a different UPC for each of the various sizes
of a product, a different UPC that would cover all of the various colors
your product comes in, the various styles, and whatever else distin-
guishes your product. All of this information that is captured on the
UPC is entered into a central computer. These databases are then made
accessible to anyone that is willing to pay for them.

And as you can imagine, everyone pays for it and why wouldn't
they? The UPC tracks the product from the first step to the last. These
UPCs are entered into the mainframe computer at each and every step
of the process. It is logged in when it is ordered. It's logged in again
when it is actually packed. Then it is logged in again when it is shipped.
What more would you want if you were the manufacturer of something? That's only half of the story, however. Look what it does for the
retailer. The computer logs it in when you actually receive it. It is logged
in again when you actually sell it. And then when the item is restocked,
it is logged into the computer once again. Once you have all of this
information, that is only the start of it. What you do with the information is even more important. All of the information gathered using the
UPC is then utilized to generate a report to show what products are
hot (selling) and what products are not selling. Then another report can
be generated to show what inventory will be needed. And after you
order that inventory, a new report can be issued to monitor the progress
of those orders.

If I am a producer, the UPC allows me to know exactly how much
I will need to produce so I don't have to worry about building up large
inventories. On the other side of the business equation, if I am a retailer,
I know exactly what is selling, and I don't have to worry about a large
inventory either. And more important, to a retailer, that means that it
does not have to drastically slash its prices in order to liquidate all of
the inventory that is sitting instead of selling. The UPC has given retailers the key to the magic kingdom, more sales with less stock. How
do you spell P-R-O-F-I-T?

One way to think about the UPC is that it takes the guesswork out
of product expectations. Producers, manufacturers, shippers, and re-

tailers now all know exactly what to expect. Having the appropriate expectations lowers cost to everyone—the producer, the manufacturer, the shipper, the retailer, and ultimately the consumer as well.

The effect of this little bar code doesn't stop with this dramatic impact on price alone. Think of the ripple effect. Because of bar codes, retailers do not need as much square footage for inventory now. Less square footage for inventory means wider aisles. So when the mother comes down the aisle with her stroller, you no longer have to fear for your life. Also because retailers know what's selling, you can also bet that you will have a better selection of goods. And because retailers no longer have to spend hours upon hours, not to mention dollars, analyzing sales trends and inventory trends and shipping concerns, all the money that is saved can be used to hire a clerk so you can check out even faster. And it's all possible because of that simple little bar code. Technology is truly amazing. The next time my wife and I are frantically looking for a price and all I can find is that dumb bar code, I'm going to hold my tongue. Because after all, when I finally do find out the price, that bar code has most likely made it cheaper.

The Business Risks Have Changed

The UPC and the creation of Just-in-Time inventory has combined to solve one of the greatest risks businesses faced over the past half-century, namely inventory risk. And it's not just inventory risk that is changing. All of these mergers and acquisitions are creating bigger, smarter, more sophisticated companies; and as a result the risks in the business world are also greatly changing. A quarter-century ago businesses had commodity risk, interest-rate risk, and currency risk. These three risks alone, which were out of the control of even the strongest-willed chief executive officer, could bring even the best-run business to its knees. Today these risks have almost disappeared. Thanks to an innovative financial market where you have hedges and interest-rate swaps and a futures market, business can now actually make money when commodities, interest rates, and currencies go against them. These risks have been greatly diminished.

Fifty years ago, one of the biggest risks and challenges that a business faced was wage risk. In other words, if you couldn't control salary and wages, your business would fail. Today this is hardly a risk at all. The reason is the creation of the temporary employment market. Today when employers need help, instead of entering into a long-term and costly commitment with a new full-time employee, they can instead hire temporary help. This wage risk in businesses today has been greatly reduced.

Back 20 years ago another one of the big business risks involved research: Did you spend enough on research? Could you find the right research people? And were you doing the right research? Today companies have learned to leverage their research, and they are doing more than ever dreamed possible. How? With research alliances. Even business competitors are joining together to combine their research dollars to make them go even farther than anyone could ever go alone. Thus alliances have put the research risk on the back burner as well.

And finally, let's not forget the granddaddy of all risks, pension risk. Nothing would keep a chief executive officer or chief financial officer up at night more than the thought of how in the world they were possibly going to find the money to pay all of those pensions when everyone retired. Well guess what? That risk has been solved as well. When businesses shifted from a defined benefit to a defined contribution system, the pension risk was shifted from the business to the individual employee.

So in this New World order of megamergers and global acquisitions where companies no longer have to worry about inventory risk or commodity risk or interest rate or currency risk and they don't have to worry about wage risk or pension risk or research risk, you may be asking yourself just what risk does business face today? Or looked at another way, what is the single greatest business risk for the next decade? That's easy—the answer is intellectual capital risk. In other words, your employees; or in plain and simple terms, your people. Remember, the Stone Age came to an end, but not for a lack of stones. Likewise business profitability will come to an end, but not for a lack of employees, but rather for how they are used. After all, we still throw stones don't we?

The one thing that becomes even more important to the ultimate success of any business as it becomes bigger (global) and more complex is that its most important asset is its intellectual capital. And as such the biggest risk any company will face is its intellectual capital risk. In this New World order, people-friendly companies will win. If you are investing in a company that is not people-friendly, first you have "brain drain"—all the good people leave—then the stock price goes down the drain as well. Do you really want to own a company you wouldn't want your daughters to work at? I don't want to, and I don't!

Quality Is Job One

It only stands to reason that if the most important asset that a business has is its people, then you need to create quality jobs in order to retain quality people. And that is exactly what is happening today. Over this past decade the highest job growth in the United States has occurred where the highest-paying or highest-quality jobs are as well. Those professions would be business and investment professionals, doctors, lawyers, and other professional occupations. The lowest-paying jobs on the other hand saw the lowest growth in new jobs; these range from bartender to hairdresser to retail clerk. The average-paying jobs, those in the area of construction, manufacturing, and transportation, witnessed average job growth. Looked at another way, if people are becoming your greatest asset, there will be a tendency to create the best jobs that you can for them. After all, doesn't everybody want a quality job?

There is a price to pay for these quality jobs, however, and that price is education. As the quality of the job increases, so does the educational requirements to do that job, which in turn lifts the educational level of the entire workforce. Consider the trends in the United States. Over the past decade over half of all of the new jobs that were created have been created for people with at the very least a four-year college degree. Meanwhile college graduates still account for less than one-fourth of the total workforce in the United States. This trend also has a trickle-down impact. There were fewer jobs created for people without a high school diploma in this past decade than at anytime in the history of the United States.

This improved quality of job growth and job creation in the United States is partly a reflection of its position in the high-technology global-economy picture. If the United States hopes to retain its economic advantage, it must continue to implement highly sophisticated technologies. And you guessed it—these highly sophisticated technologies require a highly educated workforce. Also think about the impact that the ever-changing, ever-developing technology revolution will continue to have on job quality. As more and more technology is created and more and more innovations are implemented even faster than they are today, businesses will quickly realize that the only way that they can successfully continue to incorporate all of these new innovations and improvements is with highly educated employees who will require a high-quality job. For both individuals and businesses alike, education will become essential to their survival.

Smarter Employees Mean Smarter Workers

As more and more quality jobs are being created and filled by highly educated employees, another thing is happening. You see, a more highly educated workforce is a smarter workforce, and a smarter workforce tends to figure out a better way of doing things. Economists call that productivity. The gains in productivity can be traced back to a smarter workforce.

It's not just a smarter workforce that makes a company more productive; rather it's the combination of a smarter workforce and a more experienced workforce, which when combined delivers a one-two punch for productivity. The workforce in the United States today is both highly educated and very experienced. The baby boomers that we talked about in Chapter 1, remember, are heading to that half-century mark. They are educated now, they are highly experienced, and they will become the most productive workforce ever. There are more 50-year-olds than there are 20-year-olds in the United States workforce today. The successful businesses will have to capture the right combination of talent from both of the extremes on the demographic front. Here's why you can't forget about the 20-year-olds if you are a business. One of the other keys to this great upswing in productivity has been fueled by all of the technological improvements. In fact the labor force in the United States today has more and better capital equipment than any labor force ever in the United States. From computers to telecommunication equipment, the innovations have been mind-boggling. But guess what? The 20-year-olds more rapidly embrace the use of this new technology than the 50-year-olds. While the 50-year-olds certainly have the experience, the 20-year-olds have the edge in embracing, using, understanding, and reaping the rewards of new technology. You would simply be amazed at the number of business executives in the United States today that are over 50 and couldn't send an e-mail to save their life. In fact when they hear someone's computer speak the most recognized message in the world today, "You've got mail," those business executives are looking for the mailman.

Senior Worker Power

Even though many of these older workers have been slow to adopt technological changes, their experience is priceless. The innovative companies that are smart enough to continue to tap this vast resource will no doubt be the most productive companies and the most profitable companies of the next decade.

And in the United States it's not just the 50-year-olds that will have an impact. Watch out for the 65-year-olds as well.

Congress finally adopted the Senior Citizen's Right to Work Act. This act revokes the earning limit that was set for any senior citizen who was also a recipient of Social Security. The Social Security Earnings Limit Test was part of the original Social Security Act, which was adopted way back in 1935. The original law stipulated that recipients would lose all of their benefits if they had any earnings. Over time that was amended to apply a penalty of $1 in benefits for every $3 a recipient earns over $17,000 for all workers aged 65 to 69.

There were close to 1,000,000 workers aged 65 to 69 who had their benefits reduced. And of those 1,000,000, 30 percent lost all of their benefits, and another 20 percent didn't even bother to apply for benefits because they earned more than the limit. The law served as a penalty to any senior citizen who wanted to work. In reality, it was an additional tax on senior citizens' earnings. What was truly unfair and made no sense at all was that it only applied to salary-and-wage income. Investment income was not counted. So these outdated laws of Social Security in essence used to say that someone that makes $500,000 a year from their investments doesn't have to give up one penny of their Social Security benefits. However, someone that has to get up every morning and work to make ends meet by earning an additional $20,000 will have their Social Security benefits reduced.

That's all ancient history now. The adoption of the Senior Citizen's Right to Work Act means that thousands upon thousands of senior citizens will be increasing the number of hours that they work and will now be seeking better-paying jobs because they will not be penalized. This change is long, long overdue. When the law was created in 1935, the United States was in the midst of the Great Depression. The somewhat hidden agenda of the law back then was to actually encourage older workers to leave the workforce completely to make room for the younger workers. Times have changed, and so have demographics. Now the United States is in desperate need of the additional manpower that the senior citizens can provide to the changing demographic landscape. But more important the business or industry that can quickly embrace these gray-haired Albert Einsteins that have seen it all suddenly will create a corporate culture with more wisdom than they would have ever dreamed possible. The closer each baby boomer gets to retirement, the more important the role of the senior citizens becomes.

Stay Home and Work

If one of the keys to a successful business in the next decade is it strategy toward incorporating senior citizens into its workforce, the other would be developing a strategy to let not just the senior citizens but also a good deal of their workforce work from home. Like everything else, we decided this needed a fancy name, so we call it "telecommuting." Telecommuting means you get to work from your home. Over half of the 500 companies that comprise the Standard & Poor's 500 Index have increased the ranks of their telecommuting employees. There are currently 12 million employees in the United States who work from home at least one day a week. Those 12 million employees communicate by phone, by computer, and live on the Internet. Two short years ago there were fewer than 8 million telecommuters.

The move to telecommuting is happening not just because workers are demanding it but also because it makes great financial sense for the individual businesses as well. Even if the employer provides home office equipment and even furniture, which most do not, that cost is still much, much less than the ongoing investment of keeping up and maintaining an entire office building.

Not all jobs lend themselves to telecommuting. Positions that require a lot of meetings and face-to-face interaction obviously will only work in the traditional on-site situation. But positions that focus on record keeping or independent research or creative positions such as writers or artists all could easily be converted into telecommuting positions.

While I am in no way an environmentalist, the ramifications of telecommunications for our environment are also staggering. In fact maybe the environmentalists should focus on this issue instead of protesting free trade. Anyway, here are the numbers. If 25 percent of the workforce in the United States telecommuted to work only one little day a week, more than 3 million gallons of fuel would be saved. That equates to over 32,500 tons less air pollution. It's good for workers, and it's good for the environment; and businesses that aggressively adopt telecommuting will find that it's good for business as well.

The Perfect Retirement Job

Not only will successful businesses understand the business importance of telecommuting; they will also understand the importance of demographics, which is creating an aging workforce. Astute businesses will quickly realize that they must change the way they attract, compensate, and retain workers who are at or nearing retirement. In essence they must stop the way their employees currently think about retirement. All of this is because of the unstoppable demographic trend that is leading to a rise in the share of the U.S. population that is over 55. Employers are now being forced to develop a strategy regarding the incentives that they give for retirement; and if they are going to survive, they must adopt flexible schedules for older workers. Employers must push the envelope and think outside of the box. When they see workers aged 55 and over, employers need to consider reducing both hours and responsibility in order to keep those employees happy and on the payroll.

While it should come as absolutely no surprise to you, in today's very tight labor market, firms are looking for ways to retain their employees. What is even more mind-boggling is that in the future, firms will have even greater needs and greater incentives to keep older workers. No successful business can afford to ignore the baby boomer generation as it moves toward retirement age. Successful businesses must learn to abandon their traditional swinging door policy for retirees. Even though not many businesses today are changing, it is becoming clearer and clearer that the implications of enticing more workers to delay full retirement are much greater than most businesses first realized. Consider the fact that in the 1970s and 1980s the share of the U.S. population aged 45 and older remained flat for over 20 years at just under 30 percent. In the 1990s the aging baby boomer generation increased that share to almost 35 percent. Even more relevant than the implications of an aging population is the segment of the population preparing to retire, the 55 to 64 age group, and the share of those that are 65 and older. Population projection puts the share for both groups at over 25 percent by 2010. This would be an unprecedented increase from under 20 percent in the 1970s.

This is an extremely tough concept for most businesses to grasp because they view most demographic issues as a snapshot, a point in time, and they miss the big picture. You see, if you took a snapshot of the demographics in southern Florida today, some businesses would be convinced that people in southern Florida are born Cuban and die Jewish. That's because the youth there are from Cuban descent, whereas the numerous retirees are of Jewish descent. If you fail to look at trends and just look at where we are today, you can see how easy it would be to conclude that people in southern Florida start out Cuban and end up Jewish. By the way, you would be dead wrong!

Now even though most employers may not be aware of the uncertainties regarding future workforce size, they all recognize the harsh reality that the pool of workers for most jobs continues to grow older and that a large number of experienced workers are nearing retirement age. Employers simply cannot replace the human capital of older workers, especially those with skills and expertise that can only be gained through work experience. Businesses are also going to become extremely reluctant to lose their employees who have gone through formal education and training programs at the firm and provided by the firm. And you've guessed it—it's those older employees who are nearing retirement age who, because they most likely have been with the firm for many years, find themselves in this category. Thus businesses cannot afford to let their long-time employees simply walk out the door. The loss of these long-time employees is becoming a major risk. One of the reasons for this increased risk is global competition. Firms need to keep their productivity at a level where their business can continue to expand and to grow. And it's these experienced workers that are pushing the productivity levels to new records year after year.

But enough about the business aspects, what about the employee? Why should any workers who are at or near retirement age not retire simply because their employers need them? There are fewer and fewer incentives available to keep people wanting to work. Remember, as we discussed in Chapter 2 regarding the poor savings rate in the United States, we touched on the demographic forces that kick into place when an entire population is turning 50 and nearing retirement age. When you are over 50 and nearing retirement age, more than likely both your home and your vehicles have been paid for. In addition your children are either already through or almost through college. And don't forget about the impact of the record "bull" stock market. This record bull stock market has skyrocketed the value of individual retirement accounts (IRAs) and 401(k) retirement accounts, and most stock options (unless you're with a dot.com company, which most 50-year-olds are not) are also in the money. What this all means is that many employees nearing retirement do not have the same fear that their parents had regarding maintaining their same comfortable standard of living after they retire.

All this doesn't mean that higher wages and salary cannot be used as an incentive; it simply means that higher salary and wages don't automatically mean an extended commitment by an employee nearing retirement. In fact, in many respects just the opposite is happening. Higher salary and wages, which lead to greater employee wealth, lead to the desire for greater and greater amounts of leisure time to enjoy that newfound wealth.

During the next decade the successful businesses will realize that they must go way beyond traditional salary-and-wage increases if they expect to cope with the aging baby boomers who are going to dominate the U.S. workforce. Instead of only using salary and wages to induce workers to stay past the traditional retirement age, they must use other forms of compensation as well. One approach will be the continuation of a trend that is already beginning, and that is the increase in benefits, specifically health care benefits. This is one area that still worries and concerns most people close to retirement; thus a top-notch health and dental and eye and prescription drug program will convince many people to stay who might have been on the bubble about retiring or staying.

Good businesses will not stop there. They will continue to think outside of the box and push the envelope even further. They will not look at all things the same way, like the little boy to whom, once you give him a hammer, the whole world looks like a nail. The successful business of the future will allow these older employees more flexibility than most traditional businesses are comfortable with. If they want a shorter workweek, give it to them. If they want fewer functional responsibilities, give it to them. Another approach is that businesses will create a series of projects just for these older workers. This flexibility is going to be key. Older workers will quickly switch jobs and go to a competitor if it provides them with a more flexible lifestyle.

Isn't it simply amazing how the world has changed? It used to be that businesses were ready to push retirees out the door, and retirees had very, very little, if any, leverage of any kind. Today all of the bargaining power is in the hands of the retirees, especially when one considers that as each day goes by, the retirees become a larger and larger share of the labor market.

As the workforce grows older, the successful business will be the one that sees the great benefits in taking whatever steps are necessary to retain its pool of experienced workers and to attract other experienced workers. You may be finally nearing the perfect job. Your employer will let you decide how much you want to work and what you want to work on!

Don't forget the economic impact of all of this as well. The longer these retirees stay on the payroll, the more disposable income that they have to spend and to travel all around the world to see their grandchildren. We very well may be witnessing the most affluent group of retirees with the greatest spending power ever. Maybe that's why the planes are so crowded.

Planes, Trains, and Automobiles

It is only fitting that I'm actually writing this part of the book on a plane on a Monday morning on my way from Chicago to New York. Anyway, let's shift gears and focus on the specific sectors that will be generating the greatest activity in this merger boom, starting with the transportation sector. The title of John Candy's comedy movie *Planes, Trains, and Automobiles* is perfect for what the transportation sector can expect in this upcoming merger-and-acquisition boom.

During the next decade the airline sector will continue to merge and to consolidate, with most of the activity being global in nature. This sector is still in the process of attempting to recreate itself. The decade of the 1990s could be characterized by the airlines strategizing on how to get more people on each flight. After all, this was a pretty simple equation. The more people you could cram on each plane, the lower the fares could be, which would encourage even more people to be crammed on a plane. This strategy actually helped boost revenue. Market gurus extrapolated these trends and said that there would be gigantic planes with very, very crowded conditions. There is a problem however when you extrapolate trends and numbers. The problem is that people who extrapolate numbers and take them to the extreme are being misled by what I refer to as the Elvis factor. You see, in 1970 there were 210 Elvis Presley impersonators registered in the United States. By 1977 that number had ballooned to 5,075 Elvis impersonators. Some businesses went on to extrapolate that by the year 2000 one out of every five Americans would be an Elvis impersonator and that the largest economy in the free world would be totally dependent on Elvis's popularity. I don't think so. They were wrong on Elvis, and they are also wrong on these overcrammed and jammed-in plane trends.

In the decade ahead, just the opposite will be happening. Service and luxury are replacing low fares as the way to get more passengers on board. This can take the form of better-quality food, more leg-room, better and more comfortable seats, personal television screens, Internet access, and so on. The success of the industry will be to capture the business traveler. Even though the business passenger accounts for less than 20 percent of ticket sales, it is responsible for over 50 percent of the sector's profit. If you have to be somewhere because of a business meeting, you will get there regardless of the price of the airline ticket.

Focusing on the business traveler instead of on the low-fare passenger will also help airlines in another way. Low-fare passengers file the majority of claims for damaged and lost luggage. Thus the refocus away from this group could actually save money.

This strategy has profound ramifications for merger activity. If the industry shifts to the business traveler, it must develop a global airlines sector that services the businesses that must go global as well. Business travelers would pay up in cost for the airline that could take them anywhere in the world. And that is exactly where we are going to end up. Cross-country mergers will be the order of the day for at least the next decade.

Let's move on to the second part of John Candy's movie, trains. The conventional wisdom is that because there has already been a rash of railroad mergers and all of these mergers resulted in service and performance problems, there is no case for future mergers. Conventional wisdom is wrong.

I will be the first to admit that Burlington Northern's acquisition in 1995 of Santa Fe Pacific did result in major service disruptions and created an inefficient operation. This fact however will not stop mergers.

I would also agree that the 1996 merger of Southern Pacific and Union Pacific was an unmitigated disaster that caused extensive service delays and generated congestion everywhere. In fact, it was so bad that it is estimated that this disruption cost the economy of the western United States over $3 billion. Again this fact will not stop mergers either.

And I will also admit that the merger of CSX and Norfolk Southern was the granddaddy of all railroad merger screwups. In fact the proposed date of the actual merger was even postponed in order to guarantee no service problems. But this ill-fated merger even went one step better. CSX and Norfolk Southern promised that their guarantee of uninterrupted service along with their productivity and efficiency gain would actually result in fewer trucks on the highway, because CSX/Norfolk Southern would actually be attracting freight away from the road.

Well, I'm sure you remember what happened. The minute the merger was finalized, both of the companies had major problems. The computer system failed to integrate, there were crew shortages everywhere, and all of this added to more congestion and much slower average train speeds. And guess what? Instead of taking freight off the road as promised, this merger is doing just the opposite. And the reason is very simple. Because of the problems at CSX/Norfolk Southern, customers were being driven to use truck transportation because the train transportation was so unreliable. Want proof? United Parcel Service moved over half of their railroad-carried freight off the railroad and on to trucks. But you know what? This doesn't matter either. It will not stop future mergers.

The only thing that does matter is that every year the railroad sector watches its market share shrink as it continues to lose share to the trucking sector. The only possible way for railroads to compete with the trucking sector is to merge and consolidate. Railroads have been losing market share to the trucking sector for years. This trend is not going to reverse itself. The fact of the matter is that the trucking sector offers better flexibility, which means improved customer service, than any railroad can hope to achieve. The railroad sector must wake up to the fact that it is no longer the key driver of the U.S. economy that it was 100 years ago. With that fact staring you in the face, your only option is to merge.

Let's move on to the final aspect of John Candy's movie, automobiles. The automotive sector will be pushed to the merger altar for very different reasons than planes and trains. Consumers will continue to demand more and more innovative designs and gadgets and will be willing to pay for them. The problem is that in order to respond to these new high-level demands, the sector and individual companies must have extensive research-and-development efforts in order to continue to feed the pipeline on this new product-innovation binge. And the only way to get there is through mergers. There is an ever-shrinking talent pool of truly creative automotive designers in the workforce. If you can't hire them, automakers will be forced to simply buy the entire company they work for simply to acquire the research-and-development capability.

Telecommunications Explosion

While the transportation sector will certainly witness an uptick in merger activity, it will be nothing like what we are going to witness in telecommunications over the next decade.

Ever since the passage of the landmark Telecommunications Act of 1996, big-time mergers have been the story of the day in the telecommunications industry. It's extremely important to understand that the motivation behind mergers today is much different from what it was yesterday. Historically, telecommunications mergers happened because one company wanted to buy up their competitor so they could gain market share. That's not the case today. It is rare to see companies merging that currently compete with one another. Many of the mergers involve companies that before the passage of the Telecommunications Act enjoyed government-protected monopolies (for example, local phone companies). Others involve companies that again prior to the Telecommunications Act were not allowed to expand into other parts of the industry (for example, long distance carriers).

Telecommunications companies will continue their aggressive mergers for three fundamental reasons. The first reason is to expand their network. This is the most basic and fundamental principle there is in telecommunications. If you are in telecommunications, you always want to have the most expansive network possible. That will never change, so it will always serve as fuel to mergers.

The second reason is the convergence in the sector. The telephone is converging with cable television. Meanwhile cable television is converging with Internet service providers, and these very same Internet service providers are converging with telephone companies. When one distinct service converges, the firms that provide those services converge as well. They do that to gain the much-needed product expertise regarding the new service, and they also do it for economy-of-scale reasons.

The third and final reason is that it is cost efficient. In other words prices will fall. And don't forget government regulators love it when the mergered entity can provide its service at a lower price. This price break will come from a confluence of three factors. First, these larger firms, because of their size, scope, and financial strength, will have lower cost access to the capital market. Remember, bankers like to lend money to really big companies that have lots and lots of assets on their books. Second, capital investment will increase. The development of new and costly network infrastructure is a large financial pill to swallow. The merged entity is much more likely to make this major capital investment. This in turn will accelerate the speed of the development and implementation of new and improved telecommunications products and services. These products and services increase competition, and increased competition puts downward pressure on prices.

Third and finally, prices will fall because of the major cost reductions that can be achieved. These major cost reductions are the result of one simple fact—economies of scale. You see, what I am talking about regarding economies of scale is the concept that when fixed costs of equipment and computer systems are spread over more and more customers, the overall cost per customer comes down. How this is actually accomplished is that the merged company spreads the cost of buildings and facilities, equipment, computer hardware and software, customer service and billing systems, marketing, sales, advertising, personnel, and legal all over a larger base of customers. And once accomplished the actual fixed cost to each customer goes down.

As the lines continue to blur between telephone companies, cable companies, and Internet service providers, there will be a blur as these individual companies rush to merge with one another.

Financial Services Boom

Believe it or not, for as good as it's going to be in the telecommunications sector for mergers, it's going to be even better in the financial services sector. The financial services sector will witness the greatest boom of all sectors in merger-and-acquisition activity. Let me start by giving you a better frame of reference as to the overall scope and magnitude of the financial services sector, one of the broadest sectors in the market today. It encompasses the traditional commercial bank that you are familiar with; it also encompasses investment banking firms, and insurance companies as well as mutual fund and other asset management companies.

The foundation for this merger boom in financial services companies is in two landmark regulatory changes that took place in the past decade in the United States. As the decade of the 1990s began, interstate banking laws were dramatically changed to such a degree that true interstate banking companies were now a reality. This change enabled commercial banks to expand their geographic market and service boundaries. Because these old interstate-banking laws had been on the books since the Great Depression, this actually represented the first opportunity for these commercial banks to expand their business beyond their original state boundary. And you guessed it, the quick way to take care of all of this pent-up demand for geographic expansion is through mergers and acquisitions. As an interesting side note to interstate banking, did you ever wonder why such major interstate commercial banks as First Union and Nations Bank ended up in North Carolina of all places? That's easy. It's because North Carolina has almost always allowed its commercial banks to expand anywhere else in the nation, but on the flip side it prohibited banks from other states from doing any business within the state of North Carolina. This gave North Carolina a leg up on the rest of the country regarding interstate commercial banking.

As the decade ended, the second major legislative change occurred—the repeal of the Glass-Steagall Act. This act had restricted the cross-ownership within the financial services sector among commercial banks, investment banks, and insurance companies. This law had also been on the books since the Great Depression.

In 1999 Congress repealed the Glass-Steagall Act of 1933, which created a "wall" between the banking and the securities industries. Congress enacted the Glass-Steagall Act in response to the stock market crash of 1929 and the Great Depression, in which a third of our banks failed at the same time our stock market collapsed. The goal of the act was to create a separation between the banking industry and the securities industry. Congress later adopted measures to create a similar separation between the banking and the insurance industries as well. That may sound like a wise separation. But over the years, study after study failed to prove its underlying assumption—that banks speculating in the stock market with depositors' money led to the Great Depression.

Two forces have been combining to pressure for repeal of Glass-Steagall. First, this act has put the U.S. financial services sector at a competitive disadvantage globally because in most industrialized nations, banks are able to offer one-stop shopping, that is, banking, securities, and insurance. It is impossible for the United States to compete if it can offer only one-third of the services other global financial services firms can offer global consumers.

Second is the influential force of the time-starved baby boom generation. As the boomers head into their fifties, they want things made simple and convenient for them. In other words, they want and will demand one-stop shopping. They don't want to go to one place for a savings account, another place to buy individual securities, another place for life insurance, another place for mutual funds, another place for home owners insurance, and so on. The boomers want the opportunity of going to one place for all of their financial services needs. And with the repeal of Glass-Steagall, now they will get it.

This change will dramatically alter the financial services sector landscape as insurers team up with banks, who team up with securities firms, who team up with local banks, who team up with mutual fund companies. Better keep a scorecard handy—the names are going to change quickly as merger mania is about to reach new heights.

When it is all said and done, the firms that evolve as a result of the repeal of Glass-Steagall will be better positioned to compete in the global arena. If you want proof of the impact that these legislative changes had on the makeup of the sector you need look no further than the megamergers that have already occurred—from the Citicorp and Travelers deal, to the Morgan Stanley with Dean Witter deal, to the Bank of America with Nations Bank deal, to the First Chicago with Bank One deal, to the Alliance with Sanford Bernstein, to Old Mutual (London) with United Asset Management, to Caisse de Deposit (France) with

Nvest, to ING's acquisition of Aetna's financial services group, to Union Bank of Switzerland with PaineWebber.

However, just because the regulatory landscape had changed to allow these blockbuster deals to occur doesn't mean that they will in the future. The fact that the legal obstacles have been removed only gets you halfway there. If there are not solid fundamental business reasons for the merger, it won't happen. The reason that I believe that the next decade is going to see unprecedented activity in mergers and acquisitions is the strong fundamental business reason that serves as encouragement to mergers in financial services. Actually there are five such reasons.

First is leverage. The exact same comprehensive database of customer accounts information could be used to determine who would be the most likely prospects for different products or services. It also may give access to information that would better help banks evaluate their risks to clients and potential clients.

Second is scale. Consider the case of a bank that lends money to the retail market through either consumer lending or mortgage lending. Both of these functions require a significant marketing and branding commitment. And they require significant customer support and servicing operations. Adding new customers adds very, very little variable costs while at the same time it spreads all of these fixed costs across a wider customer base. And remember, these fixed costs are extremely high in the financial services sector because of their commitment to top-notch information technology systems.

Third is revenue growth. Financial services sector profitability is pretty easy to understand. It is typically driven by a strong economy and low interest rates. In order to continue profitability, however, you must have revenue growth. And the way you get revenue growth is to sell more of what you sell. And the easiest way to do that is to cross sell other financial services to your existing customers. And the best way to acquire those other financial services to cross sell to your clients is through a merger.

Fourth is competition. The financial services sector is a true global sector. When you find yourself in a global sector, you have competition not only between domestic financial services companies but also from foreign financial services companies as well. European financial services firms and Asian financial services firms want to increase their presence in the United States. Meanwhile U.S. financial services firms want to compete overseas. And to be successful in this highly competitive global market, you must have the size and the scope that can be acquired only through major mergers and acquisitions.

Fifth and finally is securitization. Before securitization, here's how the financial services sector used to use your money. You would begin the process by depositing some money that you saved into your commercial bank or savings and loan. Your bank then used your money and turned around and made loans to other people or other businesses. And while this process is still in place today, each year it is getting smaller and smaller, being replaced by securitization.

Let me step back and briefly explain exactly what securitization is. It begins by a bank loaning you money. What the bank does next is combine your loan with other loans it has made to other individuals and to businesses, thus creating a "pool" of loans. Next it creates a financial security that is backed by the principal and interest that you as well as all of the other individuals and businesses in your loan pool pay. This financial security is sold to a wide range of institutional investors like me. Numerous financial institutions, commercial banks, savings and loans, insurance companies, mutual funds, pension funds, investment banks, and the U.S. federal government actively participate in the purchase of these securities. Let me show you the magnitude of this thing. Securitization is only 20 years old, but within the next decade it will account for over 50 percent of all lending.

Let me explain why this fuels mergers. Securitization breaks down the barriers to entry for financial services firms that want to figure out a way to put various loans to work. In other words, it increases competition. Think about it: A relatively small firm can set up shop, make loans, secure them, and quickly sell them to someone else. It is no longer necessary to have a large network of local branches to raise deposits and then turn around and make a loan. The more competitive a sector is, the more it will merge. In addition to these five reasons there is one basic overriding principle. Larger financial services firms will be less risky. They will be able to diversify across nations, across regions, across all product lines, and as a result they will be less likely to suffer when any one regional economy hits a bump in the road.

DR. BOB'S NOTES . . . TOP 10 THINGS TO REMEMBER!
Chapter 5

10   The only possible way for railroads to compete with the trucking industry is to merge and consolidate.

9   As the lines continue to blur between telephone companies, cable companies, and Internet service providers, so too will there be a blur as these individual companies rush to merge with one another.

8   A smarter and more experienced workforce combines to push productivity higher.

7   Larger financial services firms will be less risky because they will be able to diversify across nations, across regions, and across all product lines, which makes them less susceptible to any one regional economic downturn.

6   The ultimate success of any business as it becomes bigger and more complex is that the most important asset it has is its intellectual capital (people). Thus the biggest risk that any company will face is its intellectual capital as well.

5   The way you manage the global company is that you don't manage it at all. You simply regionalize it.

4   If European governments reform their labor, financial markets, and corporate governance issues, then mergers in Europe will skyrocket.

3 Successful businesses will be the ones that see the great benefits from taking whatever steps are necessary to retain their pool of experienced workers as well as to attract other experienced workers.

2 Mergers and acquisitions will be supporting and encouraging even more global trade than we have today.

1 The global merger-and-acquisition boom will be driven by increased competition, no pricing flexibility, and the need for scale in order to go global.

Chapter 6

Sectornomics™—Turning Trends into Strategies, Picking the Sector Winners

The key to success isn't much good until one discovers the right lock to insert it in.

Tehyi Hsieh
Chinese philosopher, educator (1948)

I t is my hope that the first five chapters of this book that focused on global trends and developments have given you the keys to success for investing in our complex global marketplace. However, simply having the key, as Tehyi Hsieh puts it, is only half the battle. Now you have to figure out what lock to put it into. In this chapter I am going to show you not one lock but five separate locks into which you can insert your keys. Each of these locks represents a sector that I feel will benefit the most over the next decade from the global trends and developments that we have uncovered and analyzed.

Why Just Sectors?

Right about now you may be saying to yourself, "Wait a minute! Don't just tell me about some sector. I want to know which individual stocks to pick or which individual country or region I should be investing in." And the way the world used to work, you would have been right in wanting to know these things. In fact, historically a stock's price was determined by exactly those three things: First, the individual fundamental factors regarding the company; second, the sector that the company was in; and third, the country or region. At any point in time any one of these three factors could play the dominant role in determining where the stock's price was headed. But at the end of the day they all pretty much seemed to have about equal influence and impact on the price of your stock. What that meant for you as an individual investor was that you better pick the right region; then you better pick the right sector; and then obviously you needed to pick the right company. In this New World order I believe the rules of investing are changing. The single most important decision you will make in investing is the sector you are in, not the country or the individual stock. While it will always matter what country you are investing in and what stock you are investing in, I firmly believe that the single most important factor to determine the success of your investment will be the sector in which you are investing.

It's the Sector, Stupid!

With the recent presidential election in the United States still on the minds of many investors around the globe because of the controversy surrounding it, I thought that it was time to dust off one of the most famous one-liners in U.S. presidential politics—"It's the economy, stupid." It was actually former President Bill Clinton's close political advisor and strategist James Carville that made that catchy one-liner famous. Well, I've taken the liberty of revising that famous presidential campaign quote to "It's the sector, stupid."

The combination of our global marketplace with technology is providing the fundamental one-two punch of why sectors are skyrocketing in importance. Again, think of the global markets and economies as now all being connected. And remember, it doesn't matter how they are connected, the only thing that matters is that they *are* connected. Markets and economies may be connected by economic ties, as the United States and Canada are. Or maybe it's political ties, such as China and Taiwan. Or it can be psychological or emotional ties that make absolutely no rhyme or reason. Take, for example, a bank in North Carolina that has no exposure at all in Russia. However, when Russia defaults on its debt and the banking sector is hit hard because of it, this poor seemingly unrelated bank in North Carolina that has no economic or political ties to Russia finds out that it still can't escape the global markets because it is tied emotionally. You see, what's really happening here is that there is nowhere to hide. Think of the automobile manufacturer in Japan that is hitting on all cylinders after the Japanese economy has turned the corner and consumers are buying big-ticket items. Then along comes Ford Motor Company in the United States issuing a warning about its profits and the demand for its products. Because of technology this information is immediately available around the globe to every investor and every potential investor. And when this occurs, you can bet that all automotive stocks around the globe will be under pressure. Why? Because investors will fear that if it can happen to an automobile company in the United States, it can certainly happen to one in Japan. And of course all of this happens at the snap of a finger because of the technology revolution and the information explosion. That means that before the Japanese automaker can prepare a response, its stock price has already dropped because of something that someone said in the United States. So in this case, even if you picked the right country to invest in and even if you picked the right company, all of a sudden you find out that because of our global markets, it's the sector, stupid.

And it's not just the simple globalization of our markets and economies that are causing a rise in the importance of which sector you choose. There are three other developments that also support the heightened importance of the sector allocation.

My Cost Is Your Cost

The first development is the integrated pricing and cost structure that is evolving around the globe. Think of how this works with the price of oil. No matter where you are located around the world, you are going to be paying about the same for the price of oil. So what does this mean for sectors that are heavy users of oil? I believe it means two things. First, the region or country you are located in is much less important; you are pretty much strapped with the same price of oil. Second, it doesn't matter which company that you invest in; all of the companies are pretty much paying the same price for this oil, so it will affect them all pretty much the same way. Now individual businesses will still attempt to remove themselves from the rest of the pack in the sector by maybe entering into the futures market to buy oil or by putting on a financial hedge against the price of oil or by negotiating some sweetheart of a long-term contract. However, at the end of the day these short-term strategies tend to cancel themselves out over time for these individual companies, and what is left is that the entire sector faces the same cost together. Thus all companies in that sector tend to move together either up or down, depending on what's happening with the cost of oil.

Watch how this works with the airline sector, one of the biggest consumers of oil for jet fuel. When the oil price goes up, it doesn't matter if you are Lufthansa, Singapore Airlines, or American Airlines; you will be paying more for your fuel. And with fuel being one of the largest and most important components in an airline's financial picture, all the airlines will tend to move together either up or down as this cost component moves. And remember, this will happen regardless of the company you invest in, and it will happen regardless of the country or region of the world you are investing in as well. This uniform cost and pricing structure places even more importance on individual sectors.

Do You Recognize Me Now?

The second development that is driving the importance of sectors over regions or countries is the explosion of mergers and acquisitions that I discussed in the previous chapter, especially in the case of all of the cross-border merger activity that is going on. Why, you almost have to keep a scorecard. The names are changing so quickly that it's getting difficult to recognize whom you are investing in. When a company from one continent merges with a company from another continent, which continent are we supposed to worry about for this new merged company?

Let's stick with our oil industry example, and watch how this phenomenon will impact your investments. Take the case of the recent merger between oil industry giants British Petroleum and Amoco. On the one hand we have British Petroleum, a company with 56,000 employees located in London, England. British Petroleum was always looked at as a European company. Now on the other hand we have Amoco, a company with 43,000 employees located in my hometown of Chicago, Illinois. Amoco was always looked at as a U.S. company. With their merger they have in essence lessened the importance of the country's or the region's risk (either Europe or the United States) and increased the sector risk. I do not see this trend reversing itself.

Now this is not meant to imply that all of these megamergers will make the country's or the region's risk disappear. That is not the case because companies will always be subjected to country or regional shocks that can move their stock price. What it does mean, however, is that the more we see cross-border mergers, whether it's a European company with a U.S. company or a Japanese company with an Australian company or any combination you want, the impact will be the same. With each passing cross-border merger the significance of individual sectors becomes all that more important.

We Make Money the Same Way

The third development is commoditization. As more and more products and services become commoditized, you will find more and more companies making their profits the same basic way. What this really means is that the revenue (money) that a company takes in is becoming similar across sector lines regardless of what company you are in. Now companies still have numerous tools at their disposal to differentiate themselves. First of all, they can sell a lot more than their competitors, and this will make their revenues and profits rise. Or they can figure out how to cut costs better than the rest of their competitors so that they are able to make more money based on the revenue that comes in the door. The one thing that they can't change very well is what the sector will be able to charge for their products or services.

Sticking with our oil sector example, here is what I mean. Let's say that you were smart enough as an investor to pick the most cost-effective, cost-efficient, highly productive oil company of them all. In other words it is able to make more money than anybody else is with every dollar that comes in the door. Now along comes the Organization of Petroleum Exporting Countries (OPEC) cartel, and they decide to increase the production of oil by millions of gallons per day for whatever reason. Remember, when you are a monopoly like OPEC, you don't need a reason. Thus when OPEC does this, the increase in oil supply immediately drops the price of oil around the globe, which in turn drops the price that oil companies can now charge around the globe. When this happens, the price of all oil companies' stocks go down. It does not matter which individual oil company you own. The market couldn't care less that you own the best, most cost-efficient, most productive oil company of them all. The only thing the market cares about is that it is an oil company, that the impact will be on the entire sector, and that the impact will be negative. As revenues become more and more commoditized in terms of what individual companies can charge, all of a sudden it is the sector and all of the companies that comprise it that face the same price pressures. It is not the individual company that really matters the most.

As the rules of investing change in the new high-tech global marketplace, we have to be flexible enough to change with them. An investor who buys two entirely different companies in two different and remote parts of the world in order to diversify risks may be in for a surprise in this New World order of ours. You see, a decade ago maybe that diversification strategy was fine. But going forward, that investor may be shocked with the results if these two different firms in two different parts of the world happen to be in the same sector. What that investor is about to find out is that it is becoming increasingly more difficult, if not impossible, to achieve diversification in your investments by the classic method of geographical location. And even picking different companies may not provide you with any diversification if those companies happen to be in the same sector.

The implication for investors is quite obvious. In our New World order there will be less and less reliance on the regional asset allocation of your portfolio. And while picking the right stock or company will always be important, maybe in the decade ahead picking the right sector will be more important. The rules of investing are changing right before our very own eyes. While some things will not change, the three dominant factors that will drive a company's stock price will remain the same; the individual fundamental factors of that company, followed by the sector that company is in, followed by the region of the world in which that company is located will remain the same. What is changing in our global marketplace is the relative importance of each of these factors. Think of the ramifications of this seachange. You could pick the right individual company in the right region of the world, but if you happen to pick the wrong sector, your stock price goes down and you lose money. So you got two right (company, country) and one wrong (sector). That's a batting average of 667, which in baseball terms would put you in the Hall of Fame with the highest batting average in the history of the game. However, from an investment perspective you just struck out because you forgot that the most important thing is the sector.

Let's look at the flip side for a minute. Suppose you find yourself investing in the wrong company and in the wrong region of the world. You can still be successful and make money if you picked the right sector. Even if you are not in the best company or in the best region, you can still turn a potential investment strikeout into a homerun if you are in the best sector.

I have dubbed this new investment strategy theory *Sectornomics.* Now I am sure that you are familiar with macroeconomics and microeconomics, neither of which need any explaining. And whether you live in the United States or abroad, you are probably familiar with the term "Reaganomics," which was used to explain then U.S. President Ronald Reagan's economic programs. Sectornomics is my discovery of what may go down as one of the most important investment strategies in the decades ahead.

Because I discovered it, I get to define it as well. My formal definition of Sectornomics is "the *sector* that you invest in will have the greatest *economic* impact on your investment's performance, even greater than the individual company that you invest in or the region of the world that you invest in." There you have it. William Shakespeare contributed 1,500 words to the English language. I humbly would like to introduce just one word to our investment language . . . Sectornomics. That's one down and 1,499 to go; I better get busy.

Let's take this newfound investment strategy of Sectornomics and put it to some practical use. Let's translate all of the global trends and developments we've discussed into specific strategies that highlight individual sector winners.

PHARMACEUTICAL SECTOR

Investment Strategy #1: We're Not Getting Any Younger

Well, there is one thing that you will have in common with everyone who reads this book, myself included, and that is that none of us is getting any younger. In fact the demographic trends in the United States along with the rest of the industrialized nations are all showing the same trend line. These countries are getting older.

In the case of the United States the aging process is being driven by a confluence of three demographic forces. First, the baby boomers are finally making their way down the age spectrum to the later years of their lives. These baby boomers (myself included) are finally getting older. Second, the United States now has longer life expectancy, and as a result of this the oldest age group is growing. Consider that back in 1971 when I graduated from high school only 3 percent of the U.S. population was over 75 years of age. Today it is 6 percent—double. Third and finally, don't forget that the birthrate is declining as well. When you put all these together it creates a population in the United States that is quite simply getting older. Again, when I graduated high school, the median age in the United States was actually under 30 years of age at 28.2 years. Today it stands halfway to 40 at 34.9 years. This demographic shift has tremendous positive ramifications for the demand for drugs and new treatments in the pharmaceutical sector, especially when you overlay the fact that the rest of the industrialized world looks just like the United States. In other words, the rest of the industrialized world is getting older as well. The significance of this shift is staggering for the pharmaceutical sector. If you gave them a blank piece of paper, they couldn't draw the demographics up any better than they are going to be for the next decade. The more people that move from their fifties to their sixties and seventies, the more drugs are going to be sold. The older you get, the greater your dependency on various drugs. Also the older you get, you develop new aches and pains each day that open up the opportunity for someone to sell you even more prescription drugs. Here's an extremely important point to remember. Not only are we getting older, but there are more of us as well.

Obviously the aging demographics will be a boom for the pharmaceutical sector. However, that boom gets turbocharged because life expectancy is expanding and people are staying around longer than ever before. And the more old people there are around the world, the greater the demand for the drugs, which are the profit drivers of the pharmaceutical sector.

A Never-Ending Supply of Drugs

It's not simply the demographics that make the pharmaceutical sector a great place to invest; rather it's also how demographics will influence other factors. Now keep in mind that the pharmaceutical sector is one of the main reasons why life expectancy is expanding. Through its research and development efforts, the pharmaceutical sector has developed outright cures for some diseases and the ability to strictly retard disease in other cases. All of this leads to two factors. The first is more obvious—if you had a disease, you are now able to lick it with these new drugs, and thus you will be living longer. The second factor is more important—the longer you live, the greater the likelihood that you will contract other illnesses or diseases. And guess what? That same pharmaceutical company that kept you alive is waiting in the wings to sell you something else for whatever ails you. What a business! The more things the pharmaceutical companies can cure you of, the more time you have to potentially catch other things so they can cure you again and again and again.

Think of the case of the 65-year-old that today is able to take medication to slow down a rapid heart rate and prevent a heart attack. Twenty years ago that wasn't possible, and that person most likely would have died of a heart attack. Today because of the medication people take, they can expect to live another 20 years or so—from 65 to 85. Besides a longer and happier life, think about what's also in store for this person—arthritis, high blood pressure, low blood pressure, high blood sugar, low blood sugar . . . you name it. It's a fact that the longer you live the greater your chances are of developing these problems. And the more people that develop them, the more profitable the pharmaceutical sector can become.

Also don't forget the role that research is playing in this never-ending supply of drugs. Drugs are being created today to cure things that as little as 10 years ago seemed impossible. And it's not just the new things; it's the improved things as well. Virtually every drug on the market today is a candidate to be replaced by a new drug that, due to the advances of medicine, will work a little bit faster or a little bit better or maybe with fewer side effects. The potential is limitless, especially when you realize that virtually everything can be improved.

It's an Annuity Business

Every company and every business around the globe strive to make their business more like an annuity. In other words once you have your clients, they keep coming back year after year (annual = annuity), and investors then look at your business as a annuity with very little risk because you have developed such a loyal client base.

If you were the maker of widgets, for example, let me explain how you would annuitize your business. Instead of trying to sell all of the widgets that you produce every single year, you would like to find someone who would enter into a longer-term contract to buy your widgets. Finally you hit the mother lode. You find three different companies that agree to enter into long-term contracts for the next 10 years; and combined, these three companies will be purchasing over 90 percent of the widgets you make every year. You have just succeeded in annuitizing your business because for the next 10 years you have already sold (annuitized) over 90 percent of what you are producing. Your only business risk is what to do with the other 10 percent each year. What would you rather invest in: a widget company that each and every year for the next 10 years has to figure out who is going to buy all of its widgets or a widget company that every year for the next 10 years has already sold over 90 percent of its widgets? That's a no-brainer; you would pick the widget maker that has locked in long-term commitments for over 90 percent of its widgets. In other words you would pick the company that has annuitized its business. If you got this question wrong, I want you to stop reading, put this book away, and go put all of your money under your mattress because you shouldn't be allowed to invest.

Alright now, how about this? Instead of trying to find which businesses, if any, around the globe have been able to annuitize their business, how about finding an entire sector of the market? Well, look no further because the pharmaceutical sector is the closest thing that you are going to find to an annuity business.

You see, unlike companies that manufacture widgets, pharmaceutical companies manufacture drugs. And drugs, unlike widgets, are absolutely necessary for an individual's health for various health reasons. The pharmaceutical sector doesn't require that the economy expand rather than contract to sell its products like the widget maker does, and what's going on in global economies and global markets is completely irrelevant. And while many expenditures in your life are optional, such as clothes, cars, cosmetics, and even widgets, you will be buying your prescription drugs to keep you healthy—they are not an option.

But wait, it gets even better. Once you purchase your prescription drug, chances are you are locked into a repeat purchasing cycle. Once you are given your prescription for high blood pressure, you most likely will be taking that medication for the rest of your life. You have become an annuity for the pharmaceutical sector. And even if you are not taking something for some life-threatening reason, chances are you will still be a repeat customer. Many of the prescriptions that are filled today lock you into becoming a guaranteed repeat customer. Just think back to the last time that you picked up a new prescription drug. Chances are that on the label it said "good for two or three refills." Thus when you are finished using the drugs, you call the pharmacy or take the empty bottle in for a refill. Oh and by the way, you have to pay for that refill. Once again the pharmaceutical sector is annuitizing its businesses by locking in guaranteed repeat business. Can you imagine how successful Apple Computer would be if, for example, every computer sold had a label on it "Good for three refills"? And when you are finished with this computer, simply bring it to the dealer and it will sell you another one.

The pharmaceutical sector is as close as it gets to an entire sector being annuitized. Now I will admit that, unlike my widget example, individuals are not bound by some legal contract to continue to buy the product. They do have a much more important contract, and that is a health contract. If you want to remain healthy, take the drugs. If you want your health to slip, don't take the drugs—it's that simple. You don't need a lawyer to get you out of a medical contract; all you have to do is quit buying the prescription drugs. If I had my choice between the two contracts, I'd take the medical one every single time. I'm an optimist, however, and I believe that most people want to live longer, happier, healthier lives. And if I'm right, which I believe I am, that means they will never break their medical contract, which in turn means that the whole pharmaceutical sector is turning into an annuity business.

Faster, Me Matie, Faster

No matter where we find ourselves today, whether it's on a plane or on a boat or in a car, everyone wants everything faster. And no matter how fast you get your Starbucks coffee or your McDonald's Big Mac, you still feel it should have been faster. Watch how this need for speed is going to benefit the pharmaceutical sector.

The entire pharmaceutical sector has a huge commitment to research and development. After all, that is their lifeline to new products and in turn to new profits. Watch how the process currently works in the United States. A pharmaceutical company will receive a patent for a certain drug. That patent protection is good for 20 years. What it effectively means is that none of your competitors can make your drug. Now from the time you receive your patent, it takes you approximately 10 years to develop, to test, to receive approval from the Food and Drug Administration (FDA), and ultimately to bring your new drug to the marketplace. Thus, by the time you bring your new drug to the market, you really have only 10 years of patent protection left to make your profits and to recover all of your research-and-development costs.

A streamlined review-and-approval process from the FDA is in essence expanding the patent for the pharmaceutical sector. Back in the 1980s it took an average of almost 36 months (3 years) for a new drug application to be approved. In the 1990s that time had worked its way down toward 24 months (2 years), and today it stands at 12 months. Going forward, I expect this process to be streamlined even more. Why? Two reasons: First, the explosion in new technology and medical measurement and testing devices has made the FDA more productive than it has ever been. Technology is letting the FDA do things both faster and with a higher degree of certainty because the amount of information it can analyze is greater than ever before.

Second, the FDA allows terminally ill patients to use experimental drugs in the hope that it can help them. Thus using real, live, terminally ill patients instead of laboratory rats provides the highest quality of testing and research possible. Thus I believe that these two forces, technology and the use of experimental drugs, will combine to improve the time of the FDA's process to drug approval to less than six months in the decade ahead.

Think of what this can mean for potential profits for pharmaceutical companies. It used to take 10 years to develop, test, receive FDA approval, and finally bring a drug to the market. And 3 of those 10 years were tied up in the approval process of the FDA. Again, what all this effectively meant is 10 years of patent protection, not 20.

Watch what happens to a company's patent protection now that the FDA process is streamlined. It will only require 7.5 years, not 10 years, to develop, test, receive approval, and begin selling a product. Now a company has 2.5 more years of patent protection. Instead of having only 10 years left, it has 12.5. This extra 2.5 years is like riding the gravy train. All the cost associated with a drug has already been absorbed, and now it is simply a cash cow making profits. And the government has just given the patent holder an extra 2.5 years! I love this country!

The Urge to Merge

And finally, don't forget how the merger mania boom that I discussed in Chapter 5 will uniquely impact the pharmaceutical sector. There are three major influences to fuel pharmaceutical sector mergers. The first, which is not unique to the pharmaceutical sector, is the desire to merge with competitors to simply increase market share. This merger in investment banking industry terms is called a "horizontal" merger. Think of it as two virtually equal companies, on the same horizon if you will, joined together. The extreme desire for more and more market share will create more and more horizontal mergers.

The second influence is intellectual property. Remember how I pointed out the heavy commitment that is needed for research and development and the fact that research and development is like the cash register of the future? Well, any firm with a strong stable of new products is a likely candidate for a merger. Think about it: If a company can't compete with you, it will instead buy your intellectual property when it buys you. After all, that is the American way—if you can't beat 'em, buy 'em.

The third influence will be pharmaceutical companies trying to leverage their business by merging with pharmacy benefit managers. That's right, the exact same pharmacy benefit managers that choose which drugs will be reimbursed and at what level and under which health care benefit plans. Now again in investment banking terms, this is called a "vertical" merger. Unlike the horizontal mergers where you are buying a company equal to you, in this case you are buying a company above you, or "vertical" to you, if you will—a company that can have a great influence over the profitability of your company. I look for the lines to really blur between pharmacy benefit managers and pharmaceutical companies in the future, which should mean a more predictable stream of revenue and profits. After all I can't imagine any pharmacy benefit manager that a pharmaceutical company owns that would be dumb enough not to recommend the drugs of the pharmaceutical company that owns them. Can you?

TECHNOLOGY SECTOR

Investment Strategy #2: Pretty Soon the Only Road Will Be the Information Superhighway

It continues to amaze me that there are investors still not willing to jump on the information superhighway by investing in technology. These are the same investors who smile when they finally see the light at the end of the tunnel until they realize it's the train coming the other way!

I quite frankly think that three simple facts say it all. First, computers are still the single largest category driving economic growth around the world. Second, the semiconductor market will double twice in the decade ahead. And third, there are more people getting online than ever before, and we are still just scratching the surface of the abundance of opportunities that will be created by the Internet. If you step back and consider where technology has come from, sometimes that makes it easier to realize where it is going to take us. Sometimes we forget that technology is, after all, still an evolving industry. Think of where we are today with the Internet that has created the cyberspace generation. The Internet would have never been possible if it weren't for the personal computer. After all, if we didn't have personal computers everywhere you looked, how would you surf the Net? And in turn, the personal computer could have never happened if it weren't for the development of the minicomputer. And there would have never been the need or the drive to create a minicomputer if we didn't have that big old mainframe computer that started this whole ball rolling in the first place.

It's this exact evolution that feeds the volatility in the technology sector that makes investors nervous. Think about what happens: With each shift or evolution there are major, major disruptions within the technology sector as it tries to recreate itself. Spending on technology is usually erratic during this time as business is trying to decide what to buy. When spending is choppy, profits become unpredictable, and the technology market is extremely volatile. And with every major shift or evolution first we will experience the downside. We will always take a step backward in technology before we take the next giant step forward. And that is simply because the older technology that we are leaving will always be able to decline faster than the new one will be able to grow. But remember what happens with each and every one of these shifts. The new technology market is always several times bigger than the old technology market that we just left. Think about this: The minicomputer market was way bigger than the mainframe computer market. And in turn, the personal computer market was way bigger than the minicomputer market and so on and so on and so on.

As technology continued to expand with each evolution, it touched more and more people; and the more people it touched, the more productivity boomed. With each dramatic shift not only did technology simply get bigger and bigger, but technology was really creating a new foundation for productivity. And it was this productivity boom that was the main fuel for the profit and the stock market boom that we are witnessing.

Now all of this didn't happen easily or without any pain. You see, this technology and productivity boom meant that people would lose their jobs as companies became more productive by integrating technology. And it is these exact efficiencies today that are moving the economy forward. Technology in a sense has created the most efficient and productive businesses in the history of time, and these productive businesses are in turn driving the economy.

Think about what's happening to the U.S. economy for a minute. The U.S. economy, which is the single largest economy in the entire world, has witnessed the greatest economic expansion ever over the past decade. Historically, when an economy sets off on a record tear for an entire decade, it is typically jump-started by one of three sources. First, they acquire some new territory; in other words, they got bigger, which in turn made their economy bigger. Well, that's not the case with the United States—it didn't add any new state in the past decade. In fact the last state, Hawaii, was added way back in 1959. Second, if it isn't new landmass, it's usually some new natural resource from your old landmass that fuels your economic explosion. Well, that wasn't the case with the United States either; there was no new discovery of major natural resources, such as coal or oil or the like. Third, if it isn't new landmass or new natural resources, then it has to be population. Sorry, that's not it either; population growth has been relatively flat in the United States. If it's not population growth or land growth or some new natural resource, what has caused the record economic expansion in the United States? The answer is quite simple—technology. Technology will have a greater influence on the economy than natural resources, people, or the land they live on.

Young and Old Demographics Converge

Watch how demographics is going to play a key role in technology. Younger workers in the workforce today have in essence grown up with computers. As a result these workers are much more willing to embrace any new technology that comes along. In fact, this younger workforce is utilizing technology in their businesses and everyday lives, and they are thinking of more and more innovative uses for the Internet as well as for any other technology they can find. Thus, watch what is happening at the workplace. As the older generation is advancing through the workforce toward retirement, they are being replaced by a new generation that was born with a computer in their crib; they are extremely computer literate, and they will drive technological change to the next level at the workplace.

Meanwhile, don't write off these older workers (after all, I'm one of them). Even though a majority of older workers are still somewhat skeptical and maybe even a little afraid of technology at work, there is still hope. Also regarding older workers, don't forget it's not just technology. Older workers in general simply do not like change, and people that do not like change do not like experimenting with new things. And the new thing just so happens to be technology. Anyway here's why there is still hope. Currently in the United States more than one-third of senior citizens are experimenting with the Internet. The reason has nothing to do with technology. It is quite simply that if you want to stay in touch with your family, you better get on the Internet. Instead of writing a letter asking someone how he or she is doing and then waiting a week to get a reply, you can go online, send an e-mail, and find out today. Also these senior citizens are quickly finding out that if they have any hope of communicating with their grandchildren, they better get online because that's where the grandchildren are.

Technology has lessened the impact of your children leaving home for college. I can speak from experience here. All you have to do is go online and send an instant message, and it's like your daughter is up in her room instead of away at college hundreds of miles away. Now the more savvy these older workers become on the Internet at home, the more likely they will be ready to embrace new and improved technology at work as well.

When these older workers converge with the younger generation on technology in the workplace, you better hold on because the sky's the limit.

Bandwidth Will Help

One of the problems with technology, especially with the Internet, is it is still way too slow. Even though it has improved our lives tremendously, the Internet remains a major source of frustration for Internet users in their own homes because it's too slow. The reason in technical terms is bandwidth. Bandwidth determines how much and how fast information can get to you. Think of it like a hose. If your house was burning down, would you want to try to put it out with your half-inch garden hose that can only let so much water through at a time, no matter how far you turned the faucet on? Or would you rather have a five-inch fire hose that shoots the water out so fast it will knock you down? Well, bandwidth for Internet users at home today is like the garden hose. What they want is a fire hose.

The reason for this is because bandwidth technology has simply not been developed as quickly as some of the other technological advancements, and one of the reasons is that almost all businesses and major organizations maintain their own computer network. When you have your own computer network, you have greater bandwidth, which allows the Internet to work faster. Did you ever wonder why when you are surfing the Internet at work when you are supposed to be working, you can fly all around the Internet? Then when you try it at home, it is so slow and takes so long to move from one website to another. It's not because your workplace has better computers; rather it's because the computer network at work has broader bandwidth.

Most people, myself included, access the Internet at home the old-fashioned way. We are using the telephone line to access our Internet service provider. Thus if you think about it, we are really using this old telephone network system that was in place for years before the Internet was even thought of. All of that is about to change. New and improved technologies are continuing to evolve within the telecommunications industry. In addition, Internet access through cable or through digital subscriber lines (DSL) and even satellite is also becoming available, and all of these advancements have one thing in common—they all broaden the bandwidth, which removes the number-one source of irritation to Internet users at home. And when you remove this source of irritation, technology demand will hit another new high.

It's the bandwidth problem that causes that little hourglass to pop up on your computer, while you have to sit for seconds that seem like hours anxiously waiting for it to get you to the next website. Once you remove this irritating time lag, popularity will soar. How popular do you think the remote control television would be today if it had the same bandwidth problem? Picture this: You are sitting back in your easy chair watching some sitcom and you decide to change channels to check out what's happening in the market on CNBC (hopefully you are tuning to CNBC see if I'm the guest cohost on *Squawk Box*). Instead of changing channels when you press the button, the screen goes blank and a little hourglass pops up as you wait for the electrical signal to connect. When it finally does connect you to CNBC, you have just missed the insightful comment I made to Mark Haines. So you angrily hit the remote control button again to go back to your sitcom. Instead of taking you instantly back, the screen goes blank again, and the hourglass pops up again until it's good and ready to change channels for you. By now you are so frustrated that I'm willing to bet you are ready to throw the remote control through the television screen. That's the exact same level of frustration that most Internet users at home are faced with.

What is going to happen in the future? When the bandwidth improves to the point that you can surf the Internet as quickly as my younger daughter, Stephanie, can surf the cable channels on our remote, watch out. Stephanie can access 80 different channels in under a minute—it will make your head spin. I'm still convinced she goes so fast she has no idea what's on any channel; she just does it because she likes to see me shake my head in disbelief. Bandwidth will do exactly that for the Internet. Oh, and don't forget how much more productive this will make us at home. The quicker we surf the Net, the more time we have to do other things. It also has productivity ramifications in the workplace as well. The number-one reason why employees do their personal shopping on the Internet at work is not because they are bad or lazy or dishonest employees, but because it's faster at work. When you can do it as fast at home as you can at work, employees will be freed up from doing their Internet shopping chores at work and instead actually spend more time doing what they get paid for.

Don't Forget Biotech

When I discuss technology as being one of the best sectors to invest in, I am talking about biotechnology as well. Many investors think of biotechnology as a sector unto itself. That is wrong. Biotechnology is simply one of the industry components that make up the overall technology sector. The biotechnology industry is actually a marriage between biology and technology.

The latest and greatest fruit to be born from this is called *genome*. Genome is a map of DNA (deoxyribonucleic acid), which is the very structure of an organism. This is commonly referred to as the mapping of the DNA. Genes are actually DNA particles found on chromosomes. Genes contain the blueprint for building all of the proteins that make up an organism.

The best way to understand how DNA is organized is to think of it as individual bricks to build a house. How those bricks are put together and how many are used will determine exactly what the house will look like. DNA, however, isn't bricks; it's actually sugar—four different sugars that interact with each other in specific ways. These four sugars are called nucleotide bases and are classified as (A) adenine, (C) cytosine, (G) guanine, and (T) thymine. These four letters tell us everything with regard to the mystery of life. When they are linked together, they become a piece of DNA. There are over 3 billion bits of information on one single strand of DNA.

Twenty years ago it was estimated that humans had 100,000 genes. That total was revised down to 80,000, then down again to 50,000. Now that we have a map of DNA, we know that there are only 30,000 genes.

Because of this lower number of genes, some investors are shying away from biotechnology. The reason is because the fewer the genes, the more complex their reaction will be with one another. This will make developing a drug or a cure to offset this complex interaction much more difficult.

Think of it like the electronic circuit breaker in your house. If you have 20 circuit breakers and the power goes out, you can locate and solve the problem pretty quickly. If you had 50 circuit breakers, it would be even easier to locate the problem. And if you had a separate circuit breaker for every outlet, let's say 200, you would locate the specific problem immediately. On the other hand if you only had one circuit breaker, it would be much more difficult to locate the problem. It's the same with genes; the more genes, the easier it is to find, isolate, and solve problems; the fewer the genes, the harder the problem solving is.

I think that this concern is misplaced. The lower number of genes will not stop biotechnology from being a great place to invest because biotechnology is the marriage of biology with technology. It's the technology side of the marriage that will save us. Think of it this way: We have been trying to unlock the mystery of life forever; and now in the year 2001 we finally unlock the key by mapping DNA. The fact that we finally did it today doesn't mean that we are smarter today. After all, I'll take Albert Einstein, Charles Darwin, Enrico Fermi, Galileo Galilei, Isaac Newton, and Jonas Salk over all the scientists in the world today combined. So if we aren't smarter, how did we do it? you are asking. With the advances in computing power. You see, we have these big honking computers that can process all of the information you ever dreamed of at the speed of light. No human could ever process the 3 billion bits of information on a single strand of DNA. Our computers today will process 3 billion bits of information as easy as taking a walk in the park.

Because of this computing power explosion, we will be able to slice and dice every one of millions of options that the 30,000 genes have to offer. And our computing power will help us locate the problem, just like the circuit breakers in your house help you locate the problem.

Think of what the future holds. Because of human genome advancements we will someday be able to develop a drug or a treatment that will replace the one problem gene that is responsible for your medical disease with a new healthy gene. The potential is limitless. There is no disease today that cannot be cured with the proper human genome advancements.

There was another startling development besides just the lower number of genes. The genetic difference between humans and other creatures was much smaller than anyone had theorized. In fact now that the sequencings of the genome of both humans and the laboratory mouse are complete, scientists were shocked to discover that of the 30,000 genes, humans only have 300 genes that mice do not have. That means our genetic structure is 99 percent the same as that of mice. Who knows, when John Steinbeck wrote his classic novel *Of Mice and Men* back in 1937, maybe he was trying to tell us something. Mice and men, biology and technology, convergence is a powerful force.

Technology and Telecommunications Converge

I believe that as we embark on the next decade, the current division between the technology sector and the telecommunications sector will continue to blur; and as these two sectors converge, it will become harder and harder to tell one from the other. Nowhere is this dichotomy more prevalent today than with the Internet. If your access to the Internet is "wired"—in other words, you have to plug it in—it's considered technology. On the other hand, if your access to the Internet is "wireless," then all of a sudden the Internet is no longer technology; it is now telecommunications.

The future of the Internet and maybe even the future of technology in my opinion will be wireless. And the reason is convenience. Remember that once we get someone hooked on something like the Internet, they want it all the time. And the only way to have it all the time, no matter where you are, is for it to be wireless. To understand this issue of technology versus telecommunications and to get a sense of the potential of "wireless," one has to look no further than Asia.

China is the largest, most dominant country in all of Asia, and it has the most people as well. In China mobile phone subscriptions are beating out Internet subscriptions by a whopping six-to-one ratio. But wait, it's not just China. This trend is happening all throughout Asia. In Korea mobile phone subscriptions are beating out Internet subscriptions by a five-to-one ratio. In Taiwan it's a four-to-one ratio. And even in Hong Kong mobile phone subscriptions are still outdistancing Internet subscribers three to one. Now think about this: With all of the new technology and technological advancements, what will happen when all of these mobile phone users become Internet users because of wireless technology that will enable them to quickly, cost-efficiently, and reliably access the Internet through their mobile phones? Is it a technology revolution or a telecommunications revolution?

Let's refocus on China for a minute. China currently has about 8 million Internet users. Let's take a closer look at the demographics of these 8 million Chinese. Over half of them are actually college students. And a majority of these college students don't even own a computer. The way they access the Internet is by using a personal computer at school. And don't forget what it was like when you were a college student; you don't have any money. The average college student in China earns under $200 a month.

Meanwhile look what's happening on the Chinese wireless mobile phone front. China has over 50 million mobile phone subscriptions. Mobile phones in China are used by China's wealthiest consumers. So now consider the dichotomy between those who use the Internet and those who have mobile phone subscriptions. The Internet users are college students with no money. The mobile phone users are China's most influential and wealthiest consumers.

For a real peek at the future, consider this: Because of their heritage, tradition, culture, and pride, Chinese consumers do not like to buy things on credit. The typical Chinese consumer has little, if any, use for a credit card. The major reason that shopping on the Internet in China has been a real bust is that in order to shop online you need a credit card. What do you think will happen to Chinese shopping online when the following development occurs? Chinese consumers who access the Internet through their wireless mobile phones can purchase anything they want online; and instead of using or needing credit cards, the purchase is simply billed to their mobile phone bill. Was it technology or was it telecommunications that finally got the Chinese consumer to shop online?

TELECOMMUNICATIONS SECTOR

Investment Strategy #3: We're All Connected

Now that I have convinced you that the lines will blur between technology and telecommunications and that it will be difficult in the future to tell one from another, there simply could not be a better lead-in for my next investment strategy—the telecommunications sector.

Possibly the most interesting aspect of telecommunications is the dramatic changes that the sector has been through and the changes that will continue to force this sector to keep evolving. Talk about a growth industry! In the early 1900s, each American made an average of 38 telephone calls a year. Currently, Americans each make 2,325 calls a year . . . that's a 60-fold increase. Buying a telephone company that was more like a utility was once thought of as an old boring investment. Suddenly that is changing. Now you buy a telephone company that is more like technology. The basis for this sudden evolution is quite simple—the rules have changed; and when the rules change, businesses respond accordingly.

In the United States the rapid changes began after the adoption of the landmark legislation called the Telecommunications Reform Act. This act, which was adopted in 1996, absolutely turned the industry upside down and in essence threw out all the rules. Local phone companies were then allowed to compete with long distance phone companies by providing long distance as well as local phone service. Meanwhile long distance phone companies were now freed up and allowed to compete in the local phone market. In one fell swoop the walls that had been erected to separate local phone carriers from long distance phone carriers came tumbling down. Competition exploded as everyone poked into everyone else's business. And now companies have to look over both shoulders to see who is going to compete with them.

These major regulatory changes were not confined to the United States. The sweeping changes that were affecting the telecommunications sector were also evident in Europe. In Europe the fuel for change was the World Trade Organization. The World Trade Organization forced European governments that have state-owned telephone companies to sell off their ownership and privatize them. The landscape in Europe changed from a nationalized telecommunications sector to a privatized one. Suddenly all of the telecommunications companies have either been completely or partially privatized, or as I like to think of it, they have been either completely or partially freed. It's simply amazing what happens to a business when a government no longer controls it; why it actually thinks like a business. It wants to become more productive and more efficient. In addition it looks for other business opportunities to expand its services beyond its traditional national border. All of the telecommunications companies all throughout Europe that never, ever, ever had to worry about any competition are all of a sudden being bombarded with competition all throughout Europe. And it's not stopping there. Telecommunications companies in Europe are looking at expanding into the United States. Meanwhile telecommunications companies in the United States are looking to expand into Europe. And this same synergy is happening around the globe, from Asia to South America. Once the rules changed, the telecommunications sector became a true global industry.

The Lines Are Disappearing

The national boundary lines are not the only lines that are disappearing within the telecommunications sector. One of the most sweeping changes going forward will be the continued merging of functions. The lines between key functions are disappearing faster than national boundaries.

The functions that I'm talking about that used to be separate are these. You would get your phone calls over the phone line; you would get your cable television over the cable line; and so on, and so on. These lines will soon disappear. It doesn't matter if you are sending voice, data, pictures, or video; you will be able to do it all over the same network. As this occurs we will also witness improvements in both the capacity and the speed within the telecommunications sector.

When I was growing up, the telecommunications sector was pretty simple; it was phone calls. Eventually it evolved to faxes as well so that you could actually send both voice (phone calls) and data (faxes) over the same line. This was considered quite a network. The telecommunications network over the next decade will be a network of live videoconferencing, interactive games and activities, and movies of your choice to download. Of course it will also carry data; however, instead of simply faxes, it will be complex mountains of information. Oh, I almost forgot, it will still carry your voice for the old-fashioned phone call.

Just as the lines are disappearing between functions, they are also disappearing between competing services. Local phone companies are becoming long distance phone companies. Local phone companies are becoming cable companies. Local phone companies are becoming Internet service providers. Local phone companies are becoming satellite-paging companies. In short, everyone is becoming everyone else. And because of the competition, once this process begins, I do not believe it will reverse itself. The reason is that if your competitors can offer local, long distance, and cable at one stop and you can't, you will quickly find out that you are at a competitive disadvantage. When the move begins to "one-stop shopping," it means provide one-stop shopping or be prepared for consumers not to shop with you at all.

Also don't forget the role that demographics is playing in this convergence. Consider what's happening in the United States. The baby boomer demographic trends have created a demographic force that during the next decade will move from their fifties to their sixties. As this occurs the boomers want life to be more simple. This has always been one of the guiding principles of my wife, Cheryl; maybe she has been preparing me for this all my life and I never knew it. Her words of wisdom are, "Less is more." And to the boomers "Less is more." Less bills to pay is more time to play.

Do you really think these baby boomers are going to stand for getting a different bill every day? One day, they get a bill for local phone service. Then the next day they receive a cable television bill from the cable company. Then a few days later they receive a long distance phone bill from their long distance phone service company. Then it's a bill for their pager from the satellite paging company and a bill for their Internet access by some new start-up Internet service provider. I don't think so.

In the decade ahead not only are the lines between functions disappearing, but services and functions are being bundled as well. The telecommunications sector clearly understands my wife's guiding principle . . . less is more!

A Whole New Ballgame in China

Possibly the single most fundamental reason why telecommunications will be a good investment in the next decade is what is about to happen in China. The recent World Trade Organization agreement between the United States and China will bring sweeping changes to many industries, none as dramatic as what will happen to telecommunications.

This was truly a landmark event for the telecommunications sector. Before this agreement China very severely restricted the sale of telecommunications service, and no company outside of China could invest in telecommunications within China under any circumstance. This landmark agreement for the very first time opens up the telecommunications sector to the full array of services and to the direct investment in telecommunications businesses in China. Consider how these landmark changes will alter the face of telecommunications in China forever.

First, look at the scope of services provided. The golden goose, if you will, regarding China telecommunications services is the corridor between Beijing, Shanghai, and Guangzhou, which represents over 75 percent of all domestic traffic for telecommunications service. China will open that corridor immediately. Then over time the rest of the geographic restriction will be lifted for the remaining somewhat rural parts of China. In three years the paging services restriction will be lifted. In five years the mobile phone service ban will be lifted, and in six years the local phone service ban will be removed as well. Anyone will be able to provide any telecommunications service anywhere in China.

Second, remember that before this agreement foreign investors were forbidden from investing in telecommunications services. Now China will allow up to 49 percent foreign investments in every type of telecommunication services. The floodgates will open, and capital will flow into China like never before.

Third, China will become a member of the Basic Telecommunications Agreement. That means that China will implement the principles of the Basic Telecommunications Agreement, which will encourage competition, especially in regard to pricing. Also China will not be able to regulate technology. Under this agreement China has no voice whatsoever regarding technology, which means that foreign telecommunications suppliers can use any technology they choose to provide telecommunications services.

In many ways this may be one of the most far-reaching agreements from an investment perspective in the past one hundred years.

The Future Is Wireless, Not Plastic

One of the greatest films of all time was released in 1967. The film was *The Graduate*, starring Dustin Hoffman. One of the most memorable lines in the history of film comes from this movie when the graduate, Ben (played by Dustin Hoffman), receives words of advice from a family neighbor, Mr. McGuire (played by Walter Brooke). Mr. McGuire surprises Ben with a piece of unsolicited and mysterious advice. "Plastics," Mr. McGuire says. Ben is at a loss. "There's a future in plastics," Mr. McGuire repeats, urging Ben to "think about it."

As I recalled that famous line, I was thinking that if they were to release a modern-day version of *The Graduate*, I am willing to bet that Mr. McGuire's advice would not be plastics . . . it would be "wireless."

Of all of the networks, the wireless communications network has the greatest potential for growth. Don't forget what networks do. They create unlimited new opportunities. By connecting things together, networks increase the number of potential contacts; and the more contacts there are, the more services and products there can be as well.

There are two guiding principles regarding the value of networks. The first is Moore's Law. Moore's Law states that computer power doubles every 18 months with no increase in price. The second law is Metcalfe's Law. Metcalfe's Law states that the more people that are hooked up to a network, the greater its value.

Watch how Moore's and Metcalfe's laws are now feeding off each other in wireless communication. The declining cost of technology has dramatically reduced the price of mobile phones, which in turn increased their affordability, which meant that more consumers bought them. And the more people that are on this mobile phone network, the faster the technology spreads.

Consider this example. You have a wireless telephone network. Your network has only 10 customers. Each of these 10 customers talks to each other one time a day. So the total calls in your network each day is 100 calls (10 customers each making 10 calls . . . $10 \times 10 = 100$). Now watch what happens when your wireless network acquires just one more customer. By adding one customer, your customer base increases by 10 percent (1 customer is 10 percent of 10 customers). Now look what happens to the number of calls. You have 11 customers calling each other the same one time a day. Now you have 121 calls per day in your wireless network (11 customers each making 11 calls . . . $11 \times 11 = 121$). So the number of calls in your network has just increased 21 percent (21 more calls is 21 percent of 100 calls). Now remember, the more calls that are made the more money you make. Is this wireless network a great concept or what? You increase your customer base by 10 percent, and your calls increase by over 20 percent. I think even I could make money in this business.

In the United States, for example, back 15 years ago there were fewer than 100,000 mobile phone users. Today in the United States there are close to 100 million mobile phone users. That's a 100-fold increase in 15 years. And on a global basis the wireless mobile telephone network simply continues to grow at an even more rapid pace. The wireless mobile telephone network will shortly surpass the number of televisions in the world, which stands at about 800 million. It will then surpass the number of fixed telephones, which currently stands at 900 million. Wireless mobile telephones will become the world's largest network. And what's extremely interesting is that usage cost is not slowing down this network. The average mobile phone user pays approximately 40 cents per minute. The average fixed line user pays about 10 cents per minute. Even with the higher cost of making calls with the wireless mobile phone, mobile telephone subscriptions are doubling every two years; and in most industrialized nations fixed-phone penetration is actually trending down for the first time.

Consumers are using their mobile phones at the office and at home, even when a substantially cheaper fixed line is close at hand. The next time you go to an airport, watch the number of people on their cellular phones when there is a cheaper pay phone on the wall behind them. Another interesting thing about mobile phones is that most customers will have more than one mobile subscription. Each family member has their own mobile phone. That's the way it is in the Froehlich household. I have a mobile phone; my wife, Cheryl, has a mobile phone; and both of my daughters, Marianne and Stephanie, have their own mobile phones. Why if they could figure out a usage for pets, I'm sure our dog Fred, a miniature Schnauzer, would have a mobile phone as well. Contrast this to the fixed phone line, where there is typically only one per family.

For a glimpse of the future, perhaps you should look at Finland.

After all, Finland is the world's most advanced and most sophisticated telecommunications market. In Finland a mobile phone is not a luxury, it's a necessity. And to the youth of Finland, it is their personal connection with one another, no matter where they are and no matter what time it is. To not have a mobile phone in Finland as a youth means that you are out of the loop and cannot be communicated with whenever and wherever the urge strikes. The impact of this is unprecedented. In Finland 20 percent of the households have a mobile phone, but they do not have a fixed phone. Nokia, which is Finland's wireless telecommunication powerhouse now, accounts for over 20 percent of all of Finland's exports. To give you some frame of reference, that is more than the entire paper and pulp industries combined, which historically have led Finland's exports. Do you want a look at the future? We're already seeing it in Finland. The future is wireless . . . as Mr. McGuire would say, "Think about it."

FINANCIAL SERVICES SECTOR

Investment Strategy #4: It Doesn't Hurt to Save

And while you are at it, think about the demographics in the United States as well as the demographics of the rest of the industrialized world that all point to an aging population base. This aging population base bodes well for a savings boom.

Remember, as you get older you enter into your peak earning years. And many of your major costs then, namely your children and your mortgage, will account for a much smaller portion of your paycheck. Put in simple terms, these demographic shifts mean that people will have more money to save. There will be an explosion in savings rates not just in the United States, but in the rest of the industrialized world as well. And when people have more money to save and invest, this is quite obviously bullish for the financial services sector.

But it's not just the increase in savings rates that will fuel the financial services sector; it's lower interest rates as well. And this will come about as a result of the increased savings rate also. Increased savings will improve the balance sheets of most businesses and most individuals as well. As businesses improve, they need to borrow less and less money for current operations. Thus if less money needs to be borrowed, the demand is going down, which will send interest rates down along with it. Over the next decades demographics are going to lay a tremendous foundation for the financial services industry, first, by increasing savings rates around the world and, second, by lowering interest rates. Financial services companies tend to do extremely well when people give them money and interest rates are low. And don't forget the ripple effect that these low interest rates have. Lower interest rates after all encourage economic expansion. When it costs less to borrow money, you can do things that before you maybe couldn't afford to do. As the economy expands and grows because of lower interest rates, businesses are healthier financially and individuals are healthier financially as well. This is very bullish for the financial services industry because it will mean fewer and fewer credit problems, bad loan problems, and bankruptcy problems for both individuals and businesses.

The More Money You Have, the More You Make

Recall for a moment how the financial services industry has evolved. From a historic perspective, the obvious industries within the financial services sector were pretty segregated. Insurance companies, for example, concentrated on and made all of their money from insurance. Banks, on the other hand, concentrated on and made all of their money from banking. However, in the United States the repeal of the Glass-Steagall Act in essence deregulated the entire industry.

What this has the effect of doing is pushing some subindustries into other subindustries. For example, everyone now looks for a new and improved product line. Banks now offer mutual funds. Nonfinancial firms are becoming banks. The crossover and explosion in mergers and acquisitions has created financial services firms that now provide a wide range of various financial services to solve your various financial problems.

Think of what this shift and expansion of products has done to the way financial services firms will make money in the future. Because they will be doing a number of different things, they will make money in a number of different ways.

They will make money from fees that are levied as a percentage of a transaction. They will also levy fees that will be a monthly, quarterly, or annual charge. In addition they will earn fees based on the amount of assets that they are managing for either an individual or a business. The only common thread in all these is that you have to have the money to make the money.

Size will become even more important in the financial services industry in the next decade. The bigger you are, the more assets (money) you control. The more assets that you control the more potential fees that you can earn from what will soon become what seems like a limitless supply of services and products, all for a fee of course. It's always a good idea to invest in a company that has more and more ways to make money than ever before. Think of the bank that could only charge a fee for banking service. The upside was somewhat limited. Now that same bank has fees for mutual funds and for selling insurance products. And before you know it, they are actually making more money from nonbanking activities than from banking activities.

High Anxiety

For the foreseeable future there is another very important trend that will bode well for financial services. When you are in your twenties and thirties, you don't tend to worry too much about retirement. When you are in your fifties and sixties, you worry a lot about retirement. It's a central source of anxiety. Will you have enough money to retire comfortably? This added anxiety will bring even more money into the markets, which will further fuel financial services companies. One of the reasons for this anxiety overload is that as you get closer to your retirement, the reality sets in that you are the one ultimately responsible for your financial well-being, not your employer.

This shift began, remember, when companies starting shifting from defined benefit pension plans to defined contribution plans. From a business perspective, moving to a defined contribution plan had several benefits. First, there were dramatically fewer regulatory and administrative costs to be burdened with. Second, you had much greater flexibility in terms of how you wanted the plan structured. But third and most important, you have now shifted all of the financial risk of this pension plan to the individual employee. It is no longer a business risk—it is a personal risk. This is where the anxiety kicks in. If the plan falls short, you have no one to blame but yourself. So your anxiety over your pension plan will drive you to save some money somewhere else just in case your retirement costs more than your pension can afford.

As if this isn't enough anxiety, baby boomers also have the constant threat of the demise of Social Security. Confidence in the ability of Social Security to provide any portion of future retirement needs is dwindling fast. From year to year or month to month or day to day, first Social Security is going broke, then it's fixed, then it's going to be privatized, then it isn't. The only thing for certain is the uncertainty regarding Social Security. And remember, the question isn't just will the money be there when you retire, but how much will be there. Hardly a day goes by that someone somewhere doesn't threaten that Social Security is going to reduce the cost of living adjustments or that Social Security is going to raise the eligibility age for retirement benefits. And then you get the idea from left field that they are going to include all of your Social Security benefits as taxable income. I do not expect these topics to be dismissed any time soon. The longer they stay around, the greater are the prospects for major cuts and massive reductions in the levels and programs of Social Security benefits. All of this chatter causes even more anxiety. Anxiety causes people to think even more about saving and investing. All of this anxiety is bullish for the financial services sector.

And if that doesn't cause enough anxiety, in the United States there also is the concern of what the aging population will do to the Medicare and Medicaid entitlement programs. These are extremely complex political, social, and financial issues that will not be solved anytime soon. Because of their complexity, they are extremely difficult to understand. Most people in the United States know that Medicaid and Medicare have something to do with providing medical coverage to old people. And now on top of every thing else to worry about, their medical coverage could be in trouble as well. I think we just uncovered another source of anxiety. Faced with the threat of now possibly having to pay for their own medical expenses, what do you think the baby boomers will do? You guessed it; this Medicaid/Medicare anxiety will again push baby boomers toward more and more supplemental savings programs that they can tap if needed in their retirement. Who knows, maybe anxiety is even more important than lower interest rates for the financial services sector.

Give Me Some Advice

Within the financial services sector and possibly the real winners, as a result of all of this investor anxiety, are the full-service brokerage firms. While all of financial services, regional banks, money center banks, insurance companies, investment banks, brokerage firms, and asset managers will benefit from the increased trend toward saving and investing, no one will benefit from this anxiety attack more than the full-service broker will. All of this investor anxiety about needing a plan and having a plan and sticking to a plan will all be extremely bullish for the brokerage community. It's amazing that when consumers become worried about something, all of a sudden it clicks with them that they need financial advice. They are facing possibly the most critical issue in their lifetime, their financial well-being for the rest of their lives. Do you really want to do that without the advice of a professional? I don't think so!

In addition to anxiety working in the brokers' favor, there are three other developments that are pushing consumers to seek financial advice. The first development is the *complexity* of the markets. It's not just about stocks and bonds any more. If you say stocks, I say domestic or international? And before you can answer that question, you are hit with large-cap, mid-cap, small-cap, or micro-cap? And while your mouth is still open, you are asked whether you want growth style, value style, or blended style? What sector do you want? What type of interest-rate exposure are you willing to take? What type of currency exposure are you looking for? And while you are at it, how about some puts, calls, options, swaps, covered calls, forwards, leaps, and spiders? We haven't even gotten to what you are interested in buying yet.

The markets have turned into an extremely sophisticated and complex global market that never sleeps. Every single minute of every single day, some market somewhere is open for business. Finally more and more investors will come to the realization that they are in over their heads and ask for financial advice.

The second development that is pushing investors to brokers is that they are worried about *keeping up their success*. You see, a decade ago when they were 15 years away from retirement their spouse humored them by letting them be in charge of their 401(k) retirement account so that they could feel like they were on Wall Street. Well guess what? A decade later that $50,000 account has grown to a couple hundred thousand dollars. All of a sudden it isn't a little hobby that doesn't really matter. Now we are talking about real serious money. Now, the spouses are not going to be so happy to let "Weekend Willy" call the shots on a couple hundred thousand dollar retirement portfolio based on some information from an online chat room. There is more to investing than simply making money. You also have to figure out a way to keep the money that you make. It's the full-service brokerage firms that are best equipped not only to help you make money, but also to protect your downside risks as well.

The third and final development is the fact that as you get to retirement, instead of having more time on your hands, you find that you actually have *less free time*. From visiting the grandchildren, to leisure activities, to social clubs, to volunteering, to part-time employment, to recreational activities, your time simply disappears. What is even more important is that time is extremely valuable and precious to you at age 60. At age 16, time is never a real concern because you have your whole life in front of you; there will always be time to do certain things. Suddenly at age 50 and age 60, you realize that there are now more years behind you than in front of you; and that makes your time very, very precious. When time is precious, you will guard how you use it. Would you rather see your grandchildren play tennis or try to figure out why the stock price of the stock you sold is wrong? Do you want to spend your later years giving back to the community by volunteering in a hospital, or do you want to volunteer to try to figure out the ramifications of the capital gains distribution you just received and were not expecting? Demographics is going to force people to place a higher value on time than they ever have before. And when you do that, something has to give. I am willing to bet because of this and other developments along with good old anxiety that investors will be running for financial advice in droves.

Transparent Pricing

There is one final trend that will be developing, and it has to do with transparent pricing. Transparent pricing simply means that you will be able to see the prices. Remember, if you will, that a financial services product is an intangible thing. In the most pure sense it's a promise under certain terms and conditions, whether it's insurance to pay for your car if you are in an accident or it's paying interest on your checking account. These are intangible things until you actually receive them. However, in order to provide these intangible things, the financial services industry requires a great deal of investment in tangible things like employees and buildings and vehicles and furniture and computers and so on and so on. All of this tangible overhead requires some hefty profit margins over which the overhead can be spread.

Watch the role that technology is playing in this. Technology in general and the Internet specifically are forcing all of the financial services sector to put their cards on the table. Ten years ago if you wanted to compare insurance rates, you probably had to go to three different brokers in three different parts of town to get estimates. Not any more. The Internet has exposed everyone's prices online in real time. There is no place to hide any more. Everyone's price is out in the open for everyone to see. Pricing has become transparent.

There is an extremely important side benefit to all of this. Consumers generally choose their financial services firm based on the combination of three factors: safety, price, and service. Watch what is happening to each of these factors. First, regarding safety, with the continued explosion of mergers and acquisitions the financial services companies are becoming bigger and bigger. Bigger financial services firms can spread out their cost to a larger base and thus become more profitable. Larger financial services companies can also withstand a temporary economic shock from any part of the world better than a small company can. Thus the safety factor has almost been commoditized. It's tough to distinguish yourself in terms of safety.

Second, there's the factor of pricing. Now with transparent pricing everyone will be moving to price products within a range of everyone else's price. Soon price will not be a factor because all prices will soon be in the same ballpark.

Third, that leaves us with service. The only thing left to distinguish you as a financial services firm in the future will be service. In fact it will all come down to service and convenience. The successful financial services firm will have every type of product their customers will ever need: checking account, savings account, mortgage, automobile insurance, life insurance, mutual funds, and a full array of business services as well. In addition they will need to combine the bricks (branch offices) with the clicks (online presence).

The financial services sector is about to embark on a tremendous run over the next decade. The only firms that will be around to finish the race are the firms that realize it's the "services" in the financial services sector that will determine the ultimate success or failure of every company that comprises the financial services sector.

ENERGY SECTOR

Investment Strategy #5: Plug It In and Turn It On!

Make no mistake about it; we clearly live in a high-tech "wired" economy. We sometimes forget that the most basic premise for the high-tech economy is not technology but rather the fuel that keeps technology running . . . namely energy. When you combine the explosive growth of energy-consuming technological devices with the industrialization of emerging economies and countries from even the most desolate spots around the globe, you will witness a decade of explosive growth, opportunity, and profits for the overall energy sector.

Because we have quickly integrated it into our everyday life, we sometimes forget about the energy consumption that happens all around us. Why, in my office alone, I have three separate television monitors for nonstop business news programming. In addition, I have a dual-screen Bloomberg terminal and a Reuters terminal, as well as my own dual-screen desktop personal computer. And that doesn't even account for my private printer and two telephones. Come to think of it, I probably use as much electricity in my office as some third world countries do.

You know I've often said that some of the best investment opportunities are right in front of us and we simply do not recognize them. I want you to pay attention to how you start your next day, and watch the opportunity that this holds for the energy sector.

Here's how I started my day today. I got up and brushed my teeth with my electric toothbrush. Remember when we used to use manpower to brush our teeth? Not anymore; that's one for energy. Then my wife, Cheryl, buzzed my hair using an industrial-strength electrical barber razor. When we were first married, Cheryl would cut my hair in the garage using scissors. No more scissors for me; that's two for energy. I then used my electric nose hair trimmer. Is this out of control or what? I'm not even going to tell you how those nose hairs got out before electric trimmers; that's three for energy. Standing next to me in the bathroom, Cheryl dried her hair with her electric hair dryer while the electric roller was charging. I remember when we used towels to dry our hair and spongy rollers to make curls. Not anymore . . . let's see that makes it four and five for energy. I made my way downstairs to my study, unplugged my laptop computer, which was recharging at the same time my cell phone was recharging. That's six and seven for energy. Meanwhile Cheryl turned on our gas fireplace. Remember when we used to use logs in the fire? Not anymore, now I'm a gasman; that's eight for energy. Next I pressed the electric garage door opener—no lifting of a garage door for me; I simply press a button and electricity does it for me. That's nine for energy, and I haven't even left the garage yet. Now remember, this is one house in Naperville, Illinois. When you think about my neighbors doing the exact same thing and all the people in Illinois and all the people in the United States and all the people in Europe and all the people around the world, it suddenly becomes so clear that energy will be a great investment. For without energy, we can't continue to expand into technology. And while technology may be the engine to drive the future growth of economies around the world, remember that all engines need fuel to work, and the fuel for this engine is energy.

The real future upside to the energy sector, however, will not be fueled merely by developed and industrialized countries like the United States, but rather by the continued advancements in the emerging markets and economies around the world. Think of this potential in terms of the two Ts—telephones and televisions, two things that most people (myself included) in the industrialized world simply take for granted.

The United States has a phone line for every person in the country. The same can be said for Hong Kong. In Japan, Singapore, New Zealand, and Australia, there is one telephone for every two people. Here's where it begins to get interesting, however. Take the case of China where there is only one phone for every 60 people. Can you even imagine what will happen to energy demand when China's telephone penetration approaches that of the United States? And it's not just China; the other major population hubs in Asia are in even worse shape. Pakistan has only one phone for every 83 people; India has one phone for every 95 people; and Indonesia has only one phone for every 151 people. As these countries evolve, think of the magnitude of the increased energy demand that will be associated with that advancement as well. Here's one final thought to ponder: It's actually hard to believe in this day and age that today in North Korea there is only one phone for every 796 people. Needless to say my two daughters, Marianne and Stephanie, who have their own phone line that they share in addition to their own cellular phones, wouldn't last a minute in North Korea.

Let's shift for a minute to the other T, televisions. Again the United States is the world's leader with 80 percent of the population having televisions. Japan is a close second with 70 percent of their population with a television set. Japan is followed by Australia with 60 percent, New Zealand with 50 percent, Hong Kong with 40 percent, and Singapore and South Korea with 30 percent of their population having televisions. As these countries continue to evolve, the penetration of televisions will evolve and grow as well. And remember you have to plug these televisions in so you can get a picture. If you are looking for a clearer investment picture of what could happen, consider this: In China and Thailand only 20 percent of the population have televisions. Meanwhile in Malaysia, Indonesia, and the Philippines only 10 percent of the population have televisions. In the population hubs of India and Pakistan less than 10 percent of the population have a television. As these emerging economies become industrialized, televisions will become a way of life, and the demand for energy will be the food that feeds that way of life. Once these people use their televisions to tune into CNBC's *Squawk Box* with Mark Haines, they will be hooked and will never be without a television again. And in case you were wondering just how far we have to go, in Afghanistan only 12 people per 1,000 have a television. That means that only a fraction over 1 percent of the entire population have a television. Who knows, maybe my subinvestment theme should be televisions.

It All Started with Oil and Gas

Both oil and natural gas are fossil fuels, formed hundreds of millions of years ago when small sea creatures and plants were buried. During these hundreds of millions of years between layers of rock and sand was this plant and sea creature matter. Finally the extreme heat and pressure from the earth's core turned this plant and animal matter into oil and natural gas. There has always been a great deal of overlap between the oil and the natural gas industries due in large part to the fact that the exploration of both of these forms of energy is hidden deep under the earth's surface. The overlap begins and ends with exploration.

The natural gas industry has been deregulated, while the oil industry has not. In the United States, for example, businesses can buy and sell natural gas on the open market. This open competitive market, however, has yet to reach the consumer, who really doesn't have a choice because most natural gas companies still have exclusive distribution agreements.

Here's an interesting perspective: More than 50 percent of the oil used in the United States is imported. Thus the reliance on the Persian Gulf oil producers remains extremely high. On the other hand only 15 percent of all the natural gas that is consumed is imported, and all of that comes from Canada. Global demand for both oil and natural gas will grow at unprecedented levels as the underdeveloped nations around the world compete with the United States and the rest of the industrialized world for oil and gas.

In an effort to prepare for the newfound demand, companies are looking for ways to become more efficient and more cost-effective. Both of those objectives are being achieved with major consolidation through which companies can both get more efficient and control their costs. Exxon has merged with Mobil to form the world's largest oil and gas company. In addition, British Petroleum has joined forces with Amoco and then also acquired Arco. And the beat goes on globally as well. Total acquired Petrofina, which then gobbled up Elf Aquitaine.

Also as more and more companies are searching for new supplies of energy they are focusing on both remote and politically unstable areas of the world that are still pretty much untapped. There are both more risk and higher costs associated with this strategy, which is also fuel for mergers among oil and gas companies.

During the next decade I expect oil and gas companies to spread their merger nets a little bit wider and to start acquiring electric utility companies as well. With deregulation in the electric utility industry in high gear in both the United States and Europe, especially the United Kingdom, oil and gas companies will seize this as an opportunity to broaden their revenue base. It's a pretty basic investment principle—the more diverse your revenue base is, the greater the likelihood of more stable revenue streams. Stable revenue streams equal stable earnings, which in turn lead to higher stock prices.

It's Electric!

World energy demand will more than double over the next decade. At some point during that decade, emerging and developing countries led by China will actually consume more energy than the developed industrialized countries. And electricity will be the single fastest-growing industry with the brightest prospects for growth in Asia and in Latin and South America. And there is plenty of room to grow. Today, in 2001, 80 percent of the world's available oil remains in the ground, as does 95 percent of the world's natural gas supply.

The electric utility industry was actually invented over 125 years ago by Thomas Edison, so it's a whole lot younger than the hundreds-of-millions-of-years-old oil and natural gas supplies. Edison's vision was to provide electricity from a central station and to distribute it to individual homes. And that is exactly what he did back in New York City on September 4, 1882, when Edison's Pearl Street Station went into use supplying electricity to light up 400 light bulbs for 85 customers. And thus the electric utility industry was born.

Distribution of that electricity both back then and today is only half of the equation. You see you have to produce it as well. A majority of all electricity that is produced is created by burning fossil fuels, the same fossil fuels we just discussed—oil and natural gas with the addition of coal. These fossil fuels actually are burned to turn water into steam that moves the blades of an engine that spins the generator that actually produces electricity. Electricity can also be produced in hydroelectric facilities. In these facilities, water turns the turbines that spin the engines that in turn produce electricity. The overwhelming majority of all electricity, however, is produced by burning fossil fuels.

And of the fossil fuels, coal is the clear leader. In fact coal accounts for 55 percent of all the fuel that is burned to create electricity. Natural gas is 10 percent of the fuel, hydroelectricity is 10 percent, and oil is 5 percent. The remaining 20 percent is fueled by nuclear energy. There has not been one single new nuclear power plant opened in the United States since the Three Mile Island nuclear accident in Pennsylvania in 1979.

Now one of the reasons that I think you are going to see a real merger-and-acquisition consolidation between natural gas and electric companies is because they are converging anyway. Think about it: Coal accounts for 55 percent of all fuel burned to produce electricity. Coal is a dirty fuel; burning coal emits polluted particles, which require an extensive and elaborate environmental system of scrubbers to clean these particles before they are transferred into the air. Natural gas, on the other hand, is a far cleaner fuel to burn. As electric utilities begin the transition from coal to natural gas, I look for them to not only use but actually buy natural gas companies. After all, the best way to control a source is to own it.

This convergence is leading to a global consolidation within the electric utility industry. Mergers and acquisitions have been accelerating since the middle of 1990 when both the United States and Europe got very serious about deregulation. This happened especially in the United States, where government regulators began breaking up electric utility monopolies because businesses and consumers alike were complaining about high electric bills. Finally in 1996 the Federal Energy Regulatory Commission in the Untied States ordered utilities to open up their electric lines to competitors for sale of wholesale electricity.

In 1999 Pacifi Corp of Portland, Oregon, was the first U.S. utility acquired by a foreign company when Scottish Power of Glasgow, Scotland, bought it. Other energy companies from Europe have been making acquisitions in the United States, and U.S. electric companies have been making acquisitions in Europe as well.

Among all of this merger mania and deregulation focus, something went almost unnoticed in the Untied States. In 1996 California became the first state to deregulate electric utilities at the retail consumer level.

The California Crisis Unwrapped

I am keenly aware that for any individual to consider energy as a viable investment opportunity, they must first be convinced that the electric utility disaster that occurred in California will not be repeated elsewhere around the United States or elsewhere around the globe for that matter. What went wrong with retail electric utility deregulation in California anyway?

First and foremost, as investors you need to remember that deregulation works. This debacle in California will not stop the deregulation of electric utilities across the United States. This problem is not about deregulation but rather about the misguided public policy approach to implement deregulation in California. The fact that the California electric utility industry is in chaos is not the result of deregulation. Everyone would agree that seat belts, for instance, are good things. But suppose that someone decides to put the seat belt on in such a way to support her sore neck? If the car gets into an accident and the passenger breaks her neck and dies from the injury inflicted by the seat belt, does that mean we should outlaw seat belts? Absolutely not! Likewise, the fact that the misguided California deregulation is in chaos does not mean that deregulation, when properly implemented, is bad as well.

If you think about the groups that influence public policy debates in California, it should come as no surprise that this got screwed up. About a third of public policy is driven by consumer advocates, a third by the environmentalists, and the final third by movie stars. It's a wonder, serving that diverse group of constituents, that anything ever gets done right.

Anyhow, in my opinion, California electric utility deregulation was doomed for failure from the very start in 1996. Three separate components of this deregulation combined to guarantee failure, California style, if you will. First, it all started with the trees; everything always starts with the trees. Instead of looking at these massive "white elephant" power plants, Californians wanted to look at trees (don't we all). So the discussion began that if the state would deregulate the electric utility industry, these utilities could buy electricity at the wholesale level from a facility in some other state. Are you getting the picture here? Let some other state cut down the trees and build the power generating plant, and then these California electric utilities would buy some of this electricity and then turn around and sell it to the retail electric consumers in California. Everyone was excited about deregulation and the free and open markets and the fact that they could save the trees as well. There was one small glitch, however; California doesn't trust the utilities. So the state in its infinite wisdom decided that its electric utilities were freed to go into the wholesale electric market to pay wholesale prices for electricity. However, the retail prices that they could turn around and charge the ultimate California consumer would be frozen—no rate hikes allowed. That's not deregulation, that's half deregulation. It's deregulated at the wholesale level, but it's certainly not deregulated at the retail level. This causes retail consumers to be out of touch with reality, which is exactly what is going on in California. Think of it this way: What if they deregulated gasoline stations the same way? In other words gasoline stations were freed to buy gasoline anywhere they wanted at the wholesale level; however, the price that they could charge you and me at the retail level was frozen. Think of how out of touch that makes consumers. Suppose the price of gasoline skyrockets to $5 a gallon. So now this local gas station buys gasoline at $5 a gallon at the wholesale level. However, they are frozen in the amount they can charge you and me—it still only costs us $1.75. So you pull up in your gas-guzzling sport utility vehicle, aware that the price of gasoline is $5 per gallon, but you only have to pay $1.75. Do you think that your driving habits will change? Absolutely not. Heck, you will jump into your gas-guzzling sport utility vehicle just to drive one block to buy your Starbucks coffee. Because California deregulated at the wholesale level and froze prices at the retail level, the retail California consumers are out of touch with reality and will not change their consumption patterns. For the laws of supply and demand to work, you have to use them both. Consider this strike one.

The second component that virtually guaranteed failure was long-term power contracts, or should I more appropriately say the lack of them. Remember again the distrust that California has for the utility industry. Because of this misfound trust, the state would not allow any electric utilities to enter into long-term contracts to purchase power. The reason was that they felt if the utilities were allowed to structure some long-term contract, it would end up being some sweetheart deal for the utilities and their investors, and somehow the poor California electric power consumer would get the short end of the stick. As a result that meant that California utilities were forced to buy all of their electricity on the "spot" market by paying the current market rate. Now back in 1996, maybe this ill-conceived logic didn't appear quite so bad. That was because back then in California if you had to go on the spot market to purchase a megawatt hour of electricity during peak demand, it went for a little under $10. At the height of the crisis four short years later, the cost of buying a megawatt hour of electricity during peak demand in California skyrocketed to an astounding $350. Now don't forget that to make matters even worse, those utilities were not allowed to pass one cent of that additional cost on to the ultimate electricity consumer in California. Do I hear strike two?

Third and finally, in a mind-boggling approach that you can only find in California, here's what they did next. After really sticking it to the utilities on the first two matters by not allowing them to pass on any cost increases at the wholesale level to the retail consumer and forbidding long-term power purchase agreements, the state finally decided to give the poor utilities something; and when they did, failure was guaranteed. Because the California electric utilities were being asked to walk away from their power generating plants and instead to purchase power on the open wholesale markets, the state decided to give the utilities something for these big power generating plants. The state agreed to richly compensate the utilities for what they defined as "stranded assets." But wait, this is just the start. California, in an attempt to make peace with the electric utility industry, valued those assets at a much greater value than fair market value. But hold on, it doesn't end there either. California didn't want to pay for all this, so they decided that any new entrant (competition) to the California utility market must pick up part of the cost of these stranded assets. Would you like to guess how many new electric utilities came to California to do business and increase competition after deregulation? You guessed it, a big fat zero! And the reason that there is no new competition in California is because once these new competitors are strapped with these old stranded asset costs, they simply can't compete on a price basis. Strike three, you're out!

Consider this as proof. Less than 1 percent of California residents have switched retail electric utility suppliers since deregulation. The reason that there are not any choices since deregulation is because of the price disadvantage new entrants are placed in.

Despite what's happening in California, deregulation of electric utilities can work and will work. In Texas and Pennsylvania, both very large states, deregulation has been extremely successful. And the father of all electric utility deregulation, Great Britain, is a wonderful example of how it can work. After deregulation was implemented in Great Britain, almost one-third of all Britains switched to a new retail electric utility supplier.

The deregulation problems in California are unique to California; they will not spread to other states, and they certainly will not spread to other countries like Europe, where electric utility deregulation is progressing nicely.

Global Differences

It will be extremely important in the decade ahead to watch how the world's industrialized powers, the United States and Europe, reconcile their different energy agendas.

In the United States that agenda is being driven by the dot.com and technology explosion, while environmental issues have fallen off the table. In Europe the agenda is completely reversed. It's the environmental concerns that are driving the energy agenda with the so-called new economy in the back seat and nowhere near being a driver.

In the United States over 10 percent of electricity consumption is

Internet driven. If you think about it, the Internet is configured around software that runs on hardware, neither of which runs without electricity. And it's not just some electricity; it's electricity all the time. This Internet-driven consumption is very, very demanding. As both of my daughters, Marianne and Stephanie, have informed me, it's "24/7." I had no idea what the heck they were talking about, like it was some zip code that was missing the last two digits, until they explained 24/7 to me. It means 24 hours a day, 7 days a week. In other words "24/7" means all the time. I wish they would just say that. The Internet is causing people to stay hooked up online 24/7, which means electricity will be used 24/7 as well. This influence of the Internet on electricity consumption will force the issue of electricity power supply in the United States.

Meanwhile in Europe the agenda is not being driven by the Internet but rather by the "trees." The concern and the focus in Europe regarding energy is the environment. Because of this overriding concern for the environment, the future of energy will be much different in Europe than it is in the United States. The future landscape will be dominated by some combination of solar power, windpower, and biomass, with the brightest future being windpower. You see, solar power is still a pretty inefficient source, which doesn't bode well for the high-efficiency need of an electric utility. Meanwhile biomass, where you plant fast-growing trees, cut them down, and burn them for power, also has hit a stumbling block. Quite frankly there is a shortage of land available for forestry farming in Europe. Which brings us right back to windpower. Governments in Europe have been providing substantial financial incentives for windpower, which has resulted in wind farms springing up in Germany and Spain as well as in selected parts of Scandinavia. I just hope the wind doesn't stop blowing just when you're trying to log on to the Internet.

Asia's Power Surge

To get some idea of how much electric capacity will need to be added around the world, one needs to look no further than Asia. Over the past 30 years the trends have been going straight up in terms of kilowatt-hours of electricity consumed by each person. In China consumption of kilowatt-hours of electricity per person has gone up over 400 percent. In Hong Kong it's up 300 percent. In Singapore it's up over 600 percent. In Thailand and South Korea it's up over 1,000 percent. That's only half the story, however. It's when you compare electricity consumption to that of the United States that you get a feel for the potential of the future.

Electricity consumption of a kilowatt-hour of electricity per person in the United States currently stands at approximately 12,000 kilowatt-hours per person. In Singapore it's 8,000. They are at only 66 percent of where the United States is today. Hong Kong currently stands at 5,000, which means that they are merely at 40 percent of the U.S. consumption pattern. And China is currently under 1,000 kilowatt-hours per person, which is only 8 percent of that in the United States. As these countries become more and more industrialized, they will consume more and more electricity, and their kilowatt-hour consumption patterns will look more and more like those of the United States. As this demand evolves, we simply may not be able to build the power generating plants fast enough. I hope you can turn it on after you plug it in!

DR. BOB'S NOTES . . . TOP 10 THINGS TO REMEMBER!
Chapter 6

10 The uniformity of cost and pricing places even more importance on individual sectors.

9 The more things the pharmaceutical industry can cure you of, the more things you could possibly catch in the future so they can cure you again and again.

8 Consumers are using their mobile phones at the office and at home, even when a substantially cheaper fixed line is close at hand.

7 With each cross-border merger, the significance of individual sectors becomes all that more important.

6 Anxiety causes people to think even more about saving and investing, thus anxiety is usually bullish for the financial services sector.

5 In telecommunications, lines are disappearing between both functions and competing services.

4 The combination of the explosive growth of energy-consuming technological devices with the industrialization of emerging economies and countries will fuel unprecedented growth in the energy sector.

3 The future of the Internet and maybe even the future of technology will be wireless.

2 Facing possibly the most critical issue of their lifetime, their financial well-being for the rest of their lives, investors turn to financial advisors (stock brokers) for professional advice.

1 Sectornomics means the *sector* that you invest in will have the greatest *economic* impact on your investments' performance.

Chapter 7

The Principles of Investing in Long-Term Trends While Living in a Short-Term World

Since time is the one immaterial object which we cannot influence, neither speed up nor slow down, add to nor diminish, it is an imponderably valuable gift.

Maya Angelou
Author, poet, film director, and civil rights activist (1993)

Now comes the hard part. You have a good understanding of the global trends and developments that will drive our markets. And you are even equipped with a couple of investment strategies that should benefit from those trends. The problem is that we live in a short-term world and these are long-term trends. The single most important ingredient for the success of these trends is time. And as Maya Angelou so aptly put it, "we cannot influence, neither speed up nor slow down" time.

The investment dilemma that you are about to face is one that I refer to as the blizzards and icebergs. It's the classic battle of how to invest in long-term trends if you live in a short-term world. You see, I am a firm believer that you can classify every investment event that drives the market into one of two categories. You guessed it—either blizzards or icebergs.

Blizzards are the investment events that take a relatively short time to impact the markets. The lag time between the event and the market impact is measured in weeks or days or hours and sometimes even minutes. That's what it's like to live in a short-term world. Now when these events do occur, both you and the markets are bombarded with what seems like a blizzard of information about the event. No matter where you turn, everyone is talking about it—the taxi driver, the waitress, every television channel, every newspaper article. Why, chances are your children could even be doing a current events school project on it.

Let me give you a couple of examples of blizzard-type investment events. It could be an economic release that shows that producer prices were higher than expected this month, so now inflation is back and that will be trouble for the market. Or it could be an interest-rate hike or an interest-rate cut. Or it could be an earnings release that, depending which company it is, could move the entire market either up or down. Oh, let me give you one last example, it's my favorite blizzard, an Alan Greenspan speech! Investment blizzards, just like real live weather blizzards, are very difficult if not impossible to predict. And when the blizzard finally hits, either the weather or the investment blizzard, it's already too late to do anything about it.

Now on the other hand, we have the iceberg investment events. These iceberg investment events take a relatively long time to have any impact on the markets. The lag between the time we recognize the investment event and the impact on the market is measured in years and even decades. Even though as investors we can all see the iceberg clearly coming, we will question the impact it will have on the markets. The reason is that the market, in essence, only sees the tip of the iceberg. Examples of these iceberg-type investments are the evolving demographic trends around the globe that I told you about in Chapter 1 and the globalization of economies and markets that I told you about in

Chapter 2. Other examples would be the technology revolution I discussed in Chapter 3, followed by government downsizing in Chapter 4 and the corporate restructuring, merger-and-acquisition boom I pointed out in Chapter 5. From an investment perspective the interesting thing about icebergs is that unlike blizzards they are relatively easy to predict. In fact you can actually see the investment iceberg coming for years before it hits you. The problem is that most investors are so focused on the short-term blizzard of the week that they fail to recognize the long-term iceberg investment trends that will impact our markets for decades to come.

Through the years I have developed a series of investment principles that can be used as a guide to help you invest for the long term, even though we live in this short-term world. These are my six principles of investing.

Principle #1: Fear and Greed

As a student of the markets for over a quarter of a century, I have uncovered the only two elements that drive every single investment decision that we make. Now that doesn't mean that we don't continue to try to kid ourselves with other reasons. We will talk about price/earnings ratio as the reason that we are buying or selling. Some of us will even say that our asset allocation models are out of sync, so we have to make some changes. Others will hop on the old bandwagon that you are buying or selling for diversification reasons. Well guess what? That's all a bunch of baloney. Investors buy and sell stocks or buy and sell bonds or buy and sell mutual funds based on one of two things: fear and greed. And that's how the short-term blizzards get you every single time. You can almost take this one to the bank: The markets always tend to err on the extremes. In other words the markets will never be as good as they look in the short run. And conversely the markets will never be as bad as they look in the short run. The reason is that the market always errs at the extreme. If things look too good to be true, they probably are. If things look too bad to believe, they probably aren't. You know why—fear and greed. Investors who have a short-term focus watch the market go up and up and up until they can't take it any more; greed kicks in and they jump into the market with both feet. That's when reality sinks in, and the investors find that things are never as good as they look and the market corrects itself.

These are the same investors who watch the market go down and down and down; and after convincing themselves that it will eventually go to zero, they are overcome by fear and they sell. You guessed it; as soon as they sell, the market turns and heads back up, recouping all of its losses. Remember, things are never as bad as they seem. Fear and greed work the other way as well. The market goes up and up, and fear makes you jump in because you are afraid you are missing this market high, even though the fundamentals don't look good. On the other hand when the market's going down and down, greed can kick in, making you decide to lock in your gain and sell out. The reason fear and greed are so important is that they both contribute to the market going up and down.

Long-term investors don't rely on fear and greed. Long-term investors realize that fear and greed might determine the short-term volatility of the market, but the long-term direction is determined by global investment trends, not fear and greed.

Principle #2: You Are Going to Lose Money . . . I Guarantee It!

It never ceases to amaze me the number of people that I run into all across the United States who are looking for that perfect investment—40 percent investment return with no risk of loss, guaranteed. That is not the way investing works. One of the real downsides to this record bull market that we have experienced is that investors' expectations are way, way out of whack. They think the market can do nothing but go up; and when it goes up, it will go up in double digits without any risk. Investing wasn't designed to be risk free. The key to investing is not to eliminate risk, but to estimate it accurately and manage it wisely. Those are certainly investment words to live by. Understand the risks that you are taking because every investment has some element of risk.

Let me go out on a limb now and give you a guarantee. I guarantee you that you are going to lose money in this market. That's an iron-clad guarantee, even if you understand and implement all of the global trends and investment strategies that I discussed in this book. The only decision that you get to make is how do you want to lose your money. You have two choices. First, you can sit on the sidelines trying to guess what the blizzard is telling you and miss out on all of the gain and return by trying to time the market. This is the way the short-term-world investors lose money.

Second, you can choose to lose money when you have to give back some of your gain when the market turns and corrects itself. This is how the long-term investors lose money.

The difference is that the long-term investors are able to get back what they lost over time because as they focus on the long-term trends and developments, they let their time in the market work in their favor.

On the other hand the short-term-world investor very, very seldom, if ever, gets a chance to get back the lost opportunity to make money. Why, I still know some investors who as soon as the Dow (Dow Jones Industrial average) touches 3,000 again are jumping back in with both feet. Like I said, they will never get it back. Remember, everyone has a photographic memory. Some of us, however, don't have any film. Those would be the same people waiting for Dow 3,000 again.

Principle #3: You Didn't Sell the House, Did You?

I simply cannot imagine how volatile the real estate market would be if it faced the same challenge as the stock market, battling between the short-term world and the long-term investor.

Unlike the stock market your house isn't priced every second or hour or every day. It's only priced when you buy it or sell it; after all, that's the only time it matters.

Think about this: Today as a result of the advancements in technology and law enforcement, the names and addresses of known sex offenders are published on websites all across the United States. Suppose the list is released, and little to your knowledge a known sex offender actually lives on your street. What would happen to the price of your house if it were priced like the stock market? Wham-o: The value of your home would drop from $200,000 to $100,000—if the real estate market was priced by the minute like the stock market is. And you guessed it; the short-term-world person sells the house for $100,000 and loses $100,000.

Or how about this? That 100-year flood that seems to happen about every five years (I still don't understand how engineers can get away with calling it a 100-year flood; I've already witnessed four of them, and I haven't even turned 50 yet!) comes along and floods everyone's basement. Bad news! The value of your $200,000 house instantly drops by the market to $100,000. And again the short-term-world person sells, losing $100,000.

But in time the sex offender moves out and the value of the house fully recovers and then some. Or the city fixes the drainage pond, and the value of that home also fully recovers and then some. And what about the long-term investors in the housing market? They didn't lose a single penny; they actually made money.

If only we would realize that the same principle holds true for investing. Just because your investments are priced every second and you know their value hourly, daily, weekly, monthly, quarterly, and annually doesn't mean you have to sell them. Remember, losses on paper are just that until you sell the properties. For it's only after you sell them that those losses become reality.

If we bought and sold homes based on every single piece of information about our neighborhood and our community, could you imagine the volatility in the real estate market? Yet that is exactly what the short-term-world investors are doing to our stock market. They buy and sell stocks based on every little piece of information and every little price move, which creates the volatility in our stock market.

The next time that you are worried about selling your stocks or bonds or mutual funds when there is a downturn in the market, remember to ask yourself this question, "We wouldn't sell the house, would we?"

Principle #4: The Woodshop Syndrome

Nothing puts the struggle of the long-term investor in a short-term world into better perspective than the "woodshop syndrome." The woodshop syndrome goes like this. You begin by going into your woodshop to build a chair. But after you get into your woodshop, you realize that some of your tools need to be sharpened. However, your sharpener is dull, so you have to fix that before you can begin. Now you are ready to sharpen your tools. After you sharpen your tools, you decide to keep a log of when you sharpen your tools so in the future you can figure out just when and why some of the tools get dull quicker than the others. You are really on a roll now, so you devise and develop this very simplistic but ingenious instrument that can actually assess the sharpness of your tools without running your fingers over them. Now by the time you have all of your materials and tools ready for use, you have actually forgotten why you went into the woodshop in the first place. That's the woodshop syndrome.

And that's exactly what's happening with the short-term-world investors; they have caught the woodshop syndrome, which means that they have forgotten why they are saving and investing in the first place. But instead of being distracted by sharpening tools, short-term investors are being distracted by one of the most popular blizzards . . . interest rates. Will the Federal Reserve Board move interest rates up? Will the Federal Reserve Board move interest rates down? Will the Federal Reserve Board keep interest rates the same? Will the Federal Reserve Board change their bias to tightening? (What the heck does that even mean?) And don't forget about the other blizzards: What impact will this or that economic release have on the next Federal Reserve Board meeting? And did you hear what Alan Greenspan said at his luncheon speech yesterday? And so on and so on. Some short-term-world investors have become so fixated on interest rates that they have forgotten why they are investors in the first place.

The reason that you save and invest is to improve the quality of your life. Now "quality of life" means a lot of different things to a lot of different people. It may mean sending your child to the college of his or her choice, or retiring at age 60, or buying your dream home.

Interest rates have absolutely no bearing on why you save. Think about this for a minute: Whether interest rates go up or down, shouldn't you still be saving to send your children to college? And whether interest rates go up or down, shouldn't you still be saving and investing for your retirement? And what about your dream house? Regardless of where interest rates are, if you still want a dream home, you have to save and invest for one.

Short-term-world investors are lost in the blizzard of their woodshop, while long-term investors never forget why they are investing regardless of the blizzards outside. Please be careful that you don't get caught up in the woodshop syndrome. By the way, where did my hammer go?

Principle #5: There's Only One Way to Make a Billion Dollars

As the number of millionaires continues to grow and grow around the world, the new focus will eventually become being a billionaire. Now the next time that you are sitting on the sidelines of the market trying to guess which way the blizzard is blowing so you can decide whether or not to invest, I want you to remember this story about working and investing.

There are two different approaches you can use to accumulate $1 billion. You can either work to accumulate your $1 billion, or you can save and invest. If you decide to work for your $1 billion and not save and invest because of the short-term blizzards, here's what you would have to look forward to. Let's assume you were lucky enough to land a job that paid you a whopping $100 an hour. And even better, you don't have to pay one single penny in taxes—no federal taxes, no state taxes, no local taxes, nothing, not one thin dime. So that means that you get to keep the entire $100 per hour. Let's take this one step further and suppose that you get really motivated and work 12 hours a day every single day of the year, all 365 of them.

So you earn $100 per hour, work 12 hours a day for 365 days a year, and you don't have to pay a thing in any taxes. Do you have any idea how long you would have to work to accumulate $1 billion? What do you think—maybe 10 years at 12 hours a day, 365 days a year, or would it be more like 15 or even 20 years?

You better sit down for this answer. If you earned $100 per hour, tax free, and worked 12 hours a day for 365 days of the year, you would only have to work 2,283 years in order to accumulate $1 billion. And that's assuming that you could find a job paying $100 an hour, tax free, and that you could work 12 hours a day for 365 days a year.

I'm not sure I like this option. I'm tired just thinking about it. Let's look at saving and investing to accumulate $1 billion. If you began with one lonely dollar bill and were somehow able to save and invest so that dollar doubled (compounded) each day, how long would you have to save and invest to accumulate $1 billion? Remember now, on day one you have $1, on day two it compounds (doubles) to $2, and on day three you have a whole $4. So how long would it take to get to $1 billion if you started out with one lonely dollar—10 years? 25 years? 100 years? 1,000 years? 2,500 years?

Well, you really better sit down for this one. If you were able to double your money every day, starting with $1, after only 31 days, you would accumulate $1,073,741,824.

Now I realize, as I'm sure you do, how unrealistic it is to think that in my working example anyone could actually find a job paying $100 an hour, tax free, and would be able to work 12-hour shifts every day of the year for 2,283 years. Likewise I know that it is equally impossible to find an investment that would double your money daily, but it is a great illustration of the power of compounding. Time helps your investments through compounding. Essentially, as your investment builds interest, it is added to your principal, in this case $1. It is then reinvested so you generate interest on both your original principal and the added interest. Time is your greatest ally if you stay invested.

Principle #6: Is Everything a Buy?

Okay, if you are going to stay invested, you still have to figure out where to invest. And I hope that the fact that you've gotten this far along in the book means that you have a pretty good idea about which sectors to invest in. However, you still need to pick some individual stocks within those industries.

Investors look to the high-paying, high-flying whiz kids of Wall Street, the research analysts, for a clue about what to do and which company to buy. Seeking professional advice is a prudent thing to do as an investor. However, the advice you need is not from a research analyst's report on the Internet, but from a financial advisor (a stockbroker, for those of you like me who are from the old school). If you get your investment advice off of the Internet, you might as well ask a homeless person where to live. There are two extremely important reasons on why you need to be leery of following any information you read on the Internet or anywhere for that matter regarding what a research analyst said or did not say.

First, the research analysts find themselves needing to please two masters: the firm for which they are working and the firm that they are covering. And when you are trying to please two masters, an inherent conflict of interest will always arise. Then one has to question the credibility of the report.

Remember now that the firm for which the analyst works is a brokerage firm. Brokerage firms make their money by getting people to buy stocks. When a research analyst issues a report telling people to sell this stock and that stock, it's not the kind of stuff that helps to grow the business. There is inherent pressure on analysts to issue positive reports. In addition to helping the brokerage firm get their clients to buy stocks, the analysts face other business pressures from their employers. In many cases there are other business relationships or potential business relationships that could be affected by the research report that they issue. These relationships could range from investment banking to strategic partnerships to getting into other lines of business.

As if this isn't enough pressure, the analysts also feel it from the companies that they follow and write research reports on. Every good chief executive officer (CEO) and chief financial officer (CFO) reads every single line that every single analyst writes about their company in every single report. How you write your research report may determine in the future whether you get the 10 minutes with the CEO or the 2-hour luncheon meeting. It could also have a strong bearing on the future answers you get from the CFO as well. Issue a negative report, and in the future you can expect tart, crisp, one-word answers like yes and no. Issue a positive report, and it will increase the likelihood that they will want you to clearly understand the story behind the numbers.

It is extremely difficult, if not impossible, to serve two masters. Because even if there is absolutely positively no conflict at all in your research report, simply the appearance of a conflict will call into question the credibility of the report. Here is what I mean about the appearance of a conflict. One of the best, most influential and most powerful research analysts on all of Wall Street is Jack Grubman, the telecommunications analyst at Salomon Smith Barney. Now in late 1999, Mr. Grubman turned positive on AT&T. On the surface you may say to yourself, so what? Well consider this: A few months later AT&T needed to select three Wall Street brokerage firms to underwrite AT&T's $10 billion stock issue (by the way, investment bankers make a lot of money on $10 billion deals), and you will never believe which was one of the three firms selected? You guessed it, Salomon Smith Barney. Conflict of interest or appearance of a conflict of interest, does it really matter? Oh by the way, I almost forgot to mention that the chairman of the board of Citigroup (remember if you will that Salomon Smith Barney is part of the Citigroup financial giant), Mr. Sandy Weil, actually sits on the board of directors of AT&T as well. I'm sure it's nothing, but did you also know that the chairman of the board of AT&T, Mr. Michael Armstrong, also is on the board of directors for another company and their name is . . . you guessed it, none other than Citigroup—the same Citigroup that owns Salomon Smith Barney, the same Salomon Smith Barney that pays Jack Grubman's salary and bonus. Is this a conflict or an appearance of a conflict? You be the judge. This issue is not unique to Salomon Smith Barney. It happens in all of the firms all the time. Only you can decide, does it matter?

The second fact that you must consider regarding research analysts is that they love to stick together. No one really wants to stick his or her neck out because it just might get chopped off. If 20 analysts are covering a stock and 19 have the same opinion and one has a different opinion and the different opinion is wrong, I'll bet you that the one who is wrong will be updating his or her resume. If however the analyst sticks with the crowd and stays in the pack and all 20 are wrong together, what are you going to do—fire all 20 research analysts from all 20 firms? I don't think so—I can already hear the excuses. Can you believe how everyone on Wall Street missed this one? We are no better off or any worse off than any of the other Wall Street firms.

Let me help to put this into perspective for you based on an analysis by Zacks Investment Research. One of the most watched indexes in the world is the Standard & Poor's 500. The Standard & Poor's (S&P) 500 is comprised of 500 different companies, whereas the Dow Jones

Industrial Average is comprised of only 30 different companies. As you would expect, every one of the 500 companies that comprise the S&P 500 index is very closely watched and very closely covered by the research analysts.

At the end of last year there were 8,000 separate research analysts' recommendations covering the 500 individual companies that comprise the S&P 500 Index. Of those 8,000 separate recommendations that range from buy to sell with anything in between, like hold or accumulate, how many of those 8,000 recommendations do you think were "sells"? Only 29 were sells—less than one half of one percent.

Do you really want to get your advice from a research analyst's report on a website? I don't think so! Remember, light travels faster than sound. This is why some of these analysts appear bright until you hear them.

The next time that you get caught up in wanting to follow a research analyst's advice that you just read on the Internet, I want you to remember these three widows fishing in a boat out in a lake. Suddenly a frog jumps in the boat and says, "Kiss me and I'll turn into a research analyst." One of the women immediately grabs the frog and puts it into her purse. The other two women begin frantically screaming, "What are you doing? One of us needs to kiss that frog and maybe it will give us some hot stock tips." To which the first woman calmly replies, "No way, hot stock tips are a dime a dozen; but a talking frog, now that's worth something!"

The Next Generation of Investors

Hopefully the younger generation will learn something from those three widows. If you think about it, the next generation of investors are probably just now turning 20. What kind of investors will they be? How different will they be from prior generations? Will they figure out the formula of how to become a long-term investor in a short-term world? Each year Beloit College in Wisconsin assembles a list of the ways in which each class of first-year students differs from their teachers and from their parents. I took a close look at that list, and as we try to figure out what type of investor the next generation will be, maybe there are some clues in those lists from Beloit College. Let's not lose sight of the fact that this next generation of investors has a different frame of mind. To begin with most 20-year-olds today have probably never dialed a phone. They have no idea how big a breadbox is. To them Yugoslavia has never existed, and they never understand why people worry about the packaging of Tylenol.

Only time will tell what type of investors they will become. As investors in the markets today, we have a role to play with this next generation of investors. You see, it is said that we don't inherit the earth from our ancestors; rather we borrow it from our children. The same can be said for the stock market. We didn't inherit the stock market from our ancestors; we are borrowing it from our children.

The next time you find yourself struggling between the short-term blizzards and the long-term iceberg trends remember this: If we gave way to the short-term world and let the blizzards rule our investment actions, what type of market will that leave for our next generation of investors? We didn't inherit the stock market from our ancestors; we are borrowing it from our children. And remember, this next generation needs all the help that they can get. After all, they don't even know if something is bigger than a breadbox.

What Has Vitamin C Got to Do with It?

As this book draws to a close, I am hopeful that the preceding pages have helped show you *Where the Money Is*. I want to leave you with one final thought, which is also the single most important thing that you need to remember. In fact much of my motivation to write this book came from this very thought: "To see what everybody else has seen and to think what nobody else has thought." I wish I could take credit for that; however, those are not my words, those are the inspirational words of Albert Szent-Gyorgyi. Albert Szent-Gyorgyi won the 1937 Nobel Prize for discovering vitamin C. And while he was actually talking about research when he uttered those now-famous words, the same could be said for investing. After all, that's what successful investing is all about . . . to see what everyone else has seen and to think what nobody else has thought. From the evolving demographic trends in Chapter 1 to the technology revolution in Chapter 3 to the corporate restructuring in Chapter 5, I hope that in some small way I have helped you to better see what everybody else has seen. And then in Chapter 6 where I turned trends into strategies using Sectornomics and Chapter 7 where I shared with you my principles of long-term investing, now you will be able to think what nobody else has thought.

Have a great day, keep a positive attitude, and please join me in resolving to remain a long-term investor in a short-term world. And don't forget to take your vitamin C! It's both good for your health and it will be your daily reminder of *Where the Money Is.*

DR. BOB'S NOTES . . . TOP 10 THINGS TO REMEMBER!
Chapter 7

10   Time helps your investments through compounding; it is your greatest ally if you stay invested.

9   The longer-term direction of the market is determined by global investment trends, not fear and greed.

8   The reason that you save and invest is to improve the quality of your life.

7   Just because your investments are priced every second and you know their value hourly, daily, weekly, monthly, quarterly, and annually doesn't mean you have to sell them. Remember, losses on paper are just that until you sell them.

6   I guarantee you that you are going to lose money in the market. The only decision that you get to make is how you want to lose it.

5   The single most important ingredient for the success of global trends and developments is time.

4   Most investors are so focused on the short-term blizzard of the week that they fail to recognize the long-term iceberg investment trends that will impact the markets for decades to come.

3 We didn't inherit the stock market from our ancestors, we borrowed it from our children.

2 Seeking professional advice is a prudent thing to do as an investor. However, the advice you need is not from a research analyst's report on the Internet, it's from a financial advisor (stockbroker).

1 Successful investing is to see what everybody else has seen and to think what nobody else has thought.

BobSpeak™

A Unique Glossary of Dr. Bob's Investment Terms and Opinions

It is safer to learn than teach; and he who conceals his opinion has nothing to answer for.

William Penn
Statesman and founder of Pennsylvania (1693)

It's only fitting that we end this journey where I began mine. I was born and raised in Pittsburgh, Pennsylvania, and it now seems fitting that we end this book with a quote from the most famous Pennsylvanian of them all, the founder of Pennsylvania, William Penn. Who knows, maybe the reason that I am so opinionated is because I was born in Pennsylvania.

Anyhow, I could not agree more with William Penn when he said, "And he who conceals his opinion has nothing to answer for." The opinions that follow are mine and mine alone. I put them in writing so you wouldn't forget them. And once in writing I will have to answer for them the rest of my life. Thank you, William Penn.

Accountant's Opinion   A letter that typically precedes a detailed financial report. It is prepared and signed by an independent accountant. However most if not all of the information was provided by the employees of the company that the opinion is about. So how independent is it? The opinion goes on to describe the scope of the financial statement and presents an opinion on the quality of the data presented. Never, ever make an investment decision on the quality of the data presented. Never, ever make an investment decision based on an accountant's opinion. Remember, your information is only as good as your source, and the source of the information is the company on which the accountant is rendering an opinion. Remember, accountants can be lied to and misled. An accountant's letter is like a letter of recommendation; if you look long enough, you will find someone to give you one.

Accounts Payable   The money that a company owes to other companies and various vendors for products and services purchased on credit. When this number is rising, it is a signal to dig deeper. A rising accounts payable number can be either good or bad. If business is growing and expanding, you will obviously buy more on credit; so in that case it's a good thing. If business is flat and you don't have much cash, you might begin to purchase more and more on credit to hide your current problems. That is a very bad thing. A rising accounts payable number on its own isn't good or bad; rather it's a sign you need to dig deeper.

Accounts Receivable   The money that is owed to a company by its various customers for the products and services that have already been provided on credit. This is an extremely critical number to watch because it is out of the control of the company. Sometimes you can get so focused on the company in which you are investing that you forget about the companies that buy the products your company makes. This number is really a measurement of the financial strength of your customer base. Any company can make sales go up if it doesn't have to worry about getting paid for the product. Always, always check this number.

Agency Bonds   These are securities that are typically issued by a government agency. They do not have the full faith and credit of the

U.S. government behind them. The most popular and well-known of these are the bonds of the mortgage associations that go by the nicknames: *Ginnie Mae*, which stands for the Government National Mortgage Association; *Fannie Mae*, which stands for the Federal National Mortgage Association; and *Freddie Mac*, which stands for the Federal Home Loan Mortgage Corporation. Even though these securities are not backed by the full faith and credit of the U.S. government from a risk perspective, they are pretty secure. I would consider them just one small notch below Treasuries, which are backed by the full faith and credit of the U.S. government. The best thing about these bonds is that at cocktail parties you can name-drop Ginnie Mae and Fannie Mae and Freddie Mac and impress the heck out of your guests.

Annuity A legal contract that is typically sold or underwritten by an insurance company. The insurance company will then make payments over time to the person who holds the contract. Payments usually begin at retirement. There are different types of annuities. A fixed annuity will pay an individual a guaranteed rate spelled out in the contract. A variable annuity pays a rate that is determined by the investment returns that are tied to the performance of the market. Possibly the best thing about an annuity is that your investment grows and you don't have to pay any taxes on it until you begin to receive withdrawals. Anytime you can avoid paying taxes, do it. Not only is it good for you, it's good for your country as well. The less money paid in taxes means less money for politicians to do something stupid with. You need to buy an annuity today!

Asset Allocation The technique of spreading an investment portfolio among the various asset classes of stocks, bonds, and cash. What used to be a relatively simple thing to do has now become much more difficult as the complexity and choices for investments have grown. Now your asset allocation will consider domestic and international stocks. And in the international stocks, how much in emerging markets? Then you need to decide do you want growth stocks or value stocks or a blend of both? Then you must choose between large capitalized stocks, midcapitalized stocks, small capitalized stocks, or microcapitalized stocks. Keep in mind that we are

Glossary

still talking about stocks. The best plan of asset allocation is to call your financial advisor.

Bankruptcy A legal proceeding in federal court for either a person or a business. The court can declare that person or business insolvent, or bankrupt, if you will. Once this happens, the individual or the business is freed from making any additional payments on all of its outstanding debts. This doesn't occur, however, without a cost associated with it. In order to get out of paying all of your debts, whether you are an individual or a business, you have to turn over and actually surrender all of your assets to a court-appointed trustee. Also, bankruptcy can be either voluntary or involuntary. In a voluntary bankruptcy you would actually start the proceeding. In an involuntary bankruptcy someone to whom you owe money starts the proceeding. The real reason why individuals use bankruptcy as an option, especially from a personal bankruptcy standpoint, is that all of the actions that are coming from people to whom you owe money stop. That means all lawsuits, eviction notices, the shutting off of utilities, and so on. This bankruptcy trustee who you turned everything over to divides up all of your stuff among everyone who you owe money to. But here's the interesting thing—you get to keep some of it as well. Now this varies from state to state; certain property is exempt from bankruptcy proceeding. Most of your personal belongings, such as your clothes, are exempt. Typically your home and car are exempt as well. All retirement accounts are also exempt from bankruptcy proceedings. The reason that we have such an increase in bankruptcy filings is not because individuals or businesses are in that much worse shape today than in prior years, but because of the lawyers. Instead of chasing ambulances to file a lawsuit, they now chase spending.

Basis Point One-hundredth of 1 percent. It is typically used in discussing the yields on bonds. So 25 basis points (bps), for example, would be equivalent to one-quarter of 1 percent. So if yields increase from 5.5 percent to 5.75 percent that would be a 25-basis-point increase; or looked at another way, yields increased one-quarter of 1 percent. I think this term was created by bond market "geeks" just to confuse investors. I think we should throw it away and simply talk about percentages. It would be less confusing, and it might even get people to invest in bonds.

Beige Book An economic release that reports on the current economic conditions. It is published by the Federal Reserve Board eight times a year. The actual report has a beige-colored cover, which is why it is referred to as the Beige Book. Each of the 12 Federal Reserve Banks—Boston, New York, Philadelphia, Cleveland, Richmond, Atlanta, Chicago, St. Louis, Minneapolis, Kansas City, Dallas, and San Francisco—gathers information on current economic conditions. The final report then summarizes all of this information. One of the reasons this is such a great release is not just because you get a sense of the overall strengths and weaknesses in each geographic region, but because it's such a comprehensive report. Every report touches on consumer spending, manufacturing, real estate and construction, agriculture, natural resources, financial services and credit, employment and wages, and finally prices. Instead of the Beige Book, I always thought it should be the black-and-red book. If things were bad (in the red, if you will), we would use a red cover. On the other hand, if things were good (or in the black), we would use a black cover. This would greatly help the investors who hate details. You wouldn't even have to read anything; simply look at the color of the cover.

Beta A technical analysis tool that measures the volatility of your stocks' return relative to the overall market, which is captured by using the Standard & Poor's (S&P) 500 Index. This is one of those terms in the investment world that half of the people misunderstand and the other half misuse. I wish it would go away. The beta is based on a three-year historical regression analysis of the return of your individual stock compared to the return of the S&P 500. Here's how beta works. A beta of 1.0 means movement exactly the same as that of the S&P 500—your stock is moving in lockstep with the index. If your stock has a beta of 1.5, that means that your stock tends to move 50 percent more than the S&P 500 in the same direction. When the S&P 500 rises 10 percent, your stock should rise 15 percent (or 50 percent more). Conversely, when the S&P 500 falls 10 percent, your stock is expected to fall 15 percent (again, 50 percent more). When your investment moves more than the overall market in either direction, it is considered a riskier investment. So the higher the beta, the higher the risk. I urge you to never place an investment bet(a) simply on this lone factor.

Bond   A type of investment or security that represents debt of the corporation that issues them. Typically the issuer is required to pay the person who holds the bond (bondholder) a specified rate of interest for a specified time, and then they repay the entire debt. Because every rate is predetermined, or fixed, bonds are also called fixed-income securities. If, for example, you have a $100,000, 10-year, corporate bond that pays 8 percent interest, here is what will happen. For each of the next 10 years, you will receive your annual 8 percent interest payment of $8,000. Then at the end of the 10th year, you receive your $100,000 back as well. Typically a safe investment; however, the biggest problem is inflation. The interest that you receive is fixed, so inflation really determines the true value of your investment each year. If you receive 8 percent and inflation is only 2 percent (it cost 2 percent more to live), your investment was really worth 6 percent ($8\% - 2\% = 6\%$). If, however, inflation jumped to 5 percent, your 8 percent bond would effectively only be yielding you 3 percent ($8\% - 5\% = 3\%$).

The Bond Belle   The nickname that Mark Haines of CNBC's *Squawk Box* fame has given to Kathleen Hays. Kathleen covers the bond market and is one of the key players on *Squawk Box*. She understands the unique relationships of the economy and the bond market better than anyone does. Also she is one of my favorite people to argue with. After all, she spends a lot of her time talking to economists, so she should be argued with. She can always be counted on for excellent insights on the Fed as well.

Bond Rating   A measure of the quality and safety of the bond. Bond ratings are given to both foreign and domestic corporations, as well as to state and local governments and international countries. There are a lot of bond ratings out there. The two biggest bond-rating agencies are Moody's and Standard & Poor's. Combined they have bond ratings for over 20,000 companies and almost 40,000 municipal bonds (which include states school districts, water districts, etc.). The rating is actually given with a letter. It goes in descending order from A to D. The higher the rating, the safer that bond is thought to be. In other words, the greater the likelihood that they will meet their scheduled principal and interest payments. The highest quality is AAA. Then it goes to AA, A, BBB, BB, B, CCC, CC, and C; D is used when the bond is actually in default, which means they are not paying you. Bond ratings change over time; they can be upgraded or downgraded. There are two things that you need to be leery of as an investor: First, if you are a company and need a bond rating, you must pay for it. In other words you are now a customer of the rating agency. You pay their salaries. They can't upset you too much, can they? There is an inherent conflict of interest in this business. Second, there are so many bond ratings outstanding that it is impossible for the rating agencies to keep track of them all. Thus by the time they get around to downgrading a bond rating, the whole world already knows about it. If you are making investment decisions based on bond ratings, you are making a big mistake. Most ratings aren't worth the paper that they are written on. If you want to focus on letters, focus on your children's report card. The report card from bond-rating agencies should be written with disappearing ink.

Book Value   An investment measurement that takes the net worth of a company (which is its assets minus its liabilities) and divides it by the total number of shares outstanding. That price is then considered a company's book value. Let's say that a company has a net worth of $950 million, and it has 37 million shares of stock outstanding. It would have a book value of $25.67 (950,000,000 ÷ 37,000,000 = $25.67). This measurement is important because you can then compare it to a company's stock price. If a company's stock price is lower than its book value, it's a bargain. In this example, if the company's stock were trading at $19.50, buy it. It's like paying $19.50 for $25.67 worth of assets. If it were cash, you would do it in a minute. Anyone would give $19.50 in cash to receive $25.67 in cash. What's good for cash is good for stocks. Follow the book value—it's better than the yellow brick road.

The Brain   The nickname that Mark Haines of CNBC's *Squawk Box* fame has given to David Faber. I believe David has the best contacts on Wall Street. David is also one of the key players on *Squawk Box*. If something is happening anywhere, anytime, this guy usually knows about it. David has a memory like a steel trap. You better not say something to him that you don't mean because he'll call you on it years later.

Brief Case Indicator   The single most important economic indicator of all time. It was developed by CNBC's top show *Squawk Box*, hosted by Mark Haines. The indicator looks at how full the briefcase of Federal Reserve Chairman, Alan Greenspan, is as he walks from his car to the Federal Reserve Board office on the day of the Federal Reserve Board meeting. Finally, an economic indicator that makes sense and that investors can actually understand. By the way, it's pretty accurate as well. I'd expect nothing less from the *Squawk Box* crew.

Business Cycle   The periodic changes and long-term patterns of economic activity. These activities are driven by employment, production prices, and interest rates. This cycle is going either up or down. When economic growth is going up, we call it a recovery. When economic growth is going down, we call it a recession. The typical business cycle was thought to last 8 to 10 years. That's why most businesses required 5-year business plans because they would get you through most of the cycle. The great debate today is, "Is the business cycle dead?" The answer is no. You cannot ever kill the business cycle. However, you can change it so it is tougher to recognize, which is exactly what we have done. Because of technology and the interconnected global market, the 8-to-10-year business cycle has been replaced by the 2-to-3-year business cycle. It's not dead. Maybe we should call it business cycle "lite" instead.

Capacity Utilization   A monthly economic indicator that measures how much industrial output is currently being used. As this rate moves up or down, it is a great sign of where industry is trying to take the economy. This number is given as a percentage; and as a rule of thumb, the closer it approaches 90 percent, the closer industrial output is to full capacity, and inflation concerns take center stage. Conversely when the number approaches 70 percent, it's a sure sign that industry is slowing to the point that could be recessionary. While I have watched this number over time, I've often wondered how much better 84 percent is than 82 percent. I don't think the absolute numbers are as important as the direction the number is heading. The importance of this indicator is the trend line, not the percentage.

Capital Gain   Determined by looking at the initial price you paid for your investment and the value of that investment today. Suppose you paid $10,000 for an investment, and today it is worth $12,000. That's a $2,000 capital gain (current value $12,000 – $10,000 purchase price = $2,000 capital gain). A capital gain can either be realized or unrealized. A realized capital gain means that you actually sold your investment and have the $2,000 difference in your hand today. You have "realized" the gain. An unrealized capital gain is one in which it hasn't actually been sold yet but if you sold it you would have a capital gain. In my given example if you don't sell the investment that you purchased for $10,000 and you still have it, you have an unrealized capital gain of $2,000 that you will realize once you sell it. In addition, capital gains can be long-term or short-term. A long-term capital gain is on any investment that you have owned longer than a year; a short-term capital gain is on anything that you owned for less than one year. Call your broker for an explanation. If you don't have a broker, get one!

Compound Interest   The amount of interest that is earned on the original principal plus the accumulated interest. It's the magic that makes money grow. When you start receiving interest on your interest in addition to interest on your principal, obviously your investment will grow much faster. The catch is that you can't touch your interest; you need to keep reinvesting it . . . no exception. And the most important element to the concept is time. The more time you give your investment, the greater the impact compound interest will have—one of the cornerstone concepts of investing.

Consumer Price Index (CPI)   A monthly economic indicator that is religiously followed by most market watchers as the key to where inflation is headed. This index is commonly referred to simply by the acronym CPI. It is supposed to be an indicator of the general level of prices. Just about everything is included in this index, from energy to food and beverages, housing, apparel, transportation, and medical care, to name a few. This index is simply not cracked up to what it's supposed to be. Quite simply it overstates inflation and makes things actually look worse than they are. While there are numerous technical and statistical issues that converge to overstate inflation, the fundamental reason that the Consumer Price Index overstates inflation is that the Consumer Price Index does not take into account the retail consumers' behavior regarding changes in prices. Think about it: When the price of peaches rises faster than the price of bananas, most consumers will simply put more bananas in their fruit salad and fewer peaches. The kids can expect bananas cut up over their cereal instead of peaches. In other words, people will actually change their buying habits because of price and will buy more bananas than peaches. That doesn't mean the consumer is spending more on food even if the price of peaches is rising dramatically. This index simply doesn't understand the psychology of the retail-price-conscious shopper. This index assumes that the consumer who wants a peach will buy a peach at any cost, when in reality that simply is not so. This index drives me bananas. I don't care about it and neither should you.

Contrarian An investor who goes against the crowd. Someone who does just the opposite of the consensus on Wall Street most of the time. Someone who sees value in a particular investment when no one else wants it. The true contrarian tends to focus on everything that is currently out of favor. The greatest contrarian investor ever is my good friend David Dreman.

Credit Card A card that is issued by a bank or other financial institution and gives the person who holds the card (cardholder) access to a specified line of credit to purchase products or services or to receive cash. The slang term is "plastic" because these cards are plastic cards. Credit cards are possibly the greatest invention ever in the financial services industry. First, you never need to worry about having cash; and second, it's like having a personal accountant follow you around on your shoulder keeping track of every penny you spend. Before credit cards, someone would have $500, and weeks later they couldn't even remember where the money went. With credit cards you get a detailed accounting every single month. All the hype about consumers taking on too much debt is a bunch of baloney. Credit card usage should not be confused with debt. After all, many consumers, myself included, pay their credit card balances off monthly; they are using them for the convenience. Who knows, maybe the future *is* in plastic.

Defined Benefit Plan   A type of a pension plan that guarantees a prespecified amount to employees who work a certain number of years. (Also known as an "I don't care about the stock market" plan. If you haven't read the book, this will make absolutely no sense to you.) In a defined benefit plan the employer makes all of the financial contributions and is responsible for investing them as well. The world is changing, and more and more companies around the globe are moving away from these plans. They will soon become the dinosaur of pensions.

Defined Contribution Plan   A type of pension plan that has no guarantees regarding what it will pay at retirement. Typically both employers and employees contribute to this plan. The employee then decides how all of the money will be invested. (Also known as the "I am a stock market junkie" plan. If you haven't read this book, you have no idea what I am talking about, so read the book!) These investments will then grow tax free. However, that only matters if you make the right investments. This type of plan is the wave of the future. It makes individuals solely responsible for their retirement assets, unless of course they are smart enough to seek the advice of a stockbroker.

Demographics   The social and economic characteristics of a nation. They are characterized by age, sex, income level, education, and occupation. In my opinion demographics are the single most influential factor on investing. They are also the most misunderstood. Unlock the mystery of demographics and you will also unlock the secrets to investing.

Dividend   A taxable payment that is made to stockholders. A dividend payment must be declared only by the company's Board of Directors. Most dividends are paid out of a company's earnings. Typically dividends are paid quarterly in the form of cash. However, more and more companies are moving to paying out their dividends in the form of their company's stock. Dividends are a good thing, and they help boost the total return of your investment.

Dollar Cost Averaging One of the simplest and wisest investment strategies around. You select a fixed dollar amount ($100, for example) to invest at regular intervals (weekly, for example), and you do this regardless of what is going on in the market, whether the market is up or down. What this strategy enables you to do is to average the purchase of your shares over the long run. Thus you will make some purchases when the market is cheap, and you will make some purchases when the market is expensive. However, on average you will be much better off than the investor who is attempting to time the market. Did you ever notice how sometimes the simplest things are also the best things? Everyone should have a dollar cost averaging plan . . . I do! Why don't you?

Dow Jones Industrial Average (DJIA) The oldest and still the most widely used measure of the overall condition of the stock market. The Dow Jones Industrial Average began way back in 1896 with only 12 stocks. In 1916 the number of stocks was increased from 12 to 20. Then in 1928 it was increased to 30 stocks, and it has remained a 30-stock average ever since. The 30 individual companies that comprise the Dow Jones Industrial Average change over time. You can be taken off or added to the list. There have been two substantial changes to the Dow Jones Industrial Average since the mid-1990s. On March 17, 1997, Hewlett-Packard, Johnson & Johnson, Travelers, and Wal-Mart were added, while Bethlehem Steel, Texaco, Westinghouse Electric, and Woolworth were deleted. Then on November 1, 1999, Home Depot, Intel, Microsoft, and SBC Communications were added, and Union Carbide, Goodyear Tire & Rubber, Sears, and Chevron were dropped. While arguments will always reign whether this is the most accurate measure of the U.S. stock market, one thing that you can't argue about is that it is still the most widely watched and widely quoted. I believe it is the single most influential and watched stock market measure anywhere in the world.

Durable Goods Orders   A monthly economic indicator. This economic release is the best barometer of future manufacturing activity. You need to think of durable goods as the big-ticket items. Technically a durable good would include any manufactured item with a normal life expectancy of three years or longer. Because the item lasts at least three years, we call it durable. Even though this only measures future manufacturing activity, I like this release because I think it is a wonderful indicator regarding consumer and business confidence. Big-ticket, durable-good items like cars and airplanes and refrigerators tend to be purchased when consumers and businesses are confident about where the economy is going. I feel that this release is much more important than it first appears. It measures not only future manufacturing activity, but also business and consumer confidence. Watch this indicator closely. I do.

Earnings   The amount of money that corporations make over a certain period of time. Two of the most popular earnings periods to look at are quarterly and annual. Earnings are the reason that corporations are in business. Earnings are also the single greatest determinant as to where a company's stock price will go. In real estate the three most important factors are location, location, and location. In investing it's earnings, earnings, and earnings.

Economic Indicator   Statistics that measure certain components of the economy. Some indicators focus on housing, others focus on employment, while others focus on inflation. There are hundreds of economic indicators to choose from. Economic indicators can be classified into three different groups: (1) Leading economic indicators, which have some predictive value, give you a clue regarding what will be going on in the economy. (2) Coincident economic indicators are occurring at the exact same time as the economic activity. (3) Lagging economic activities only become apparent well after the economic activity has occurred. There are so many indicators that measure so many things that it's no wonder economists can never agree on anything.

Employment Cost Index   A quarterly U.S. economic indicator; the best and the broadest measure of employment cost. First, it covers both salaried and hourly employees. Second, it includes employees from both the private (business) sector and the public (government) sector. Third, it includes the cost of all benefits paid to employees, such as health and insurance benefits. Fourth, it covers the widest time frame of any of the employment numbers because it is quarterly. Fifth, and possibly the most important, this is one of the indicators that Alan Greenspan closely monitors. If it's important to him, it should be important to you because it will be important to the markets. And yes, it is important to me as well. Remember, don't fight the Fed, which translated means don't fight Alan either.

Factory Orders   A monthly economic indicator that captures the pulse of the manufacturing industry. Factory orders are comprised of manufacturers' shipments, inventories, and any new or unfilled orders. This indicator has less and less relevance as we move from a manufacturing-driven economy to a service-driven economy. Very seldom, if ever, does this indicator move the markets.

Federal Reserve Board   A seven-member Board of Governors that is responsible for overseeing the Federal Reserve System. That system is in essence the central banking system for the United States and is made up of the 12 Federal Reserve Banks as well as national and state bank members. The Federal Reserve Board is commonly referred to as "the Fed." As an investor you know them best as the group that establishes monetary policy by moving interest rates in an attempt to influence economic growth. The Fed can raise rates by increasing either the discount rate (which is the interest rate charged by the Fed for short-term loans to member banks) or the federal funds rate (which is the interest rate that banks charge each other for the use of funds that have been deposited by commercial banks at Federal Reserve Banks). They do this in order to curb excessive growth in the money supply, which in turn should slow down the economy. The Fed can also ease rates (my favorite Fed action, by the way). They do this when they feel that the economy is not growing fast enough; lowering rates will ease credit conditions, which should stimulate the economy. Because the U.S.

economy is the largest economy in the world, the Fed is the most highly watched and influential central bank in the world today. We focus on it a little too much, in my opinion.

Financial Advisor   See Stockbroker.

Flat Tax   A tax system in which all levels of income are taxed at the same tax rate, whether it's 10 percent or 15 percent or 20 percent. "Flat" means "level"; everyone pays the same level, flat tax rate. In the United States this issue is being championed by Congressman Dick Armey, who is one of the best and brightest in Washington, D.C. There will be a flat tax somewhere in the not-too-distant future in the United States. When Dick Armey speaks, you better listen.

G-7   Stands for the Group of 7, which is made up of the seven largest industrialized countries in the world. The G-7 is comprised of the United States, Japan, Great Britain, France, Germany, Italy, and Canada. The Finance Ministers (in the United States it's called the Secretary of the Treasury) attend meetings of the G-7 to formulate global economic policy issues. Pay attention to what they say and do. Even though none of them are elected, they exert more influence than all of the other politicians in the world combined.

Gross Domestic Product   A quarterly U.S. economic indicator; the broadest of all indicators because it measures economic production for the entire nation. This number places a market value on all of the newly produced goods and services. Without a doubt, this is the best overall indicator regarding economic strength. Because it is released quarterly (after the quarter is over), you already have a pretty good idea about the economy from the hundreds of economic indicators that have preceded it that quarter. This is the one number that politicians know and watch the most.

Industrial Production   A monthly economic indicator that measures the level of activity in terms of the actual physical output of the key industrial components of the economy. These include the manufacturing, mining, gas, and electric utility industries. It's a pretty good indicator of how the old economy or the smokestack economy is doing.

Inventory The value of all of a company's raw materials, anything that is in the pipeline or in process, supplies that are being used in current operations, and finished goods as well. This number will appear in a company's financial statement. While this number is important from a financial analysis perspective, it is even more important from an investment perspective. A company that has excess inventory on its balance sheet most likely is facing one of two problems. Problem number one is that this is usually an indicator of a slowdown in sales. If you can't sell the stuff, it usually stays in your warehouse and is captured as inventory. This is a bad thing for investors. Problem number two is that it could also be an indicator of no pricing power. In other words customers are not willing to pay for your product. This is also a bad thing for investors. And while the inventory number is an accountant's term found on a balance sheet, savvy investors should watch this number closely because inventory doesn't lie.

IPO An acronym that stands for an *initial public offering* of a company's stock. Everyone loves to have something that they can't have; and because an IPO represents the very first time that investors can own this stock, it's usually preceded with a great deal of hype. Typically, it is an extremely volatile investment. I think this is where the phrase "Here today, gone tomorrow" was discovered. Anyway, proceed with extreme caution. This is not for the amateur investor.

The Big Kahuna The nickname that Mark Haines of CNBC's *Squawk Box* fame has given to Joe Kernen. Joe is one of the key players on *Squawk Box*. He likes to lull you to sleep thinking he doesn't know what's happening, and then he zaps you. One of the reasons I like Joe is that he is a former stockbroker. And remember, all through this book I've been telling you how smart brokers are. Well, here's proof. Oh, by the way, Joe has his master's degree from the Massachusetts Institute of Technology in molecular biology. And once and for all, he doesn't wear a hairpiece.

Lockup Period This is one of the most important things to look for if you want to invest in the initial public offering (IPO) market. The lockup period is actually a period of time, typically years, during which directors and employees of the IPO company are restricted from selling stock that they own in the company. The longer the lockup, the better it is. I like three years minimum to start. It is this provision that brought the so-called dot.com geniuses back to reality. You see, they launch a new IPO, keep a couple million shares of stock, the stock price goes to the moon, and they are multi-millionaires (on paper). Eventually investors forget about the hype and realize this company will never be profitable. They sell the stock, crushing the stock price; and by the time the lockup period is over, their holdings are worth a small fraction of what they once were on paper. Easy come, easy go. If you are going to invest in IPOs, lock 'em up, Dano!

Market Capitalization   The calculation to determine just how much money investors think an individual company is worth. The higher the market capitalization, the more investors think the company is worth. You can figure out a company's market capitalization by multiplying the number of shares of stock outstanding by the share price of the stock. A company with 5 million shares of stock outstanding with a stock price of $68.50 would have a market capitalization of $342 million (5,000,000 × $68.50 = $342,500,000). Market capitalization is typically broken down into four classes, with the following general guidelines: (1) *Micro-cap*, which has a capitalization between $0 and $300 million; (2) *Small-cap*, which has a capitalization between $300 million and $1 billion; (3) *Mid-cap*, which has a stock market capitalization of $1 billion to $5 billion; and (4) *Large–cap*, which has a capitalization over $5 billion. In theory, the smaller the market capitalization, the riskier the investment. However, history has already proven this not to be true. Some large-cap stocks can be just as risky as a micro-cap stock; the only difference is that a lot more people own the stock. Making investment decisions based on market capitalization is a waste of time.

Merchandise Trade Balance   A monthly economic indicator that measures the difference between imports and exports. When exports (things that are leaving the country) are higher than imports (things that are coming into the country), there is what is referred to in economic circles as a surplus in the balance of trade. Conversely when imports are higher than exports, there is a trade deficit. We have been taught to be concerned with deficits; thus we are worried about trade deficits. I believe that this economic release that alarms investors about the trade deficit is the most useless of all economic releases. First of all, it doesn't account for the value of what you import and export. If the stuff you export has value (like software) but the stuff you import has little value (like coffee), you will always have a trade deficit. Also this number does not account for all of the multinational companies that are, in essence, trading with themselves, not other countries. Then when you add in the distortion of currency movement, you will realize what I did long ago—this economic release isn't worth the paper that it's written on.

Money Honey   The nickname given to Maria Bartiromo by the brokers on the floor of the New York Stock Exchange (NYSE). Maria is one of the best and brightest at CNBC-TV. Her morning reports are presented live from the trading floor of the NYSE as part of the *Squawk Box* program.

Municipal Bond   An investment vehicle issued by a political entity, such as a state, a city, a county, a school district, a water and sewer district, and so on. There are more than one million different municipal bonds to choose from. There are more municipal bonds than there are corporate stocks and corporate bonds combined. Municipal bonds are typically used either to finance construction of a special project or to pay for ongoing general expenses. The great thing about those investments is that they are exempt from federal taxes. The money you make, you keep. You don't have to send any of it to the Federal government.

Non-Farm Payroll   A monthly economic indicator that measures the total civilian workforce and captures the total number of people employed in all sectors, industries, and activities, except agriculture. So I guess this means that no one cares if you work on a farm anymore. This is a somewhat useful number to get a general idea of movements in the employment market. However it gives you no clue regarding whether the corn crop will be harvested on time or not.

Ponzi Scheme   An illegal investment scheme that is actually named after Charles Ponzi, who ran such a scheme in 1920. The way a Ponzi scheme works is that all of the returns on your investment are paid to the earlier investor out of money paid into the scheme by newer investors. This is different from a pyramid scheme because a Ponzi scheme is operated by a central person or company that is lying about how the money is being invested and where the returns are coming from. Come to think of it, this sounds a little like the U.S. Social Security System.

Price/Earnings (P/E) Ratio   A measurement whereby you take the price of the stock and divide it by its earnings per share. The number that remains is its P/E ratio. If a company's stock price were $36 and it was earning $3 per share, its P/E ratio would be $12 ($36 ÷ $3 = $12). This would be considered a low P/E ratio. On the other hand, a company that has a stock price of $236 and was earning the same $3 per share would have a P/E ratio of $78 ($236 ÷ $3 = $78). To most investors this would be considered high. I think way too much time is spent worrying about P/E ratios. You should never, ever make an investment decision based solely on a company's P/E ratio. It can be one of the factors, but it should never be the only one or the dominant one. You better get used to P/E ratios going higher because the global marketplace is creating limitless opportunities for companies to grow their business; and when the business grows, the stock price grows; and when the stock price grows, the P/E ratio grows. Don't worry about it. All of this newfound concern over P/E makes me yearn for the good old days when someone in the high school parking lot who was discussing P/E was talking about physical education class, not price earnings!

Producer Price Index (PPI)   A monthly economic indicator that is very closely watched in order to determine where inflation is headed. This index is commonly referred to simply by the acronym PPI. It actually measures the level of prices that are paid for all goods produced and imported. Simply put, PPI tells you how much more it's costing to make stuff.

Prudent Man Rule   The most basic and fundamental principle for all professional money managers. Its roots actually date all the way back to 1830. On that date Judge Samuel Putnam uttered the now famous words, "Those with responsibility to invest money for others should act with prudence, discretion, intelligence, and regard for the safety of capital as well as income." Right on, Judge! Now consider this: If you invest your own money, this rule doesn't apply. You don't have to be prudent with your own money; you can make all the dumb mistakes that you want. However, if you send your money to a stockbroker, the Prudent Man Rule applies. Prudent . . . not prudent. Do it yourself . . . get advice from a stockbroker. This is a no-brainer if I ever saw one. Pick up the phone and call a stockbroker . . . it's the prudent thing to do.

Pyramid Scheme   An illegal investment scheme in which investors are promised ridiculous returns on their investments. The scheme works like this: A hierarchy is created in the shape of a pyramid. New investors who join the pyramid scheme join under others who have already joined, and the new entrants pay money to those above them in the hopes that they, in turn, will get paid from the new entrants below them. Pyramid schemes are illegal. Remember, if it sounds too good to be true, it probably is.

Registered Representative   See Stockbroker.

Retail Sales   A monthly U.S. economic indicator that captures every single sale transaction that occurred at the retail level. It is one of the most comprehensive economic releases. The following types of retail sales are included as part of this number: automobiles, building materials, clothing, drugstores, food, furniture, gasoline, and restaurants, to name a few. The reason that this number is so important is that the consumer accounts for over two-thirds of the U.S. economy. Retail sales gives you an excellent idea of just how financially healthy the consumer is. Thus it also gives you an excellent idea of just how healthy the overall economy is as well.

Sectornomics™   An investment strategy that was discovered by me and first reported in this book. What it means is that the **sector** (financial, technology, etc.) in which you invest will have the greatest **economic** (money) impact on your investment's performance, even greater than the individual company in which you invest or the region of the world. Not only is this the most important thing that I have ever discovered, it's also the only thing I have discovered.

Slash A term used by both investors and noninvestors who still carry a *Terrible Towel* around with them. They also believe that Myron Cope is the best announcer. Please note that placing a *Terrible Towel* on your investment portfolio does not help. I've already tried it. North Side rules! Go Steelers! *(Note: If you still don't understand, ask someone from Pittsburgh to explain it to you.)*

Squawk Box CNBC's financial news program that airs weekdays from 7 A.M. to 10 A.M. Eastern Time. Hands down, this is the best financial news program there is! You better drink your coffee before you turn on your TV because this show is so fast paced you better be up and running when you tune in. The show is hosted by Mark Haines. Mark is the best anchor in financial news today, period. He is an extremely bright and witty guy who really cares about the viewers understanding the market. If he leaves CNBC to manage money, follow him and send him your money. He is the only anchor on financial news today who would do as good a job answering the questions as asking them. If you think I'm biased because I am also a guest cohost, you're damn right I am! The best movies win Oscars. The best songs win Grammys. The best athletes win gold medals. And the best strategists win a spot to be interviewed on *Squawk Box*. Keep on Squawk'n!

Stagflation The economic term that was coined to explain high inflation, high unemployment, and a slowing economy all occurring at the same time. Prices are going up while the economy is going down. You don't have to be an economist to figure out that this is not a good thing.

Stagnation The economic term that was actually coined in the United States in the 1970s to describe what was going on with the U.S. economy. It is used to describe a period of very little, if any, economic growth in a country's economy. This is not a good sign.

Stockbroker An individual who is a professional investor. They invest for a living. They eat, drink, and sleep thinking about investments. They are also known as financial advisors or registered representatives. All stockbrokers must be registered before they can transact any business with the public. In addition they must pass rigorous qualifying exams administered by the National Association of Securities Dealers. Possibly one of the most important decisions you will make in your lifetime is picking your stockbroker. After all, you are picking someone who will be responsible for your financial future. In the decade ahead the stockbroker will evolve into one of the most important and respected professionals around the globe. And for all of you who don't have a stockbroker, I say thank you, because if it weren't for you, the stockbrokers wouldn't have any investment dummies to exploit to make money for their clients.

The Street   The term used when talking about Wall Street. It's the name given to the financial district in New York City. It is also used to describe the stock market as a whole. When someone says the Street thinks this or the Street thinks that, they are not actually talking about some paved or cobblestone street. They are telling you what is the consensus of the brokerage and other financial services firms. When someone says the Street is expecting a rate cut, they are telling you what the consensus is of the experts on Wall Street. The problem with "The Street" is that no one is accountable. If the Street says it's still a good time to invest and it turns out it isn't, you have no recourse other than kneeling down and actually talking to the real concrete street. Who knows, maybe all those people who appear to be talking to themselves in New York aren't crazy after all; they are just trying to get a hot stock tip from the Street.

Ten-bagger   The occasion when the stock you buy rises tenfold. This has nothing to do with baseball, where a two-bagger is a double and a four-bagger is a home run (called a four-bagger because you touch all four bases—first, second, third, and home). So if you buy a stock at $17 and it goes to $170, you have a ten-bagger ($17 × $10 = $170).

Total Return   A valuation measurement of your investment's performance. It is calculated by taking the interest or the dividend income generated by your investment plus the capital gain. For example, if your stock investment paid a dividend income of 4 percent and the value of the stock increased 10 percent (capital gains), your total return would actually be 14 percent (4% dividend + 10% capital gains = 14% total return). Not only is this the best measurement of your investment's performance, but it is the only one you should use. Anything else only gives you half the story.

Treasuries   Fixed-income securities issued by and backed by the full faith and credit of the United States government; considered by many (myself included) to be the safest investment around. There are three types of Treasuries: *Treasury bills*, which are commonly referred to on Wall Street as T-bills, are the shortest-term investments with maturities that range from three months to one year. *Treasury notes*, which are also called T-notes, are the government's medium-term securities with maturities that range from 2 years to 10 years. Finally there are *Treasury bonds*, which are the government's longest-term securities that have maturities that range from 10 years to 30 years. The beauty of Treasuries is not only that they are the safest investment around but also that the interest you receive from the U.S. government is exempt from any state and local taxes. And remember, any time you can avoid paying any taxes to anyone, do it.

Triple Witching   Occurs four times a year in the stock market. It happens on the third Friday in March, June, September, and December. On this day the options contracts and futures contracts expire on all of the market indexes. The simultaneous expirations set off heavy trading of options (single witch) and futures (double witch) as well as the individual underlying stocks (triple witch). These days are almost always accompanied by extreme volatility.

Unemployment Rate   A monthly U.S. economic indicator that captures the number of people who are currently unemployed as a percentage of the total employment market. The problem with this release is that if you are not actively seeking a job, you are not included in this number as unemployed. I'm not sure what you call it, but to me if you're not employed, you are unemployed. Economists worry that if the unemployment rate goes too low, we will have wage inflation because employers will have to pay employees more money (and this is a bad thing somehow). Anyway, that's not going to happen because of the low unemployment rate. This rate doesn't take into account the merger boom, which keeps employees nervous about job security; and employees nervous about job security don't tend to demand higher wages.

Volatility The rate at which your investment or a market index moves up or down. When an investment or market is highly volatile, that means that it is typically characterized by large price swings both up and down. Volatility is not a bad thing; it is actually a good thing. For without volatility, you would never have the chance as an investor to buy low and sell high. Investors who don't understand volatility end up buying high and selling low. Buying high and selling low is not how you make money.

Yield The amount that your investment has earned expressed as a percentage. You can determine the yield by taking the income earned on a security and dividing it by that security's price. If, for example, you had a stock that was paying you an annual dividend of $2.40 and had a current stock price of $26.00, your yield would be 9.2 percent ($2.40 dividend ÷ $26.00 stock price = 9.2% yield). It's just another way to measure how much money you are making.

Index

Learn to look at all things.

Lewis Carroll
Author (1869)

The index that follows will enable you, in the words of Lewis Carroll, to "Look at all things" that I talked about in this book.

energy sector (*continued*)
  electricity, 233–238
  global variations in, 238–239
  and lifestyle, 229–230
  oil and gas, 232–233
  and telephone/television use, 230–
    232
Environmental Protection Agency
    (EPA), 130
ERISA (Employee Retirement Income
    Security Act of 1974), 129
euro, 63–64, 159
Europe (Euroland), 63–70
  coming labor reform in, 70
  demographic trends in, 5, 34–37,
    39–40
  economic unification of, 6
  and German tax reform, 67–69
  Internet use in, 70, 98–100
  labor laws in, 110
  limited Internet potential in, 70
  mergers in, 158–160
  new shareholder focus in, 65–66
  protectionist policies in, 161
  retirement savings explosion in, 67
  stock ownership boom in, 66–67
Exxon, 117

families, two-income, 29
fast-food sector, 27–28
FDA, *see* Food and Drug
    Administration
fear, 245–246
Federal Energy Regulatory
    Commission, 234
Federal Reserve Board, 82
fertility ratio, 23
financial news networks, 29
financial services sector, 32–33, 186–
    191, 222–229
  and aging population, 222
  anxiety factor in, 224–226
  and increased savings rate, 222–223
  and need for financial advice, 226–
    227
  profitability in, 223–224
  transparent pricing in, 228

Financial System Reform Law (Japan),
    75
Finland, 63, 92, 221–222
First Chicago, 188
First Union, 187
flat tax, 131–132
Fleming versus Nestor, 150
Food and Drug Administration (FDA),
    204–205
food sector, 17–18
Forbes magazine, 29
Ford, Henry, 90–91
Ford Motor Company, 53–55
Forrest Gump, 78–79
Fox, Vicente, 85–86
France, 63, 66, 145
free trade, 160–163
frequent flyer miles, 59, 60
Froehlich
    Cheryl, iii, xiii, 218, 221, 230
    Fred (the dog), 221
    Marianne, iii, xii, 221, 231, 239
    Stephanie, iii, xii, 221, 231, 239
Fuji Bank, 76

Galactic Network, 91
GDP, *see* gross domestic product
General Electric, 117, 134
General Motors, 117
generation X, 5, 34–36
genome, 212
Germany, 9–10, 63, 92
  and end of Cold War, 122–125
  Internet in, 70
  population density in, 74
  public pensions in, 145
  tax reform in, 67–69
Glass-Steagall Act, 187–188, 223
global infrastructure, 103–104
globalization, 2, 6–7, 49–50, 160–169
  benefits of, 160–161
  and free trade, 160–163
  and management, 165–168
  as mandate for privatization, 139–
    140
  price pressures encouraging, 168–169
  regional approach to, 167–168